the gathering

To My Dear Friend and
her wonderful family, the
Jentzsch's. How grateful I am that
our paths have crossed over and
over. You were and still are a
blessing in my life! I know
you understand miracles as
we do. May the Lord fill
your life with an abundance of
them. Love You!
Anna Laurie & Brian Richardson
9/10

their hearts were whispering a plea
to be found, to be loved, to belong

the gathering

ANNIE LAURIE &
BRIAN RICHARDSON

one family's adoption story

TATE PUBLISHING *& Enterprises*

The opinions expressed by the author are not necessarily those of Tate Publishing, LLC.

Published by Tate Publishing & Enterprises, LLC
127 E. Trade Center Terrace | Mustang, Oklahoma 73064 USA
1.888.361.9473 | www.tatepublishing.com

Tate Publishing is committed to excellence in the publishing industry. The company reflects the philosophy established by the founders, based on Psalm 68:11,
"The Lord gave the word and great was the company of those who published it."

Book design copyright © 2009 by Tate Publishing, LLC. All rights reserved.
Cover design by Amber Gulilat
Interior design by Jeff Fisher

Published in the United States of America

ISBN: 978-1-61566-458-0
1. Family & Relationships, Adoption & Fostering
2. Biography & Autobiography, Personal Memoirs
09.12.11

dedication

This book is dedicated to the children all over the world with hopes as faint as whispers and whose hearts are still crying out for someone to come find them and bring them home.

table of contents

why the gathering

—Brian

In my mind I heard a tiny girl's voice in clear language plainly say, "Daddy, please send Mommy to come and find me!"

I heard the voice only once, but I remember it clearly, and it replays instantly upon demand in my mind. "Daddy, please send Mommy to come and find me!"

The journey began before this miraculous experience, but for me, it was the fuel that empowered me to send and follow a courageous and faithful woman, Annie Laurie, on our incredible gathering journey and then to become a real father, in every sense of the word, to twenty-four children from around the world.

—*Annie Laurie*

Can't you drive any faster? We only have a few minutes to get there! Oh, can this possibly be happening? It was so hard to believe that it was actually true. After twenty-three long years of searching, our little girl was about to be placed in my arms.

We walked into the attorney's office, and there she was; our long-awaited daughter. She was two days old, and the attorney who had her looked very awkward as he held that tiny bundle in his arms. She was all but hidden in her little outfit, and I carefully reached out my hand to pull back the hood so I could get my first glimpse of her tiny face. I wanted to savor every facet of that moment. We had fought with everything we had to be able to be at this place at this time. We had given what felt like our very life's blood to be able to stand in that office and have our little girl placed in our arms. It was truly a battle worth fighting for.

I couldn't take it any longer, so I asked if I might hold her. The attorney placed that sweet little girl in my arms, and I knew what heaven felt like. I looked into those beautiful eyes; the eyes that I had been searching for in little faces all over the world. But as I looked, it was not only her eyes that I saw but the eyes of all our children who had been gathered to our family over the past twenty-three years; children who came into our lives because this little girl in my arms kept whispering. The memories of the journey it took to get to this precious moment came flooding back to my mind; struggles with child and family services, the heartache of losing children, camping in the jungles of the Marshall Islands, visiting the orphanages of Vietnam, living amidst danger and sickness in Haiti, miracle after miracle ... on and on it went.

This is a true story. It's a story that must be told. Even though this happened to our family, this story belongs to all who want to believe in miracles. It belongs to those who are searching for miracles or those who hope miracles still happen today, to ordinary people.

A few years ago, my daughter, Clarissa, who first came into our home at two through the foster care program, came to me with tears in her eyes. She was now ten and had gone through many challenging times already in her life. She snuggled in my arms and said, "Mommy, please don't tell my story anymore. It makes me remember it all over again, and it hurts my heart so bad." I laid my cheek on her head and wept with her.

What could I say? How could I speak peace to this precious daughter? At the time, we were doing seminars frequently where we shared the story of how our adopted children came into our lives and the miracles that occurred in order for this to happen. Many hearts were touched and many lives were changed as we shared our experiences. How did I explain to her the power of her experience?

I looked at her and asked if we could talk about it for a few minutes. She agreed.

"Clarissa, what is your favorite story in the scriptures?"

"I love the story of Daniel in the lions' den."

"Why do you love the story of Daniel?"

"Because he had faith enough to do what God asked him to do and God saved him."

"What does that teach you in your life?"

"That I need to have faith enough to do whatever God asks me to do, and then he will save me too."

"Save you from what? Lions?"

That brought a smile to her lips but not yet to her eyes. "No, Mommy, he will save me from everything that will hurt me."

My heart began to ache all over again for this sweet daughter as I asked, "Has God saved you from everything that has hurt you right when it was hurting you?"

She looked at me, trying to figure out what I was saying to her. "No, but I am safe now, and he is going to keep me safe."

"But how do you know that?"

"Because he kept Daniel safe!"

"But, Clarissa, how do you know he kept Daniel safe?"

"Because I know the story!"

"Sweetheart, Daniel had to live the story before his story could help anyone. And then he had to be willing to have his story told. Probably millions of people have been helped through hard times because Daniel lived and then shared his story."

I could see that understanding was coming to her heart. I continued, "God has given you a powerful story that touches people's hearts every time they hear it. What if your story gave someone the power to have more faith in their life, just like Daniel helps you to have more faith? Would it be worth having your heart hurt a little and having to remember a little if it can bless their life?"

It was at that moment that my daughter stood up and looked me in the eyes. Tears were streaming down her cheeks, but she also had a smile on her face, a smile that reached her eyes. She said with a quiver to her voice but with strength too, "Mommy, you tell my story to everyone. Tell them I love God and that he has blessed me so much. It's okay, tell my story!"

So, part of the gift of this book is the pain and the memories of children from all over the world. Children who want you to know that the God they believe in is a God of miracles. They know because they were there.

This is their story.

•　•　•　•　•　•　•　•　•　•　•　•　•　•　•　•　•　•　•　•

Brian and I are the parents of these twenty-four remarkable children, nineteen of which have been adopted from all over the world. I say *remarkable* because we have asked of them remarkable things, and they have responded with loving and willing hearts. This journey has not been easy for any of us, but it has given us far more than we have received or ever could receive.

Not only have we been *gathering* children, we have been *gathering* gifts all along the way that have enabled us to do whatever was asked. I had to put those *gathering* stories in this book also, or it would be incomplete. Each experience prepared us for the next. We are very normal people who have decided that nothing is too hard if we have God's help. We have come from the same places that so many others have come from. It is a witness to me that we all have a journey to take. Each one of those journeys will look a little bit different. But if we allow him, I believe God will give each one of us the gifts necessary to come out conqueror.

I could fill this book with only the adoption stories themselves, but unless you know the people who walked this marvelous journey and how and why they were willing to walk the journey, then you only know part of the story.

For the most part, I am the one that has been the driving force behind the gathering of these special souls of ours. I will share my struggles and joys with you, and you will know me well by the end of this journey. But I want you to also know those who have supported and strengthened me all along the way. This story would not even be possible without the incredible support and love that my husband, Brian, and my family have given me. I thank them with all of my heart.

It would also not be possible if my Father in heaven had not been there every step of the way. Even in my hour of questioning his watch care over me, I have always known inside that he was there. I have included those times of struggling, for all struggle in their own ways. We are all in this together. May you find some of your own answers within the pages of this gift of love. This is simply *our* story.

But to tell you that story, I must take you on a journey back to a time when the journey was all just a dream in a young girl's heart.

it all starts

—Annie Laurie

All I ever really wanted to be as a young girl was a mother. This desire was with me every waking moment for as long as I can remember. It didn't matter what or who crossed my path, they were taken under my mother hen wings. My own mother said that from the time I was little I brought home stray animals and small neighborhood children. I would beg her to please let me keep them and take care of them. I just wanted to be their mother.

As a teenager, while other girls listened to the latest music and dreamed of fashion and careers, I was babysitting and pretending those children were mine. While other girls shopped for their makeup and jewelry, I always headed for the baby department. I spent hours picking out bottles, pacifiers, blankets, and clothes, dreaming of the day when I would hold my first baby, dreaming of the man that would someday join me in this wonderful journey of being parents.

I was six years old when I had my first boyfriend that I thought for sure would someday be my dream husband. His name was Stephen. I couldn't understand why he ran the other way when I told him he was going to marry me. Every day I chased him around the playground, desperately trying to catch him so I could give him just one little kiss on the cheek. I knew that then he would have to marry me. I never could catch him, so I had to move on in my quest. At seven, it was Scott; at eight, it was Bruce; and at nine, Jack. On and on it went, constantly looking for the one who would partner with me in the greatest dream of my life: to be a mother.

At eighteen, I was afraid that life was passing me by because I was not yet married. It was at this time that my dad, who was an officer in the army, was transferred to the American Embassy in Norway. My mother and two younger brothers went with him. I stayed home and attended a semester of college. That is what my parents thought I was doing anyway. Really, I was just continuing my search for a husband.

By Christmas, I missed my family so much I left school and flew to Norway, thinking I would stay only a few weeks. Instead, I became a nanny for an American family in Oslo, Norway. I was living my dream again, for I had two little children that I was in charge of all day every day. I was in heaven.

Then, one day at our church service, a young male American who was working as a missionary in that area walked down the hall toward me. I remember looking into his eyes as he walked toward me and thinking, *I would love to marry a man like him.*

He was the translator for our church meetings, which were held in Norwegian. I would listen to his voice every Sunday and feel like swooning. I couldn't tell you a thing he said, I just loved listening to his voice.

A few months later, he left for home. Interestingly enough, home was Utah, right where I was soon heading myself. By this time, I was convinced he was who I had been looking for all my life. I went home to find him. It took him several months to finally ask me out, but when he did, I thought I would die from excitement. Poor guy, he was about to get a taste of what he was really getting into by associating with me. It was okay, I didn't move too fast. I waited until our third date to tell him of my dreams and that I really wanted him to share in those dreams. It only took him a week or two to come around to my way of thinking. This was a very good omen for our future life together.

After he finally decided that he agreed to spend his life with me, he settled down to a nice, long engagement. I had different plans. I figured, if this was right, why not get down to business and get married. That took another few days of convincing, but he quickly came around to my way of thinking, again. This was another very nice omen for the future. We were married after a short courtship of three months. My Brian had come into my life to stay. He was everything that I had ever dreamed of. He was terribly good-looking, tall, and had the most wonderful eyes. But more importantly, he loved God as much as I did, and he was as determined to follow him the rest of his life as I was; wherever that journey would take us.

It was a short six weeks later that we found out that my long looked for dream was going to come true. I was pregnant. Brian was in school fulltime, and I worked fulltime in the data processing department at the University of Utah. We were just a little nervous about how things would all work out. But at the same time, we were both thrilled to be starting our family so soon.

Three months later, we found out that not only was I pregnant, but we were going to be blessed with twins! The excitement of that moment was incredible, as we watched the wonder of the ultrasound and saw on the monitor those two little bodies moving around inside of me. But even as we were experiencing the thrill of that moment, Brian's world went spinning. How could he possibly take care of a wife and two babies? We wouldn't have even been married a full year. Despite our concerns, Brian and I couldn't stop grinning all the way home. It was time to grow up very fast.

There was never a doubt in my mind about the sex of the twins, even though they were not able to tell us at the time what sex they would be. I knew from the beginning that it was a little boy and girl that I was carrying. We had their names picked out right from the start. We were going to have our little girl named after me and our son would have his father's name. Our little Annie Laurie and Andrew Brian were about to make their first appearance into the world and into our lives.

The closer we got to the special day of arrival, the more nervous we became. My job at the University of Utah was a great one. In fact, they had been so good to me during my pregnancy that even though I spent most of the day in the bathroom losing everything I had just put in me, they kept me on and treated me like a queen. But Brian and I had decided that there was no way that I was going to work after having children.

It was four weeks from our due date, and Brian was still a year from graduating. Since twins usually come early, we needed to do something, and do it quick. I was so large that I could not even get through the toilet stall doors anymore. Obviously that was reason enough to make some kind of change. We decided he needed to get a fulltime job that would take care of a family of four, and I needed to quit and somehow get ready for what lay ahead. Within a couple of days, Brian had a job working as the sales manager for the Logan, Utah, Deseret Industries. It would mean a move, but I loved to move, so that was fine by me.

It also meant he would have to be gone from five thirty in the morning until seven at night, but we would be able to put food on the table and diapers on those babies.

We found a tiny, two-bedroom house in the country. I loved it.

My time of giving birth was getting close. We had been in Logan about ten days, and it was now two weeks before the twins were due. We were still seeing our doctor in Salt Lake City, which was two hours from our home. Brian had taken a day off work to drive me down to my appointment, as I simply did not fit behind the steering wheel, but he was going to have to return to Logan early the next morning to his new job. As we visited with the doctor, he said my swelling was so bad that it would be dangerous to make the drive back home. He really wanted me to stay close to the hospital until the twins arrived. That night, I had a chat with God. I shared with him that Brian was leaving in the morning and I couldn't bear that. I told him I was afraid to be left alone and would he please do something about it. I would do my part if he would do his. Now, I knew from past experience that God would do his part, so I proceeded to do mine.

Brian and I went for a drive into downtown Salt Lake City to have some time together before he would leave the next morning. As we walked the streets, all of a sudden I took off running. Try to picture this. Here is a lady in a big muumuu, because that is all that would fit her, overly large with pregnancy, trying to waddle-run down the streets of town. Brian stood in shock and then started running after me yelling, "Stop, you are going to hurt yourself!" I was laughing loudly with great abandon tinged with mild insanity. I continued this erratic behavior for about half a block, at which time he caught up with me, and I collapsed in his arms and breathlessly said, "Take me home, I think I am going to die."

I had truly done my part, and that night, my water broke. I know heavenly Father works miracles and answers prayers, but sometimes I think he just has to laugh at us as we do desperate things trying to get those prayers answered.

I woke Brian up and told him that it was time to go to the hospital. He was so flustered that all he could think about was that he had to iron his shirt. After convincing him that it was not necessary to have an ironed shirt for a birth, we raced to the hospital. Now, there wasn't really a need to race, it was just what we had always heard you were supposed to do when you are having a baby, so we raced.

We arrived at the hospital early that morning. I can still remember lying there looking out the window at the early morning dawn. What would this day hold for us? The dream of being a mother was certainly going to be answered that day. Would Brian and I be able to meet the needs of these two special children?

With all of our excitement at being a mommy and a daddy, those few moments talking together were very sobering. We wanted to do this, but we wanted to do it right. We somehow wanted to create a family who, by pulling together, could weather the storms of life and yet also could experience together the wonderful joy of living in this world. It was our heartfelt desire to help our children find the strength to walk their particular journey in this life with courage and faith. How could two untried parents do this awesome thing? How could we give to them what we were just starting to learn ourselves? We decided at that time that the only thing we could really give them was our own walk with God; our own journey of faith and discovery of who we all are in his eyes.

It was a few hours later, after a very traumatic C-section due to my body not reacting to the epidural fully and having feeling come back in the middle of surgery, that we first held those two little babies in our arms. Sure enough, we had ourselves a little boy and girl. We had never seen anything so beautiful. But to my dismay, I was not able to see and hold them for very long, for they were quickly whisked away as I had contracted toxemia right after the birth. Hours later, I awoke to find out that I had nearly died. We knew that a power greater than ours had preserved my life. My first thought upon waking up was, *Where are my babies? Are they all right?* I was soon able to hold those two little ones in my arms once again. As Brian and I looked into their little faces, I knew that I was now, finally and forever, truly a mother.

* *

The reality of motherhood became very clear, very quickly, as the all-night feedings took place and my little Annie Laurie was sick much of the time. But I never ceased to look in their eyes and relish the wonders of being their mother. This is what I had been waiting for. I had spent years being everyone's favorite babysitter, but now I could play *real* house with my own children.

We were amazed how quickly their personalities began to make themselves known. Andrew was the perfect child until he turned one, and then it was as if he woke up and decided that it was his personal job to challenge the world. We were his world at that time, so we were the ones who received the benefit of this challenging. I remember saying over and over that if we could just channel all that determined energy, he would be one powerful young man. I guess we did our job fairly well, for today he truly is a wonderful young man who has the world by the tail and knows where he is going.

Annie Laurie was just the opposite. She spent the first year very sick but smiling and laughing through it all. She always had a chuckle and a giggle for everyone who would look her way. She brought joy to every life she touched. She loves to make people happy. She is still the same young woman today. Although she has lupus and has spent most of her life ill and in pain, she always has a smile and a laugh ready to brighten everyone's world around her.

. . . .

Seven months after the joyous event of the twin's birth took place, and just as I was settling into the world of motherhood, I woke up one morning so sick I just wanted to die. Yes, I was pregnant again. However, I had already had one miscarriage during those seven months, so we were just grateful I was pregnant.

We were determined this time to have a natural child birth instead of another C-section. I carried this baby two long weeks past the due date and thought I would burst. As my due date came and went, I called my mother crying that I just couldn't take it anymore. Well, I don't know what I expected her to do about it, for in those days, you didn't just make babies come because you were overdue. But I called wanting her to take care of it anyway. I am the first to admit that I never do anything the conventional way, so of course I didn't this time either. What would be more natural when you are three days past your due date than to get in the car with your parents and go on a road trip along the Oregon coast? But it sure made the time pass much more quickly.

We arrived back at the house exactly two weeks after my due date. My parents dropped me off, and as I waved good-bye, my water broke. This was before the days of cell phones, and I frantically waved at them trying to get them to come back. They didn't see me! I quickly called Brian and let him know that I was home and would he please come take me to the hospital.

Once again, we were two hours away from the hospital, as I had kept my same doctor in Salt Lake City and we were still living in Logan. We had to drive through Sardine Canyon, a steep and dangerous passage, in order to get to Salt Lake. I have to admit we took advantage of the situation and raced through that canyon. It was great fun. Halfway through, we were pulled over by a policeman. Brian jumped out and said, "I have to get my wife to the hospital, she's going to have a baby." The policeman peaked in the window, and I tried to look like I was on the verge of delivery, but to be honest, I wasn't having a single contraction. Oh well, it worked! He radioed ahead that we were on our way to the hospital, and we flew past one policeman after another.

After all that racing, I still went through twelve hours of hard labor. They then told us that the baby was in stress and that we needed to look at having another C-section. We had so wanted to deliver this child naturally, but neither one of us wanted to do anything that would compromise our baby. So after another painful C-section, a little baby girl was placed in my arms. I guess I shouldn't say little as she was over nine pounds and had the fattest little face. Her hair was two inches long and was every color that hair can be. Her dimples were incredibly deep, and she was beautiful. We named her Katie Clarice after her grandmother.

Her personality showed up from the very first and has stayed with her throughout her life. She was the peaceful child. Katie has carried the role of peacemaker in our home all her life. She also loved to laugh and was always a little mother like I had been. What a lovely day it was when Katie entered our home and our hearts.

Two years later, almost to the day, number four came along. We had moved back to Salt Lake City to finish Brian's schooling and to join the ROTC program at the University of Utah. My father had been an officer in the army, and my three brothers were also planning on a career as officers in the army. It just followed that Brian would also join the army as an officer.

This was our one and only planned pregnancy. After having a dream about a little boy, I went to Brian and told him he had twenty-four hours to decide, but I knew we were supposed to get pregnant. What do you say to that? Having another child at that point was the farthest thing from Brian's mind. He had just returned from a six-week boot camp in Washington. I had lost a lot of weight and was this tiny, cute little thing. Getting pregnant again was not on his agenda. But I convinced him to pray about it, and nine months later, Blaine Edward arrived.

He was a scruffy little boy who had mischief written all over him from day one. He was named after his two grandfathers, and he was our delight. How do you discipline a little boy who as you lecture him just grins at you? You just have to laugh at yourself and love him all the more. Fortunately, he was one of those children that although he was always doing some kind of mischievous thing, he was also very obedient. He had the gift of loving people. He was a born leader and is in the forefront of everything he has ever done.

preparation for the journey

Four children under four! Life was happening faster than we knew how to take it all in. Being parents was a great thing, but enough was enough. It was time to take a much-needed break. Brian and I promised each other that there would be no more children for a while. We were very determined on this matter.

Our little Blaine was only a few weeks old when Brian was finally able to finish school and we went on active duty in the military. Our first assignment was Armor School in Fort Knox, Kentucky. For those of us who need simple explanations, Brian played in tanks all day while I stayed home with our four little ones.

I say "stayed at home," but where we were staying was far from what one would call a home. It was a place of endurance. Kentucky was having one of the worst heat waves in their history. We lived in a two-bedroom trailer that was crawling with bugs and was so run-down that I am surprised we didn't fall through the floor or the walls. But it was cheap, and we had very little money. We had one tiny window air conditioner that sent a blast of cool air out a whole five feet, and that was it. I would park myself in front of that cooler with Blaine in my arms and the children at my feet and not move all day. We had no money for food, as Blaine was on a special formula which took all of our food money for the month, except for ten dollars. I washed our clothes in our bathtub, including Blaine's diapers.

I would sit out on the tarmac (the tank parking lot) and wait for hours with the kids, hoping for just a few moments with my husband. He would come in from training in the field and want to see us before he had to turn around and go back out. But we would never know when he would actually get in, so we would sit for hours in the heat, excited to have our ten minutes of being together. Thank goodness we were only there a few months. I don't know if we could have made it much longer living in that little house and spending our days on the tarmac.

Brian's next assignment was Fort Rucker, Alabama, where he attended helicopter flight school. This was a very poignant move for me, as I had been born in Fort Rucker while my dad was in flight school, and we lived there again during my junior high years. We quickly fell into the routine of our new life. Brian was gone all hours of the day and night. It was a very stressful and lonely time for both of us. There wasn't even a tarmac to go and sit on in hopes that we could see each other for fleeting moments.

It was soon Christmastime and all my family was meeting in Utah at my parents' house for the holidays. Because Brian was in flight school, he would only be able to get a couple of days off. I wanted so badly to be with all of our family again, for it had been quite some time since we had seen many of them, and they didn't even know our Blaine. There just simply was not enough time to drive out and back to Utah, and we only had one car, so the kids and I couldn't drive it either.

But that wasn't about to stop me. I simply came upon a different plan. The children and I would go on a Greyhound bus to Utah. I had never done anything like that before, but how hard could it be! When I mentioned this to Brian, he looked at me like I was crazy. I didn't see anything wrong with my plan. I figured we would go by bus, and he could fly out as soon as he could. That way we all could be there together, and the kids and I would have a little extra time. Sounds great, doesn't it?

The twins had just turned four a few days before that, and Katie was two and a half. Okay, Blaine was only eight months old, but I didn't think that would be a problem. He really was a very good baby. We would take as little luggage as possible, and surely there would be people to help us. I think Brian was so tired that he just didn't have the energy to argue. Besides, I was pretty determined to get there, and when I was determined to do something, I was a force to be reckoned with.

A few days later found us at this tiny bus stop in the middle of nowhere waiting to be picked up. Brian was not able to stay until we boarded the bus, as he had to get back to class. It's a good thing, because otherwise he would never have let us go. When the bus arrived, it was already full to capacity. Every seat was taken—every one! What were we to do now? We could wait until the next day to go, but there were no guarantees there would be seats on that bus either. It was the holidays! I was determined to get to Utah. I hefted our suitcase in one arm, slung our other bag over my shoulder, lifted Blaine into my arms and shuttled the three other little ones ahead of me onto the bus. I looked around trying to find a seat that maybe they hadn't realized was empty. There was nothing. I looked at the people on the bus hoping that someone would have pity on us and give us at least one seat that we all could share. No one moved. They all were staring at us, but no one moved out of their precious seat.

My four children were the only children on the bus. We shuffled further back as the driver yelled that we needed to get situated because he had a schedule to keep. I dropped the suitcase in the middle of the isle and sat down on it. I put Blaine and Katie on my lap and the twins on the floor in front of me. We drove like that for the first four hours of the trip.

By the time we made it to our first stop, Blaine had soaked both me and him. But there was no way I could change his diaper. So we just sat. Those children never made a peep. I told them I needed them to be my helpers, and they were. They were the best kids in the world. After that first four hours, the five of us were able to have two seats together the rest of the way. It felt like heaven.

The trip from Alabama to Utah was supposed to take about fifty hours with all of the stops and layovers in little bus stops across America. I had planned everything accordingly. We had just enough food to almost get us there, but I knew that we could be a little hungry at the end because my parents would have a big meal ready for us. We had so little money at this time, and the price of the tickets had used every reserve that we had. I didn't have a penny with me for food. We had only what food I brought with us. This would have been great, except we had a few miner setbacks.

On the second day, we ran into a terrible blizzard which slowed us down to a crawl hour after hour. It was now midnight, and we should have been there several hours ago. We still had a long ways to go. All of a sudden the bus pulled off to the side of the road. None of us could figure out what was going on. The blizzard was so bad that we could not see anything outside, but the driver didn't tell us to get off either. After sitting there for about an hour, the driver finally came in and told us that the bus had broken down and would not be able to be fixed until morning. But we had lucked out, for down the road a ways was a diner. It was closed, but the owner said that he would open up for us and fix us some food and let us sleep where we could.

I bundled the kids up the best I could, ready for the bitter cold. We had to bring our luggage with us, as they did not want it left in the bus. I thought for sure that someone would offer to help us, but no, we were on our own. I picked up the suitcase, threw the bag over my shoulder, picked up my eight-month-old baby, and led my children out into the storm. We followed in a line so that no one would get lost. It was about two hundred yards to that diner, but it felt like ten miles to me. I was so scared that one of my children would become lost or fall and hurt themselves. I prayed every step of the way and told the kids to keep praying until we got there and then everything would be okay.

I don't know how long it took, but we made it and made it together. Everyone else had beaten us into the diner, so all the tables were taken. But we found a corner to huddle in until we got warm again. We sat on that floor and could smell food cooking, and it smelled so good. We had run out of food sometime back, and I had no money. I did not even have the money for a phone call. Everyone around us obviously had money, for they were all eating and enjoying themselves. I pulled those four children into my arms and just kept telling them I was sorry but I had no food. They didn't cry. They didn't even ask once I explained. They just sat and watched all those mouths chewing those wonderful smells and quietly went to sleep. We awoke in the morning from our cramped position to the smell of breakfast being served. Once again, my sweet children quietly accepted the fact that we were going to go hungry. I do not remember one complaint coming from them at all. I wanted to complain. I wanted to yell at someone to please help us. But I didn't. I just got tougher right along side of my tough kids.

About midmorning, the bus was fixed, and the blizzard was over. We got back on the bus and drove the rest of the day. We arrived that night in Salt Lake City, where my dad was waiting to pick us up. Never has food or a real bed felt so good. But the best part was when I walked off that bus and my dad put his arms around me and held me. I had made it. I had done something hard, very hard, but I had done it. We had done it. It was one of those binding moments where you are never quite the same in yourself or in your relationship with those whom you have suffered with. I was so proud of my kids. We truly could do hard things and come out the other end having accomplished our goal.

As I look back, I believe this experience set the stage for so many of the journeys that we would take during our time of gathering. We knew that if we pulled together as a family, we could do anything, no matter how hard it was, and it would be worth it in the end.

We had a great Christmas. It was certainly worth the journey to get there. Brian was able to come and spend it with us, and I was so glad for he really needed the break. But now it was time to get back on that bus and come home. After hearing of our experience, Brian would not let us go home by ourselves. He called his commander, who gave permission for him to be home late after hearing the story. Fortunately, this time the trip was uneventful and straight forward. We made it home with no mishaps, and poor Brian did not get an adventure. I don't think he was sad about it.

• •

It was a standing joke at flight school that there had to be something in the water, as everybody seemed to get pregnant. We laughed! There was no way that we were going to follow the same road. We were going to have our break.

A few weeks after Christmas, I woke up with the flu. Brian asked if I could possibly be pregnant. I just laughed and said there was no way that I could be pregnant and God would never do that to us anyway, right?

After a few days of continuing to feel quite sick with the flu, I decided to go to the doctor, just to make sure everything was all right. He did several routine exams and tests. He said he just wanted to do a routine pregnancy test. I laughed again, saying there was just no way that I was pregnant but I would humor him. They told me to come back in the morning to find out the results. I'll never forget that morning. It is marked as one of the most embarrassing moments of my life.

That next morning my friend came with me to get the negative results of the pregnancy test. I was laughing, telling her how dumb it was that they always routinely have women take the pregnancy test if there is ever anything wrong, because—ha ha—there was just no way that I could possibly be pregnant. The room was packed with women waiting for their results. It was almost standing room only. I pushed my way to the front to receive my little paper that would tell me I was not pregnant, and the nurse smiled at me and said, "Congratulations." I just gawked at her.

"What?" I said with absolute unbelief written not only on my face but on my entire being. "There is some kind of mistake here, please check again!" I was really trying to remain calm, but I could feel myself unraveling. Yes, I definitely wanted more children, but not now, not yet! I loved being a mother, but there is a time and season for all things, and surely it was my season to just enjoy those I already had.

The nurse calmly checked again and then quietly—with a smirk, I think—handed me my little paper saying, "No, there is no mistake. Congratulations are definitely in order!"

I turned around, hemmed in on all sides by women waiting anxiously for their results, and I started yelling.

And I just kept yelling, unmindful of all the stares, the snickering, and the horrified looks of unbelief that someone would possibly act this way in public.

"No, No, No! It can't be true! It is not possible!"

My friend quickly grabbed my arm and dragged me out of

the room. I collapsed in the hall. My fifth baby, a little boy, was on his way.

I laugh now, but at the time, I thought life was just being cruel. Little did I know that instead of collapsing in anger and unbelief, I should have fallen to my knees in gratitude, for this was the last time that I would be able to carry a child and to know what it felt like to feel those precious little feet kicking inside. It would be the last time that I would be able to give birth and to hold my newborn in my arms.

But I didn't know all that at that point. I just knew that I was only twenty-three and already overwhelmed. I went home and wept for days and prayed that somehow this was a mistake. I could not possibly handle one more child. I was exhausted, I never saw Brian, and the overwhelming sickness that always stayed with me the whole pregnancy was just more than I could bear. But, as usual, God knows best, and instead of it being a horrible mistake, he made my burdens light. That was my easiest and most enjoyable pregnancy. I was rarely sick, and I had an incredible sense of peace, which stayed with me the entire time. The children were still who they were, but I was given an added ability to take care of their many needs. As time went on, I became more and more excited for the birth of this child. I felt that he would truly be a gift to all of us, but especially for me. How grateful I am for that time.

Shortly after finding out that we were pregnant again, Brian was released from flight school, due to medical complications. During armor training, while driving a tank, he very seriously damaged three vertebrae in his back. He was taken to the hospital, but we did not want to have surgery. We thought he had healed nicely, but the vibration of the helicopters brought the pain back with a vengeance. After almost killing his crew because his leg went numb while he was flying, we decided maybe this was not the best course to take. They sent us to Fort Hood, Texas. It was the middle of nowhere, but we would do our best to make it a home.

There was confusion over the due date of our fifth child. Both Brian and I felt it would be best to have my same doctor, as there had been complications with each birth. That meant I had to go back to Utah. I knew I'd have to have another C-section, as I had done so with all our other children. I wanted to have a doctor whom I trusted. So about two weeks before one due date and four weeks before the other, I went back to Utah to stay with my mother. I took the children with me, and we waited.

Brian was once again out in the field doing maneuvers for weeks at a time and could not get off to come with us. This meant that he was not going to be able to be with me at the birth of our child, so I asked my mother to please be there with me. Together, we got excited for the long-awaited day to come. Unfortunately, I found out that it was the second due date that was correct, not the first.

All my other births had been quite traumatic, and each had their own set of complications. However, this birth was again a direct gift from God. Everything went smoothly, and it was wonderful having my mother there with me. I was even able to watch this C-section via a mirror. I soon had my little Ammon in my arms.

I was so anxious to see my husband that six days after Ammon's birth, I hobbled onto an airplane with my now five children, four and under, and headed back to Texas to be with Brian. What a sweet reunion that was.

But after the reunion, reality stepped in. How do you parent and care for that many young children's needs? After arriving home, the full weight of what we had done, of where we were and the impossibility of my task ahead, fell squarely on my shoulders.

I still vividly remember the day that cold cereal and I met each other in a standoff, and the cereal won. I was in the bedroom changing Ammon's diaper when I heard giggling. The giggling got steadily louder, and I tried to change that diaper just a little faster. (But it was a bad one.) I had learned that gig-gling meant trouble with those four children. They were so cute together, but boy could they come up with some humdingers. The giggling was now loud laughing, and then, all of a sudden, silence. Then I heard scampering feet and more silence. That was it. I knew something terrible must be going on. I finally fin-ished the diaper, scooped Ammon into my arms and went run-ning toward where the noises used to be coming from. I stopped at the door of the family room and just stared. It became very evident what those children had been up to.

They had emptied several boxes of cold cereal from one end of the family room to the other. I couldn't believe it. Not only was it a huge mess, but cold cereal was so expensive that it was a luxury in our home. I put Ammon down and ran for a broom. As I walked back into that room again and saw the mess, the cereal won. I plunked myself down right in the middle of it all and started to cry. I threw the broom across the room and threw a major temper tantrum. I'm afraid it wasn't even very adult-like. I soon saw my children peaking around the corner. This woman sitting in the middle of the floor was their mother, right? They came in and gathered in my lap, rubbed my face, and told me everything would be okay. They sweetly said that the cereal would go away because they would make it go away. I saw tears starting to come to their eyes, so I knew I had to make this all okay. Of course that is what they were trying to do for me too. Between us all, everything was soon okay, and we ended up laughing until the tears were no longer tears of sadness but tears of joy.

It was also during this time that Brian was gone from five thirty in the morning until eleven at night. He had decided to go back to school and get his master's degree. I had no car and no friends. I was alone, and much of the time, I was like a lost little girl who woke up one day and didn't want to play house anymore because it wasn't fun. But I couldn't just put the toys away and walk away. I was their mother, and I had to get up every morning and face that truth. I think I spent most of my days and nights weeping and feeling sorry for myself. As I wept, I would hold my little Ammon, sing to him, and many times, I would be able to find just a spark of joy by looking into his kind and gentle heart. This is when the character and personality of my little Ammon came to the forefront. He has always been a child who was so tender hearted and loving. He was always the one taking treats and homemade cards to the neighbors. Especially the little elderly ladies down the road who he said had no one to love them.

Shortly after Ammon's birth, complications arose with my health. I took the children and went back to Utah to once again see my doctor. He decided to do exploratory surgery to see what was going on inside, as he was concerned that after four C-sections there might be some scar damage. Brian was not able to come with us, as he was in the middle of his graduate school and could not leave work.

I remember lying on the gurney waiting to go into surgery and wondering what they would find out. I was alone and scared, but I trusted that God was watching over me. After waking up, I received news that made me question for a time those feelings of trust. Was he really watching over me? I was twenty-five years old, and in what seemed but a moment, my childbearing years were over.

The doctor had decided that I had enough scar tissue that it warranted giving me a hysterectomy, and I had five children anyway, so why not. They had tried to get a hold of my husband, but he had been unavailable, so they had made the decision for us.

Just because a doctor says you cannot have any more children does not mean your heart feels it. Just because your body is not working the way it was meant to does not mean your spirit is ready to accept the emptiness that follows. Even during that pregnancy that I was not ready for, I could not get rid of the feeling that there was one more child to come into our home. That one more child was supposed to be my last little girl. Where was she? How was my little girl going to come to me now?

I was shattered. I was not only shattered because of not being able to have more children, but I also felt like I had lost my femininity. If those parts of me that made it possible to have children were gone, and my being a mother was what being a woman was all about, then I was nothing. I was just a shell. How could Brian even love me? Could I even be a mother to those children I already had?

I look back, and I never really doubted that God was there taking care of me, but it is hard to find that place of faith sometimes. It seems to get lost in the struggle of what is hitting you so boldly in the face at the time. But when the questioning is over and you are able to touch again that place in you that for a moment you couldn't find, God is there waiting to give comfort and speak peace. I believe it is this process of questioning and hungering for answers that brings you nearer and nearer to the wonderful understanding of how truly involved he can and is willing to be in our lives. He is there as it says in Isaiah 25:8 to wipe away our tears and in John 14:27 to bring us peace—his peace. I have spent so much of my life's journey going through this process over and over again. Facing life's challenges, questioning if and how my heavenly Father was there in that struggle and then being given the greater gift of faith in a God that truly cares about me, about all of his children.

I felt as if who I was had been torn out of me. It took me years to finally resolve that issue and to truly feel like a woman of worth again. Yes, giving birth is a profound experience, but so many have that power and think nothing of abusing it by abortion or other such things. It took years to understand that there is so much more to truly being a woman than just giving birth. Being a woman and a mother happens every day, in so many different circumstances, and we, as women and mothers, touch so many lives with our gift of love, femininity, power, gentleness, courage, and strength. No surgeon could rob me of those things, only I could. I believe part of the greater plan in all of this was to teach me about womanhood and its great power. How grateful I am for a merciful God who was willing to take a young woman and mold her into something far greater than she could possibly see for herself. But that is later in the story, for at this time, all I could see was that I was bereft of that which I thought made me *me*. I had so much to learn. Thank goodness life itself is such a personal and individual tutoring experience.

So many young couples ponder and talk about how many children they are going to have together. We were no different. We had definite feelings for at least six children. I had dreamt and felt strongly in my heart that there were six children that I was meant to give birth to. When our lives were suddenly changed in the matter of a few minutes, I was confused, frustrated, and even with those five children to love and care for, there was an emptiness in my heart that left me in tears day after day.

So many people said, "Be happy with your five children!" and I was, but those who have experienced this emptiness know and understand that literal aching of your arms to hold your child; the child that is not there. You understand the times you gather all your children around you and just know there is still a child missing. You know what it feels like to constantly be looking for just one more, because surely your children are not all here.

I knew there was still a little girl that was meant to be mine. I prayed over and over, sharing my heartfelt feelings and pleading somehow to have my little girl brought to me and somehow to fill this aching in my heart. I believed he could work any miracle. If he had parted the Red Sea for the Israelites, he could surely bring me my baby girl that I was aching for.

● ●

—*Brian*

I was working in the III Corps Chaplains Office at Fort Hood, Texas, when the call came. It was my father-in-law, and in his usual kind and loving way, he informed me that his daughter, my wife, was safely out of surgery. He continued softly, "Brian, there has been a problem, but Annie Laurie is doing just fine."

So what is the problem? my mind screamed. My thoughts were working about ten times faster than Dad was able to explain. You know how you have a whole conversation during a two second pause on the other end of the telephone line. *What could possibly be wrong, tell me that nothing is wrong with Annie Laurie.* "Brian, the doctor decided that the cause of Annie Laurie's abdominal pain was excessive scar tissue which encased the uterus, so he decided to perform a hysterectomy." He assured me that Annie Laurie would be okay, at least physically.

I entered my superior officer's office and told him the news. He was a very kind and good chaplain and already knew that my wife was in surgery. He suggested that I take a while to be alone. I walked outside with my numbness following right behind. My feelings were mixed. Pregnancies had been undeniably hard, and Annie Laurie seemed to get weaker with every one. I wanted my young wife to be healthy, and I knew with so many precious little children, our together time was very limited. Maybe now we could have the energy and time to focus on other important parts of married and family life.

I was searching for any positive thing to hang on to, but the full reality of the situation soon set in. Annie Laurie would never be settled. She loved our children intensely, but she felt so strongly that there were more. But five children ... surely that was enough.

I am grateful that we cannot see into the future, for I greatly fear that if I could have, I would not have gotten on the plane that was getting ready for departure. I guess you could call it the *gathering plane*. I had absolutely no idea of the growth journey that the two most precious to me, God and Annie Laurie, were about to involve me in.

our little girl

—Annie Laurie

We had made several moves in the seven years that followed. While in Fort Hood, Brian decided to become a chaplain for the military. We could not do that with the army, so we transferred to the navy, where they needed a chaplain badly. We were immediately sent to Rhode Island for chaplaincy training and then on to Miramar, San Diego. Brian's assignment there was to be the chaplain for the largest drug and alcohol rehab center in the armed services. That training was to serve him well in the journey that we had ahead.

At the end of our three years in San Diego, Brian was about to be sent on sea duty. Basically, that meant that we would not see him for three years. That was not the desire of our hearts, so we pursued getting out of the military completely.

Brian had been interested in being a teacher of religion on the high school and college level. We checked into it and found out that it would be available to him. We were very excited. We had been married eleven years, and we were ready for a change in our lives. We wanted a more stable life for our children, and we struggled with some of the lifestyles of the military. So, being a teacher was the perfect place for my husband.

Our first assignment was in Delta, Utah. Our children loved being close to family again, and for the first time, we felt like we might be somewhere more permanent. It was not to be.

During our time in San Diego, and now also in Delta, I was quite ill. The hysterectomy had taken care of nothing. In fact, it only made things worse. This was a hard time for all of us, and I found it very difficult to raise five children from my bed or from the couch. I also had times in the hospital where Brian had to take over and become the mom. At the time, I could not see the blessing. But now I can see what God was doing for all of us. He was creating children who knew how to care for others. They worked hard keeping the house going, even though they were still very young. They learned to take care of Mommy and be sensitive to my pain, both physically and emotionally. They also became independent as individuals and yet more dependent as a family. The importance of working together as a family was planted strongly in their hearts. We were given some of the most valuable gifts we ever received.

* *

—*Annie Laurie and Katie—our daughters*

Delta was such a profound time for us. It is where we learned so many of life's lessons that would prepare us to be compassionate and competent wives, mothers, and older sisters to children who would so desperately need to be loved and understood. We learned the power that came from uniting as a family and trusting in God.

At the time, we didn't realize fully what was going on, but we did know that Mommy was hurting and we needed to be good. We learned to cook and clean in her absence, and when she was home and not feeling well, we knew we should keep smiles on our faces and do whatever we could to help the home run smoothly.

We were off playing in our room one afternoon, when we were all summoned into the family room for what had come to be known as our family council. We sat there at our parents' feet as they opened their hearts to us. They expressed their concerns and worries about our mom's health and how it was affecting our little family. We prayed together and felt that we needed to unite together and decide what we as a family would promise to do so that God could make our mommy better. We decided that we would all continue on with our night and come back together the next evening with some ideas on what that promise should be.

The next day came and there we were, back in our family council. My dad asked us each individually what we had come up with. As we went around the circle, everyone said the same thing. It was amazing! We all felt that we should promise that we would dedicate our family to serving God and his children and we would always listen to his whisperings to serve whenever we could. So that's what we did, and we as a family, have done everything in our power to keep that promise.

Another tender memory we have is coming home from school one afternoon and Mom wasn't there to greet us. We quietly went through the house looking for her, and when we opened the door to her room, it was so dark and still. All we could hear was our mom quietly crying in her bed. We went to her and asked if she was okay. Of course our mother gave the brave reply that everything was just fine, but our little hearts knew different. Mom was hurting and didn't feel good, and so we were hurting too. But it was our hearts that hurt. It was hard to see her in pain and know there wasn't anything we could do. But wait, maybe there was. We could get the house clean and keep the boys quiet. We could make dinner and make sure our mom didn't have to worry about anything.

Even though there were days like this, we also remember our mother's valiant effort to put her struggles on a shelf and be the mom she had always wanted to be. We came home often to the heavenly smell of fresh baked bread, muffins, and cookies, which is still to this day remembered and talked about. Another fond memory brought up at family gatherings is our dinners for breakfast.

Family time had always been important to our parents, and they were always looking for ways to make it happen. Dinners for breakfast was one of those ways, and we all looked forward to it with great anticipation. We would often wake up to beautiful smells wafting into our rooms. We found we were a little more motivated to get out of bed and get ready in record time on those particular mornings. Our mom would wake up extra early before anyone else and make what seemed like a Christmas Day dinner. There would be roast and potatoes or ham and rolls. There would be side dishes galore, and even pies for dessert! We loved it! She wanted so badly to unite our family and create a true home that she would take what little energy she had and do just that. We never knew at the time what a sacrifice it must have been but realize now that these kinds of sacrifices are the very things that have made the gathering possible. It bound us together as a family and kept those ties strong. Now, as each new child is brought into our family, those ties are stretched to include them and bind them to us.

. . . .

—Annie Laurie

There were no medical facilities in Delta that could meet my needs, so, gratefully we were soon moved to a place where I could receive the help that was necessary. I also believe that there was a specific place that we were meant to be in order to find our children, and this was one of the means to get us there. We were moved to Layton, Utah.

So now, seven years had passed since the day of my hysterectomy, when my entire life was changed in a moment. Seven years of preparation to begin a journey that would show us how truly miraculous God's work is here on this earth. A journey that would try every one of us in a wonderfully heart wrenching and yet growing way. A journey defined by one who loves us and who had a plan not only for us but for many others around the world.

Our children were growing up quickly. Andrew and Annie Laurie were now twelve years old and entering the time of their life where their emotions were anything but stable. Katie was eleven and our homebody who just wanted to be within the safe proximity of her family at all times. She was in the sixth grade but chose to stay home to be schooled. Blaine was nine and still the biggest tease alive, and Ammon was the spoiled one. He had his mother wrapped around his finger, and he knew it.

They were all great kids, but each one had been through their own refiner's fire, as they had faced the possibility of a future without a mom and had kept the house running for weeks while Mom was in the hospital or in bed and Dad was at work. We had taught them, and life had taught them, that it took every member of the family working together to make a family really a family. Otherwise, it was just people of different ages living together.

In our church, I taught a group of teenage girls every Sunday. This particular Sunday I walked into my class, and I saw a young woman sitting on the back row whom I had never met before. As I looked her way, I had one of those experiences when you just know what you know and you cannot deny it. I knew she was carrying my little girl. I could not even tell she was pregnant, but I knew. After getting over the shock of having this feeling permeate every part of me, I introduced myself to her and made a valiant effort to continue with class. I don't think my teaching was at its best level that day, as all I could think of was what this all meant and what was I supposed to do about it.

That evening, I still could not get rid of the impression in my heart. I also felt strongly that I needed to call her and have her come live with us for the duration of her pregnancy. Was I crazy? What was I thinking? Was she really even pregnant, and what would she think? And what made me think that I could just call someone and say, "Excuse me, but you are carrying my baby"? Good questions, but when you know something is true and right, what choice do you have but to follow those feelings? So I did.

"Hi, my name is Annie Laurie Richardson, and I met you today in church. Do you remember me?"

She quietly said, "Yes," and then silence.

She wasn't making this easy for me. How was I going to tell her that I felt strongly that I was to be the mother of her child? *It doesn't matter how right this is, she is going to laugh in my face!* Then came the sweet whispering of peace, and I knew I had to do my part, and God would fill in the blanks.

I continued. "I have a feeling that maybe you and I need each other. Is there anything I can help you with?"

At those words, the story all came out in a rush. I found out she was indeed expecting a child, and in fact, that very day had been asked to leave her home. I took a huge chance and shared with her my feelings that she was carrying our little girl. I told her that I had not been able to have any more children, but that maybe, with God's help, this situation could be turned into a blessing for all of us. I look back on that and am so surprised that she did not burst out laughing, or at the very least, hang up on me.

Instead, she agreed that it felt like it was the truth, but unfortunately, just days before she had promised that child to someone else. She would not go back on that promise.

I talked to her parents to make sure they were okay with all of this, and the next day she moved in. Talk about throwing your family a curveball. I had not only brought some stranger into our home, but she was unwed and pregnant. They also knew that I felt her baby was ours; their new little sister. I also expected them to treat this young girl as one of the family. Is that too much to ask? To give your life and heart to someone and an idea that your mother believes in? What did I, as a mother, expect? I expected them to just get down to the business of being obedient to the will of God. Amazingly, they did.

This was especially true of my Katie, who was home with us every day. She put her whole heart into helping that young mother feel accepted. It was a struggle for her because she had so looked forward to her time at home alone with her mother. Now there was this stranger who was very needy and took her mother away every day in one way or another. We talked together, and I explained to Katie that I understood her feelings but I really needed her to step outside of herself and give. She was eleven, and yet I remember walking away from that conversation and knowing she would do as I had asked. She might struggle, but I knew that between that sweet girl and her Father in heaven, it would be done.

I guess that is how we have always been with our children.

We had made it a practice to talk to our children about all of our challenges. They pretty much knew our financial concerns, so we never had to say no on anything, because they knew not to ask. We had prayed so often about my health and they had witnessed so many answers to those prayers that they knew there was a God and that he worked intimately with our family. There was never any question in their mind that if we as parents felt we had been asked to do something, no matter how hard it was, then we as a family would do it, whatever the sacrifice and whatever the cost.

In those days, you did not get ultrasounds unless you had an emergency, so we did not know the sex of the child that she was carrying. But I knew. So, we had fun shopping for little baby girl clothes and dreaming. The young mother kept reminding me that this baby was already promised to another, but I would just smile and say, "We'll see." I knew we would get our miracle.

As the time drew near for the birth of this baby, my prayers increased, and I was more and more convinced that there was a miracle for us. Thinking to help with that miracle, I found out who the attorney was who was handling the adoption and called him to see if I could please talk to the adoptive parents. I figured that if I told them that this was my little girl and that I had been told that by God, they would then say, "No problem, she is yours."

I received permission to talk to the father. I called him and very convincingly shared with him my heart. I was all ready to hear him say that by all means please take this baby if that is how you feel. But instead, he began to weep and simply said to me, "Please, don't do this to my wife, she has had enough heartbreak already. Please don't do this!"

I sat there stunned. This is not what I had planned. Surely, this is not what God had planned. Weren't they supposed to feel the rightness of what I was saying and just quietly say okay? Where was our miracle?

I spent the next twenty-four hours praying and pleading. I

remember so clearly late that night sitting in my car in the church parking lot. It was two in the morning, and I was alone, confused, scared, and trying with everything I had to hold on to my faith. As I pounded the steering wheel and yelled and cried into the night, a story quietly came into my mind.

I saw King Solomon as he sat on his throne. Two women came and stood in front of him, one holding tightly to a baby. They each presented their case. Each of the mothers claimed that the baby was rightfully theirs. Then I heard the decree of the king. "Cut the baby in half that each mother might have a portion of the baby." The true mother stepped forward and gave up that child that he might not be harmed. The king then decreed that he now knew who the true mother was and gave the child to the mother who had been willing to give it up to save its life.

I knew immediately what I must do. I had to call that heartbroken father and give up that child.

Now, I must admit that in the back of my mind I thought for sure that once I had made this sacrifice, as the woman in the story, God would then work his miracle and I would ultimately receive my little girl. I made that call and listened to the grateful weeping of a rejoicing father and wondered.

A few days later, the young mother's pains started, and we rushed to the hospital. I helped her through her labor. I was there for the birth. I cut the cord. I gave that beautiful little baby girl her first bath, and I looked into her eyes and felt her spirit. Then I placed that little one in someone else's arms and walked away.

I look back on that time and realize that I was so caught up in what I was feeling that I paid little attention to what the young mother was feeling. I knew she was anxious to get on with life, but at the same time, this was flesh of her flesh that she was giving away, never to see or hold again. I have talked to young unwed mothers since and have much more compassion now for the turmoil that they go through in order to make this decision in behalf of their child. I so admire her compassion for her child's future. She knew that what she had to offer was not going to be enough to raise this daughter, and she did the best thing she knew how to do. She put that little girl up for adoption and chose a family that would love her as their own. In a way, that little girl had three mothers who loved her—her birth mother, her real mother, and me. We all played a part in her life and have loved her in our own way.

That night, again, in the wee hours of the morning, I was in my car, in the same parking lot, pounding the same steering wheel and yelling and crying into the night. Where was our miracle? Was I wrong in my first impressions that were so clear and powerful? How was he going to bind up my grieving mother's heart? It was at that point that a loving Father in heaven worked his miracle. I will never forget the words that came into my mind. "Because you have been willing to give up this precious little baby, I will multiply your gift of motherhood until you have no more room to hold it." An incredible peace followed those words, and I felt my heart being bound up and healed.

My tears were wiped dry, and I knew that God did not lie and he had a plan for me and my family, a plan that would bring me more joy in my mothering than I could begin to understand at that time. I did not know how that would happen; I just knew it would.

I spent the next sixteen years waiting and looking for that baby. Looking for the miracle that I felt was going to be sent to me. These were sixteen years of wondering each time a child came into our home if this was my little miracle girl—but I get ahead of myself—for with the miracle that would after sixteen years bring that little girl to me, so many other miracles were able to be performed. I have learned that he has a much greater purpose in life for us if we are willing to say, "Thy will be done."

the three vietnamese

—*Annie Laurie*

It had been five years since that night in the car when I had been given my miracle. But as so often happens when miracles come into our lives, it takes time to understand all that he has planned. At the time, I assumed that the miracle would be obvious. The miracle would surely be that we would immediately be brought another little baby girl to fill the emptiness. I knew he understood how hard it had been to give up that little girl, and surely he would not want me to suffer longer than necessary. Isn't that how it works? I was sure of it, but those five years brought one dead end after another. We were getting older, our children were getting older, and my arms were still aching from the emptiness and the longing for our little girl.

I am afraid that once again I was so wrapped up in my own sorrow and yearning to understand and accept God's will in all of this that I did not pay much attention to what was happening with my children. I withdrew into a place where I did not have to feel the pain and just tried to get on with life and expected the same from them.

We all have regrets as we struggle through the challenges of this life, and that will always be one of my regrets. I wish I had been able to see past my own grief into the hearts of my children.

During those five years, as we were trying to deal with our loss, I decided to try my hand at teaching. I had no degrees other than high school, but I wanted to be involved in my children's schooling. I applied at a new private school that was being formed, and they hired me as their junior teacher. I would teach the children who were ages nine to eleven. This was a new experience for me, but I loved it. It was a way to express who I was becoming inside. I had fifty students in my class the first year and a hundred in my class the second year. I found I had a gift for taking students who were troubled or who hated school or just were there because their mom said they had to be and filling their lives with a love of learning and a love for themselves and for God. You could hear a pin drop in the classroom as those hundred kids listened to the stories of times past. I loved watching a child, who had previously felt they were nothing, come to life as they worked as a group leader and found love and acceptance from their classmates. For me, that was what it was all about in that classroom. I wanted them to feel loved and accepted. Wonderful things happened.

After two years of doing this for someone else, I felt strongly that I needed to organize my own private school. I was scared to death. I had no degree that said I was qualified. But I guess that wasn't important to God. I knew I would have to have the total support of my family if I was to succeed. I certainly had never done anything like this before. I was just a normal lady living a normal life. What made me think that I could run, teach, and be responsible for a school that would teach other people's children?

People used to ask me how I did it. "How do you teach sixty children between the ages of ten and eighteen, in one classroom, and have them all come out with a love of learning and feeling like they have been fed in every area of their lives?" I didn't know how to answer that question back then, but I do now. Father was just multiplying my gift of motherhood like he promised; for that is how I taught. Class was just an extension of my home, and I was their mother away from home. I said that to my students often. They were my children, and I loved, taught, and disciplined them as such.

Of course, all my children were right there by my side supporting me in all that I was doing. Andrew and Annie Laurie were now sixteen. I taught the senior group of ten to eighteen-year-olds. Andrew became my classroom assistant and also taught a small group of boys with learning disabilities. Annie Laurie had a class of twenty-five students that she was in charge of. Their ages ranged from eight to twelve, depending upon their scholastic abilities. Katie, who was fifteen, had a class of twelve young ones who were five to seven years in age. My children had no formal training. They were just my children, and so if I could do it, so could they. I certainly could not do it on my own, and who I wanted with me were my children. Blaine and Ammon were thirteen and twelve, and I loved being their teacher. They were my greatest supports in the class.

As I look back at this time with that wonderful gift of hindsight, I can see so much more. Every day we went to school and worked with all types of children; children with disabilities such as ADD, ADHD, dyslexia, broken homes, failure to thrive in this modern world, and children who were brilliant and just needed direction to bring that out. We also brought together all different personalities and turned them into a cohesive group that could face life's challenges, just like the many personal and scholastic challenges they faced in class, with excitement and with hope and faith in their personal future. We did not know how to do that. We didn't even realize that we were doing that at the time. But our little family was being prepared with hands-on experience to do a great work.

But in a very sweet way, the students gave us another gift; the gift of tangible hands to hold and hearts that cared when he could not be there himself. Hands and hearts that would resemble so closely hands and hearts all over the world waiting to be found and loved.

· ·

It was now Christmas Eve of 1996, and even with all of our tutoring, we still were unprepared for what was about to take place in our lives.

I was busy preparing the big meal for our traditional Christmas Eve celebration. We were staying home as a family this year instead of going to our parents' home. All the gifts were ready, and I was so pleased because I had prepared early and could finally have a relaxing Christmas.

I heard the phone ring but didn't pay much attention, as I knew there were probably children racing from all corners of the house in order to be the first to answer it. If I was needed, they would find me. Sure enough, soon, one of my children came into the kitchen carrying the phone and saying it was for me. I didn't really want to talk so I mouthed, "Who is it?" They shook their head, letting me know that they had no idea who it was.

Little did I know, as I reached for that phone and spoke that simple word *hello,* we started a journey that has sent us around the world, opened our eyes to true poverty in every sense of the word, and brought us joy beyond measure as well as devastating heartache that sometimes stole our desire to go on living. But mostly it took our little family and put us in the way for the windows of heaven to pour out such great blessings and miracles that we could scarcely hold them all. With the answering of that phone, the miracle and gift of the gathering began!

"Hello, you don't know me, but I was told that you might be interested in adopting three little Vietnamese children whose mother was just murdered…"

I must be hearing this wrong? How could this be? They must have a wrong number. I'm not ready for this! I remember my heart wrenching inside me as I heard the story of three little children being found crawling and crying over their mother's body after the father had brutally murdered her. After the first shock passed, the trauma that they must be going through tore my heart apart. I immediately felt my arms aching to encircle them. I so wanted to bring those three little ones into our home, into a mother's loving arms.

I was told that one of the children was a five-year-old girl who, by chance, had been born the very day that my little lost girl had been born and was exactly the age she would have been. I thought for sure it was a sign. Then, there were two more little boys who were eighteen months and three years old. Once I could finally speak again, I told them I must talk to my husband and would call them back and let them know.

I stared at the phone wondering how to tell Brian what I was feeling inside. How do I tell the children? Here was our miracle. Here was the multiplying of my motherhood, for there was not just my one little girl but three children. I went to find Brian.

"No!" How could he say *no?* My mind was reeling. Brian had said *no!* He was not ready. He was afraid, and I must admit, so was I. I was afraid to pursue it and afraid not to pursue it. We were overwhelmed with the idea of how to help these little ones recover from such a traumatic beginning to their lives. Can a child ever heal from that? How would it affect our other children? Was it fair to them? What would the stress do to our marriage? So many questions, and besides, it was Christmas, for goodness sake. How do you change your life so completely in the middle of a holiday?

I called the lady back and said thank you but we just were not interested at this time, and I hung up. I washed my hands of the whole affair, and I figured now we could just put it all behind us and go on with celebrating the Lord's birth the way we always had. Right?

All night and all Christmas day, the thought of those three little ones plagued my mind and heart. I could not sleep, I could not focus on gift giving, and that meal I had so carefully created was not even tasted. I just kept running to my room with tears that I could not hold back filling my eyes. I would then drop to my knees by my bed to petition God one more time to please tell me what we should do.

Christmas afternoon, I finally could take it no longer, and I told Brian I had to call and I had to visit with these three children. I told him that would be the only way that I would know what to do. I asked if he wanted to come with me.

I couldn't help but think how on that first Christmas years ago a mother held her little son in her arms, a son that would save the world with his offering and sacrifice, a savior who loved little children and asked us to feed his little ones. Well, that Christmas night found us in a home where we knew no one, but where there were three beautiful little Vietnamese children, three of God's precious children, on our laps.

Little five-year-old Emily with her straight, black hair and sweet smile was so full of life. She giggled and laughed and wanted to be hugged and tickled over and over. What was that beautiful smile hiding? Could I help her?

Richard was three and just darling. He also loved to laugh, and I could hardly bear that his mother was not going to be able to raise him.

The eighteen-month-old was also a little boy named Rich-ley who looked terribly lost. His world had changed so quickly, and you could tell he just didn't know how to deal with it. He cried a lot. Oh, how I wanted to bring them home that minute. I was so sure that this was our miracle.

We were told they were available for adoption through the state and that we could have them, but we would have to get licensed with the state. Okay, I would do anything!

Over the next couple of weeks, we feverishly worked on getting the long arduous process of being licensed with the state completed. Once again I threw my family into chaos and into one trauma after another. Social workers came into our home, asked us questions, asked our children questions, and we had to disclose everything about us and our families. We felt invaded, put under a microscope, and exposed. But it was worth it, for we were going to finally be blessed with children, three beautiful Vietnamese children.

We had all fallen in love with them, and they with us. We never tired of hearing their laughter ringing through our home and the patter of their feet as they ran from one of us to the next. We would constantly catch each other's eye and give a look of wonder that they were actually going to be ours.

And then one terrible day, the kind of day we had never experienced up to that point and yet over the next few years we would become all too familiar with, we were called into DCFS (Division of Child and Family Services) for an appointment.

"We have decided that these children must go to someone else who can properly parent them. We have found a couple where the mother is half Vietnamese, and we feel she will be much more qualified than you to take care of their needs."

Much more *qualified!* Much more *qualified!* What makes a mother *qualified?* I would love them, I would serve them, I would teach them of a loving God who knew them personally, and I would hold them when they cried. I would be a mother! But no, my skin color and my heritage stood in the way. *Father, why ... oh, why?*

We had to say good-bye to those children, and I thought the tears would never stop.

I heard a story once about a young boy who lived on an island. He had a wonderful teacher, who he loved very much. One day it came time for that teacher to leave the island. The little boy would miss her so much and wanted to give her something that would show his love and gratitude for all she had given him. That last day of school, the teacher noticed the young boy was not there. She was very surprised as she knew how much he loved school. The next morning, as she was getting ready to leave, the young boy came hurrying toward the teacher. He held something in his hand. As he placed his gift to her in her hand, she saw a beautiful shell. It was a rare shell, one that she knew was only found clear on the other side of the island. She asked him how he could have ever found this wonderful shell, as he would have had to walk clear around the island to get it. He looked at her with love in his eyes and said, "Long walk part of gift." As tears filled the teacher's eyes, she understood why he was not there at school. It had taken him all day and all night to get that particular gift for his beloved teacher. That long walk, that great sacrifice, was part of the gift.

Part of the gift we bring to each of our children is the long walk it took to get them. Each of their stories is filled with miracles and with those serious challenges and heavy trials that took us to our limit. But also, a part of each one of those long walk experiences is the gift that God gave to us. Every gut-wrenching and heart-searing step was also felt by him, and I can't help but wonder how many of those steps were made lighter because he carried most of the burden. The gifts of love, compassion, understanding, wisdom, faith, and charity that we have been given could have come in no other way for us. My eyes fill often with tears of gratitude as understanding comes to me and I more fully understand the gift of the long walk.

But I get ahead of myself, for as we said good-bye to those three beautiful children, it did not seem like there was a gift at all, just pain, unbearable pain.

I fought for months to get those children back into our

home but only hit dead ends. I would leave school every day, and the kids and I would drive by the home that they were living in just for a chance that we might be able to get a glimpse at them. We would sit in the car and cry and dream of them coming back to us. We never saw or heard of them again.

Because we were now a part of the foster care program, over the next six months we were offered about twenty-five different children. They always seemed to fall through at the last minute. By this time, we were so raw that we finally called DCFS and said that we were through. We asked them to please not call us for any more children. Brian and I had talked about it and decided that, for whatever reason, maybe we just were not meant to have any more children. We had been blessed abundantly with the five we already had, and it was just time to get on with life. Ah! Now the peace could come!

Two days later we received a call from DCFS.

the four little ones

—Annie Laurie

"We have four children who have just been removed from their home because of drug addiction and neglect. The father is in jail. They are ages three, two, one, and six weeks. They are up for adoption. Would you be interested in coming and getting these children right now?"

Wait! What do we do now? We had finally resigned ourselves that there were no more children for us. Could we possibly open our hearts again? Could this be the miracle?

I told them I would call them back in five minutes and rushed out to tell Brian.

It was one of those experiences where it does not matter what you and your husband say to each other, you cannot say the right thing? A tangible darkness could be felt, and it literally was as if we were speaking two different languages. I finally gave up and left the room to call and tell them that no we did not want these children and ask for them to just leave us alone.

How grateful I am that God's power is greater than we are. I dialed the number, and I began to speak. "We would love to have these children. Where do we go?" I was stunned. What had I done?

They gave me directions to the shelter that they had been taken to, and we were told to please come quickly and get them to cause them as little trauma as possible. *Trauma?* Who was having trauma? I was having trauma! Did anyone care that I now had to go tell my husband what had occurred, and us still speaking two different languages?

I hung up the phone, and with fear and trembling, I went to tell Brian what I had done. Yes, we were still speaking a different language! We could not even be in the same room without conflict. What were we supposed to do? How could I know for sure? This wasn't just a where-do-I-find-my-lost-keys kind of question. With all the chaos in my mind, one thought kept coming through. Just get in the car and go and get these children. I finally decided I would do just that or I would never have peace again. We could decide later if we wanted to keep them.

In the meantime, Brian had decided the same thing, and we both headed separately out to the car where we met. After overcoming our shock at meeting face to face on the driver's side of the suburban, we just got into the car. We didn't even dare talk, as we knew there would be no possibility of communication at that point. We just headed out and were both obedient to that feeling in our hearts that we must do this thing.

At this time, our two daughters, Annie Laurie and Katie, were in England visiting with their grandparents for the summer. Andrew was off doing what seventeen-year-olds do, working and being with friends. But our two younger boys, Ammon and Blaine, were with us and wanted to go. I anxiously said yes, having no idea what we would be facing when we got to the shelter.

I remember so clearly walking into that shelter. I did not want to be there. I was screaming inside, *What are you doing?* I wanted to run. This is not what I thought it would feel like when I found my children. Where was the peace, the calm, the confidence? This was just blind obedience to a power greater than my ability to say no.

I looked at those three little ones sitting at a small table eating food, and I felt nothing but dismay at what we were doing. These children could not possibly be who heavenly Father wanted us to raise as our own.

The little three-year-old boy had a four-inch-long, curly, blond ponytail hanging down his back. His eyes looked old, like they had just had too much to deal with to be a child ever again. The two-year-old girl's hair was straggly and wispy, and her face was filthy. Her clothes looked like rags, and she just stared at me, daring me to come any closer. The little one-year-old boy was just sitting, face filthy, and with no expression on his tear-stained face at all.

I turned to the worker wanting to yell at her to just let me go home. I couldn't bear the pain I saw in those eyes. I could not bear the feeling of that shelter and knowing that they were there instead of in a safe home with parents who would care for them and love them. *I was not ready for this!* I screamed. But the scream was never heard.

Instead, the worker placed a tiny four-pound, little six-week-old girl in my arms. I could hardly hold her. She was so tiny, and it terrified me. I thought for sure she would break, and I thought, *What an ugly little thing she is. This is not what my little girl is supposed to look like.* I, who was supposed to be such a loving mother, could hardly bear to have her in my arms.

It all happened so fast. All of a sudden, we were back in

the car with those four little ones, and neither one of us could believe what we had done. We still could not speak to each other. We had done all of this in almost complete silence, each struggling inside with our thoughts and fears.

On that long drive home, the little two-year-old girl never stopped talking. She talked about how her mother hated her, how her parents fought until there was blood on her mom, how she did not want to live with them anymore, how the police had come and taken them away, and on and on. I kept looking at her in the rearview mirror, and then I would look at Brian and think, *There is no way that I can deal with this. This is not what we wanted. These children could not be ours. This is most certainly not my miracle.*

Brian and I finally spoke to each other, and all we could say was that as soon as we got home, we would drop off our two older boys and then turn around and take them back and tell them it just was not going to work.

Ah! What a relief. That felt better, didn't it? Didn't it?

We arrived home and decided we would just bring them in for a moment before heading back to the shelter. I walked into our home, and it was at that moment that a loving heavenly Father stepped in and gave us one of those sweet miracles that changes everything. I had the most overwhelming feeling of love for those four little children come over me and an absolute assurance that they were being given to me by God and that they would be ours forever. It was so strong that no matter what the future would hold, I could never deny it.

How grateful I am for that miraculous tender mercy, for that absolute assurance gave me the faith to keep going, even when that faith was tried and tried over and over again. When all would look lost, and when many would say to just give up, I would go back to that moment as I walked through the door, when I had been told those four little ones were mine. I knew what I knew, and it gave me the faith to leave the details to God.

* *

—*Brian*

It was quite an adjustment having little children in the home again, because we were at the stage of life when our youngest was nearing his teenage years. No more diapers, no more middle of the night feedings; we could sleep in on Saturday mornings. Life on the surface was pretty easy.

After a few days it became apparent that these little children had experienced some serious emotional trauma and physical neglect. I felt compassion for these young souls whose world was filled with fear. My compassion grew into care, and my care into love. I was falling in love with these little strangers. My love began to extend past the boundaries of my DNA and blood ties. Even though the workload increased and our life of ease was quickly disappearing, my love for these real, living, breathing, and feeling little people was becoming real and tangible.

* *

—*Annie Laurie*

The next three weeks were a blissful dream. How could we have been so blessed? Never have children received more attention, more love. Every day was a gift of joy.

And then we received a call from DCFS.

"We are so sorry, but you are not going to be able to keep these children, as we have found a relation who has agreed to take them. We will be there in an hour to get them. We feel that a family member will be much more qualified to take care of their needs."

Much more qualified? What makes a mother qualified? It

was not my skin color this time; it was the blood that flowed in my veins that stood in the way. *Father, why?*

We had to say good-bye to those children, and I thought the tears would never stop.

That was a hard day for the entire family. They had called us in the morning and picked the children up an hour later. Brian was at work crying his way through the day, and my two boys and I were doing the same at home.

Every minute of every day, my heart cried out the questions, "Where are you? What do I do with what I felt about these children? Are they not ours? Do you hear this pleading child of yours? Where are you?"

I look back at those times now and can truly see the hand of God in every step of the way, but at the time, all I could feel was the pain of being forgotten by one who had promised to always be there.

Eight weeks passed in a fog of wondering and despair. Then once again, we received a call from DCFS.

"The family placement that we made for these four children did not work out. Would you be willing to take these children into your home once again?"

Would we be willing? Where do we go? What do we do? Yes, a thousand times, *yes!* In the space of a moment, all those wonderings and heartaches were gone as if never there, and we rejoiced. Our joy knew no bounds, and we knew that life was sweet and that God truly was God.

It was at this point that the dream of a lifetime and the worst possible nightmare began for our family.

the journey

—*Annie Laurie*

DCFS had told us from the beginning that this was going to be a cut-and-dried case. These children would definitely be able to be adopted within six months. Their father was in jail because of drugs, and their mother had been turned in by a neighbor because of neglect and was herself addicted to methamphetamines. She had taken meth during each pregnancy and seriously compromised the lives of these children. (I will use the names that those children have now to protect them.) Benjamin, our one-year-old, was a fetal alcohol baby. Brian, the three-year-old had ADD, and the baby, Rebekah, was addicted to meth. Clarissa, the two-year-old, was so totally messed up emotionally that I wondered if her heart could ever be salvaged. These children needed a safe place to be.

We had taken them in on those terms of eminent adoption. But all of a sudden, all of that changed. They told us that reunification was the best thing for these children. Even though their parents were drug addicts, abusive, and even though they had neglected and exposed them to unthinkable situations, they would ultimately be more qualified to raise these children.

There was that word again. *Qualified!* What did it mean? What *qualified* you to be a mother, a father, a family?

What qualifies you to tell a child that you love them, that you want them as your own, and then over and over again send them away? Send them away to a place where you know they will not receive proper care, they will be told lies, and though they are loved in that place, the love is a selfish love, a love that is not really about them but about addictions, dysfunction, and pain. So much pain!

What qualifies you to bring them home again into your arms and bind the wounds, heal the hearts, answer the questions, and then send them back again? Back to more pain, more sorrow, and more questions of why?

For eighteen months, this was our life. This was the life of those beautiful children. I understand the need for visitation rights with the birthparents, but how do you help a child move on in life, to cope with the rollercoaster of feelings that are always there? How do you teach them, and how do you teach yourself? We were trying to teach them about a God of love when we, as the adults, were struggling with everything we had to understand that love ourselves.

How do you teach your other children, who are watching all of this happen, to be at peace and to trust that it is in God's hands? How do you continue every day to believe that it truly is in his hands when at every turn, from our perspective, God's will is being overridden by a government organization called DCFS?

Now don't get me wrong. I believe there are many wonderful people in DCFS. I believe they are trying to do the right thing, but the very nature of their job—families falling apart, drugs, abuse, neglect, pain, and heartache on every side—makes it an impossible job. I don't know how they do it day after day.

But for our family, this process was one nightmare after another with moments of absolute joy interspersed. These joy-filled moments are what kept us hanging on to a dream. A dream that someday, if we were just faithful enough, they truly would be ours and that feeling I had as we walked into our home that first night would be real.

We very quickly understood the pain and the incredible joy that came as it was time for another visit with the *biological* parents. We would dress the boys so handsome and do the girls' hair so pretty, hoping to somehow help them feel special in a world that made them feel abandoned. My daughters and I would cry every time as we did this. We never seemed to get over that. We would then put them in the car, and it was always a very silent ride as we drove them to their visit. It is interesting that there are roads that I still cannot drive down without weeping. As we dropped them off, I would feel as if my heart would break.

But then an hour, a day, a weekend later, I would make that same trip, and at the end would be those children. They would wrap their arms around my neck, and I would feel such exquisite joy just to have them for one more day in my life.

· ·

—Brian

By this time, my trust for DCFS had dwindled, and I wanted little to do with them. My feelings of protecting my wife and children from pain grew stronger, and I wanted desperately to break all ties with the government agency that was in reality just scrambling to help these little displaced children find some stability and love. I guess it's true that you really can't exercise your Christianity until someone is in your face or until someone does you wrong.

This time of visitations was one of the most difficult challenges of my life up to that point. It was so frustrating and felt unfair. Here we were, stepping forward to help four little children in a very heartbreaking and neglect-filled situation. But so often it seemed that the attitude expressed was, "If you don't like our decisions, we'll just get someone else to take the kids."

In retrospect, a large portion of my problems were caused by my egotistical pride. My heart was more concerned about how *I* and how *my* family were being treated. Annie Laurie's hurt was a constant, but she had the ability to see beyond the hurts and frustration. She continued to trust God.

• •

—*Annie Laurie*

How do I describe the joy that we felt the night my Brian decided to take me on a very romantic, expensive date to a very elite restaurant. We did not have a great deal of money, as my husband was a schoolteacher, so this was a rare occasion to go out this fancy. We got all dressed up in our finery and were ready to leave the house.

As we said good-bye to the children, I looked down at our little baby, she was about six months old at the time, and then I looked at Brian and he looked at me, and we both knew there was no leaving that little girl behind. We dressed her in her fanciest, fluffiest, laciest pink dress. We put a little bow on her head—we could not put it in her hair as she was bald as a cue ball—and left for our romantic date. We were like two young parents with their first baby. We spent the whole night *oohing* and *aahing* and doing whatever it took to get her to smile or to laugh. I am sure the food was wonderful that night, but all I know is that we had with us the most beautiful baby in the world, and for that moment, she was ours, completely ours.

sarah

—*Annie Laurie*

We must take another step back in time to when we were recovering from the loss of our three little Vietnamese.

At this same time, we had a troubled family who was living with us. It was a mother and her two children. The young girl, eleven, and the young boy, nine, had been coming to my private school. One day after school, no one came to pick them up. We waited for several hours but still no one came, so I finally took them home, not knowing what else to do. They did not leave our home again for nine months.

We finally found their mother late that night in the psychiatric ward at the hospital. She had checked herself in that day and had not been together enough to let anyone know. This sweet mother had suffered years of satanic, ritualistic abuse at the hands of her family. So had these children, and they were struggling to face each day. We talked to their church leaders and found out that the whole congregation had been praying that some family would step forward and be willing to take them in and help them. We prayed as a family once again, and all were in support of being the answer to those prayers. When the mother came home a few days later, we put her in a room by herself and doubled up the other kids. It would be good practice, for they would never have rooms to themselves again while living at home.

A couple of months later, the four little ones came, then left, and then came again. This little family was there for all of that, and as we struggled to help them through their trauma, I think seeing what we were going through and having to empathize with someone else's pain helped them to get on the road of healing just a little bit. I say again that God is amazing. Yes, it was hard to have all this going on in my home at the same time, but our promise was that we would help his children, and so he brought suffering children together to cry, to grow, and to learn.

It was just before Christmas, once again, when this family left our home to start fresh in their new life. I breathed a sigh of relief and thought that maybe I would have just a little bit of a breather. We were still going through so much with the four little ones, but I at least could have my plate lightened for a moment. It had been one year since that call that had started all of this by asking us to come see three little abandoned children. In that year, we had lost those three children, been offered and lost twenty-five different children through DCFS, and had this little lost family move in with us with all the myriad of issues that entailed. We had gone through the receiving, losing, and receiving again of the four little ones. We had also decided to move my private school into our home so that it would be easier to have the children with me. So, three days a week, fifty kids came to our home to be schooled, and amongst all of that, we were trying to raise five teenagers who were immensely supportive and yet had all of their own traumas going on, but most importantly, we were desperately trying to keep a marriage alive and well amongst the incredible stresses of our life.

Didn't we deserve a break?

Three days later, the day before Christmas, another blessing came into our life. A blessing that would bring challenges and, yet, would be the blessing I had asked for in many prayers, to help accomplish all that was going to be asked of us over the next few years.

As we have said, Katie and Annie Laurie went to England to be with their grandparents for the summer in order to help with their process of healing.

Our Katie was sixteen at that time. She had never really had very many friends, as she was a homebody and she and Annie Laurie were inseparable. But while she was in England, she became very close to my dad's secretary, Sarah. Sarah was twenty-five years old, but the age difference meant nothing to them. The two of them got along so well that as Katie left, they promised to see each at Christmas time.

We met Sarah at the airport that evening, and as I said hello to her, I had the strongest feeling come over me that she was here to stay and that she was to be a permanent part of our family Now, I knew that she had a family back in England, and she was twenty-five, for Pete's sake. You don't just adopt twenty-five-year-olds every day. But being who I am, I wasted no time acting on the feeling. I asked her on the way home if she had ever thought about just staying with us in America. My family stared at me, wondering what I was cooking up this time.

Sarah grew up in a little town in England called Rugby. Even though she loved her family, in the back of her mind, there was always the thought of another family with many children. Sometimes she would long for these children, wondering who they were and where they were. All she knew was that they were real.

My father, who she was working for at this time, had pictures of our children on his wall at work. It was on that wall that she found the family she had been looking for all those years. When she met our family that day at the airport, she said she felt like she had come home. She has been with us ever since.

Sarah has been an incredible gift from God to us. We would never think to take her away from her parents in England, but she has become so much a part of our family that it is as if she was born to us. In fact, many times we forget that she does not have the same growing up memories that we share. She is one of our three unofficial adoptions. She and her husband, Joseph, are incredibly loyal. Sarah has been there taking care of our children as I have traveled all over the world having to be gone for weeks and even months at a time. They have sacrificed much as they have helped to pay for some of these adoptions also. Their hearts are so much at one with ours that we have chosen to live on the same two hundred acres and share our futures together for the rest of our lives. We are their children's grandparents.

But the journey of accepting Sarah fully into our family, for all of us, was full of turmoil and challenges. She was a young woman who was very troubled and emotionally immature. The demands that Sarah unknowingly made on me as her mother taxed to the limit a marriage that was already under incredible pressure. But thankfully, God gave me, as her mother, a window into her soul. That was one of the greatest miracles in all of this, for had he not done that, I could not have given her the love, support, guidance, and mothering that she so desperately hungered for.

My other children were already struggling with all that had been thrust upon their young hearts. They so desperately wanted to support their parents in all that we felt to do. I mean, all of a sudden they had to change diapers, share rooms, have their things ruined, babysit, watch their parents cry, stay up nights with sick children, and give up any alone time that they ever thought of having. Now we were asking them to emotionally step aside as another adult came into the home and, instead of filling the role of an adult, she became another one of the teenagers, only because of Sarah's great need for love and emotional support, she robbed them again and again of their mother's already very spread thin time. They hated and loved her at the same time.

My poor Katie, who had loved Sarah so much, found herself regretting the day she ever decided to bring her home. Katie had always been my special companion because she was shy and a mommy's girl. She had received special attention from both her mom and her dad because she was so easy to spoil. But now she felt like she had lost that place forever.

We had always pulled together in hard times, but none of us knew how to pull together in this situation with Sarah. Each one of us tried, but as yet, we were unprepared for what we were being asked to do.

Now, I must say in Sarah's behalf that all she really wanted was to be a part of the family, but most especially to be my daughter. She had no idea that she was causing all this turmoil, and once she realized it, she spent the next several years working on repairing the damage. The Sarah today is a very different person from the one who stepped off that plane. She is now truly one of us and is loved by everyone. In fact, my other older children often say how grateful they are that Sarah came into our lives, as she has brought so many gifts with her. Her greatest gift in their eyes is her love and support of their parents' dream—gathering our family. When they have not been able to be there on a consistent basis because they were starting their own lives, they have been grateful that Sarah was always there at our side making things as easy as she possibly could.

So at this time of joy and heartache, we gathered one more to us that God knew would be a great blessing if we would be patient and follow his whisperings.

the journey continues

—Brian

This part of our story is especially difficult to talk about. We were doing all we could to help these little wounded children. They had seen, heard, and experienced things no one, especially children, should be exposed to. They had been exposed to pornographic movies. They were physically abused. According to their young memories, they rarely had enough food prepared for them. They lived in fear and neglect. Through all of this, DCFS often seemed to be unaware of the danger the children were in. The biological parents were struggling with addictions to meth, and I'm sure, various other substances as well.

It was at this time that DCFS decided to change the children's status from adoptive placement to reunification. We did not know what to feel, because this was a family and they should be put back together if possible. We are grateful that a governmental agency does not have the right or power to simply take children from their parents and give, place, or assign them to someone of their choosing. On the other hand, if children are really at risk, really in danger, then we believe something must be done.

The reports we'd get from the children after weekend visits were hard to hear. But these were just little children, with little children perspectives, so how accurate were these stories? The children would tell us that Mommy and Daddy had lots and lots of friends at their house. They said that lots of these big people would stay all night and sleep on the couch or floor, or even in the rooms where the children stayed. We asked, "Where were your mommy and daddy when these people were there?" Answer: "They left the people there," or, "They were yelling at each other and slamming doors, and then they left." They'd say, "We were really scared because the people were smoking a lot and being mean and loud." With these innocent reports, our concerns for their safety grew with each visit.

Now that the children are older and they openly recall, in great detail, many of the situations, our concerns for them at the time are confirmed. I wish they did not remember, but they do. They remember with their hearts, and it is to this day painful.

The children would plead with us to stay home and to please not go on a visit this time. They would be very sad on the way home. The baby would scream and just go wild in her little car seat. One time she was out of control and frantic for Annie Laurie to hold her. The other little children began to cry and just kept saying, "Let's go home; can we go home now?" "I want my bed," "Where's my Katie and Missie?" "Where's Blainey?" I remember on one occasion, Annie Laurie took the baby out of her car seat to comfort her for a moment or two. Some other person in the car next to us observed this and went berserk. She swerved within inches of our vehicle while shaking her fist at my wife for daring to have a child out of a car restraint. She reported us, and after that terrible drive home, two policemen showed up at our door and informed us of the complaint. They asked me if we had a child out of the car seat, and I told the truth but was afraid to tell why for fear of retribution by DCFS. We ended up paying a sizeable fine. By this time, we were afraid to do anything that might jeopardize the children's status with us. It was like being under a huge microscope; it was an unending nightmare.

During this time, we received a call from DCFS, but it was not our caseworker. We were informed that we had been turned in for child abuse. Apparently the biological parents called and reported that we had neglected and beaten the children. We, of course, denied the false report and invited the investigator to visit us immediately, or at any time of his choosing. We invited him to come to our home without warning, day or night. He realized quickly that this was a ploy of desperate, addictive parents doing anything they could to get their children back. I can understand their desperation. They were about to lose children to what they viewed as an unfair situation, even while knowing they lacked the ability, or even the desire, to care for their little ones.

We were put before a citizen review board, which consisted of members of the community. They, of course, found us innocent, and we were given a warning that any kind of abuse would not be tolerated. Why the warning since we were officially declared innocent? Even with the exoneration, we were treated as if we were indeed guilty. We were the ones that were trying to protect the children. I thought we were on the same side as DCFS, but now we were suspect for many things. The situation felt like a supreme slap in the face.

We kept going because we felt that we could at least make life somewhat stable and loving for four small, lost, and aching little children. Little did we realize at the time that the months they lived as part of our family would serve as a lighthouse on the far horizon. These children were soon to cross very rough, emotional waters, and they were going to need strong, spiritual memories that a safe and distant shore even existed.

This life of foster parenting was like a rollercoaster with square wheels. So often these events led to arguments, vows to just walk away, long discussions, and always pleading prayers. Sometimes peace would come, but for me, not often. I wanted to quit at least once every day. I felt unjustified anger and frustration toward DCFS constantly. Annie Laurie cried, prayed, and always looked for the good. She felt hurt almost every day with times of anger and utter disbelief at some of the decisions made concerning the children. I now understand that the more good you set out to do, the more opposition you're going to run into.

I have talked about our frustration, pain, struggle, and suffering. There are, however, two other groups of precious people who have their own story. I am not qualified to tell the story of the biological parents. They are real people with hopes and dreams and tender and deep feelings. They were so young, they tried so hard, and they loved their children, but the ultimate thief, addiction, destroyed their family and took their children away. Their addiction became their one true love and their greatest enemy at the same time. I cannot fathom their pain, hurt, frustration, and anger.

It is true that those who are most abused and tossed around are often totally innocent—the children. Their pain and confusion through the whole process must have been intense. I could not, nor can I even now, take their pain away; that is a job reserved for God.

One of the greatest miracles is that these four children, now teenagers, still pray with great faith, trust, and intensity. They are very strong and resilient people, and it is my great privilege to be their father.

We continued to report what we observed along with what the children told us, and DCFS began to listen. Hopes and plans for reunification began to dwindle while adoptive placement became the stronger direction. It seemed that the marriage had progressed into separation, and the drug abuse apparently deepened. The time had come to move toward termination of parental rights and adoption actively pursued. Even though there was a huge mountain of pain to be dealt with, and an equally large healing journey ahead for everyone involved, it seemed the battle was coming to an end.

Through all of this, were there any miracles? Absolutely, without question! It is a miracle that we made it through. After all of what I have described, our marriage was intact and even strengthened. Our teenagers developed a dimension of strength that they could not have gotten any other way, or as a great author put it, "They had poetry added to their souls." The capacity to love others was exponentially expanded for all of us. We were given the ability to take steps in the dark and hold on until the light would come. Our resolve to do whatever God asked of us, no matter how subtle the whisperings, was strengthened. But perhaps one of the greatest miracles of all is the attitude our biological children now have toward adoption. We are now blessed with twenty-three grandchildren, seven of which are adopted.

Did anything turn out the way we thought we wanted it to? Not a lot, but that was part of the miracle. We were taught the lessons that would best suit us for the darkening skies and stormy trials ahead. One of them being that when things seem dark and like they can't get any worse, they can and very possibly will. And that even though God may wait to deliver, he always comes; he always delivers. We were soon to realize that according to God's timetable we were still far from what we perceived as deliverance, and it would definitely get darker!

heart-wrenching decisions

—Annie Laurie

Finally the courts and DCFS were together on their decision about the children. It was the middle of April 1998. In six weeks, we were going back to court and going to get permanent custody of these four children. After so many ups and downs and let's-get-excited-to-only-be-crushed-once-agains, they were really going to be ours. After custody court, the adoption would be just around the corner. We could hardly believe that after all the struggles, it was finally going to happen.

I was at home that morning teaching the fifty children who came to our home three days a week for school. We had just finished devotional and were getting ready to start our history class when the phone rang. My daughter came running in and said it was Dad on the phone and that he had to talk to me right that moment. I told the children I would be back in just a minute and to take a break. I then excused myself and went into my room for a private moment with my husband.

He asked me if I was alone and could talk undisturbed for a few minutes. By this time, I was getting nervous. *What could possibly be so important?*

"Annie Laurie, I received a call today from the head office. They have asked if we will move to New Mexico in six weeks to coordinate the religious education of the youth in that area. What do you think?"

It is amazing the power a simple phone call has to change your life.

"*No! No! No!*" I yelled into the phone. "I am not moving! I will not move! Surely it isn't time for us to move. Not right now!" Could this really be happening? Everything was finally falling into place for our family. The children were going to be ours; Brian loved his job; I had my school and I loved it; our daughter Annie Laurie, at the age of eighteen, had just married, and I wanted to be near her. Everything was going well. "Please, don't ask me to move now."

"Sweetheart, please pray about it, and call me back. They need to know today."

Today? How do you change your whole life in a day? I didn't want to pray about it because what if the answer was yes? Then I would have to go.

"I'll pray, but the answer is no! He wouldn't ask this of us!"

Forgotten were the kids in the other room waiting for a teacher. I fell to my knees and wept until I thought I could weep no more, and then I asked, "Father, do we go?" No angels appeared, no loud voice or clap of thunder, just a quiet thought in my mind and peace in my heart, as I knew that we were indeed to move our family to New Mexico and that I was not to worry. God was in charge. No matter what it would look like, God was in charge.

I called my husband back and quietly said I would go. That was one of the hardest decisions I have ever made, as I knew from the very first moment the consequences of us choosing to accept that transfer. We would surely lose our four precious children. Because they were still under the jurisdiction of Utah, they would not be able to move out of the state.

After hanging up and crying more tears than I thought possible, I called DCFS and explained to them what was happening. Sure enough, they said the children would not be able to move out of state and they would call us back shortly with a plan.

I walked out to those fifty children, who had been quietly waiting and wondering. With a face stained and swollen from my tears I explained to them what had happened and why they had not seen me for the last three hours. We all hugged and cried and then gathered together to pray for a miracle.

Miracles don't always come so that we understand or recognize them for what they are. I certainly did not understand or see the miracle that was about to be brought into our lives at that time. I just knew that over the next week all of our hearts were exposed to unbearable pain and the only choice we had was to trust our Father in heaven.

The decision made by DCFS was to put those children back into their original home and give the parents another chance. We knew that there were drugs, alcohol, inappropriate sexual activities, and gross neglect going on in that home. But they were going back.

How do you prepare shattered hearts to be shattered yet once again? How do you teach them to still love God and to trust him when they are about to lose all that they have come to love and trust? How do you help to bind the wounds of your own children as they weep and search for answers from a loving God who seems to be abandoning them? How do you carry on living when your very soul has been wrenched from you and laid on the altar to be trampled, torn, and beaten until there is no will to live?

I truly respect those families who are willing to have foster children in their homes for years. They love them, teach them, and then send them home, praying that they will be safe. I am not of that same makeup.

I kept going back in my heart to that moment when I had walked through the door of my home that very first night that we brought them home. I had the impression so strongly that these children would be ours someday. That is how I had mothered them over the last twenty-two months. Even with all the visitations and turmoil, they were going to be ours forever. Now they were going back, and we were told we would never see them again. We had four days to prepare ourselves for the moment of parting.

The night we were to take them back, we gathered as a family and said a prayer with each child petitioning our heavenly Father to watch over them. They did not understand the full importance of what was about to happen. They were five, four, three, and almost two. They were too young to understand that this was more than just another visit; too young to understand that these people, who they now considered to be Mom, Dad, brothers, and sisters, were leaving them in a place they hated and were not coming back in a short while to take them home. This was permanent.

We had begged the social worker to please keep their eye on the family, to please keep them safe. They promised us they would.

So, we found ourselves, our own children included, sitting in our car outside of the parents' apartment. I knew my feet must carry me to the door, but how? I knew I must let go of that precious little girl and put her in someone else's arms, but how? I knew I was going to have to walk away once again and let someone else have the children that we had felt so strongly were ours.

As we sat there, our children kept asking us questions. They wanted to know, to have the assurance, that these little ones, their brothers and sisters in their hearts, would really be okay. We could not give them that assurance. Instead, we knew that they would not be okay. We knew we were sending them to the lion's den, and we could only hope that there was a miracle for them as great as the one for Daniel as God closed the mouths of the lions.

I placed that little twenty-two month old in her mother's arms and pled with her to please love these children enough to take care of them. We all stood there with tears streaming down our cheeks as the door closed and prayed that somehow God would step in and a miracle would occur and that this was just some kind of test. Surely the rightful mother would receive the baby in the end; that is what King Solomon decreed. Where was our savior king?

We went home that night and either threw or packed away every reminder of those children. Every reminder, that is, except one little pair of Winnie the Pooh tennis shoes that our little baby girl wore every day. On the back of the shoe, there was a little tab that would click every time she took a step. That clicking could be heard everywhere, and we always knew when she was coming. We kept those little shoes out as our sweet reminder of those we loved. I can't tell you how many times one of us would go over and make that shoe click just so we would remember.

Our two boys, Blaine and Ammon, were the ones who were home for all of this. The older children were busy with their lives, and even though they were very involved, it was these two boys who lived with it day in and day out. Their personal possessions were broken and stolen. Their privacy was gone, and they had to learn and accept an entirely different set of rules and expectations. It was hard on them. I don't think they were able to give their whole hearts to these children, as the turmoil and unrest was so great that their teenage hearts just didn't know what to do with the feelings they had to face. But even though they had closed off a bit of themselves as a form of protection, they were not immune to the pain of returning those children. Mine were not the only tears that fell.

• •

—*Brian*

This was one of the most difficult, gut-wrenching experiences of my life. How could I let these little children go into a dangerous situation? I knew their biological mother was high on meth when we placed little Bekah, who was almost two years old, into her arms. This was crazy! Nothing made sense about this decision. We were racked with sobs as we looked at our four little ones, who just stood in the doorway of that dirty apartment and stared at us. They were so tired and emotionally exhausted, so there was no crying or words on their part. They just looked at us with their little wide-eyed, innocent, inquiring looks. Their eyes were pleading with us and begging us to not leave them.

Now I understand that they were afraid to cause a fuss or say anything in front of their mother.

How could a loving God allow this to happen? Oh, I know the proper answer to such a question, but in that moment, during this trial, a proper answer did not provide the strength or the peace that was so desperately needed. How could I live without these little children? How long would I feel like a supreme traitor? How many times would I imagine the suffering that they would have to face? Where were the miracles now?

Sometimes you have to look pretty hard for miracles but ours, thankfully, were just around the corner.

emily and baby girls

—Annie Laurie

I must take a step back in time again for a moment to the time after we lost the first three Vietnamese children. We were so upset about having lost those beautiful children that a friend had called us and told us about adoptions in the Marshall Islands. She said that it was very easy to adopt and usually took only about three months to complete. At the time, we were not ready to look at this opportunity, as we were still hoping for our four little ones to come back.

But after losing the four children the first time, when they had been sent to a relative, we had gone ahead and put in our papers to adopt a baby girl from the Marshall Islands. We did not want any older children. I was looking for my baby girl. Well, a lot had happened since then, not to mention over a year and a half of time had passed. That three month time period had come and gone, and we had pretty much given up on the Marshall Islands. But now we had just given our four precious ones back to their parents, and our hearts were broken.

It seems to me that many times God lets that happen to us. He allows us to get to a place where we are truly broken hearted so that he can then step in and really work in our lives. At this time, we were indeed broken hearted, and in his wonderful way, he was about to step in and do a mighty work that we, in our spiritual immaturity, would have never allowed him to do otherwise.

"Mrs. Richardson, this is the adoption agency, and we are calling you to see if you would like to adopt a little girl. She is not the baby that you wanted, but she is eight years old and desperately needs a home."

I sat in stunned silence. No, I did not want an eight-year-old; I wanted my baby. I wanted my four children back. I said nothing. She continued.

"This little girl is living with her stepfather. He has said that if she is not gone by the time she is nine, he will use her as his object of enjoyment. Her mother would like her placed in a home as soon as possible. Her name is Emicko. Would you like to adopt her?"

As I heard her name, a very strange and wonderful thing happened. I felt that little girl's spirit standing beside me. Now, I am not saying this happened in some supernatural way, I just know I felt her beside me and that feeling stayed with me until I first held her in my arms many months later.

I told the adoption worker that I needed to call my husband and that I would call her back in just a minute. As I hung up the phone, I could feel the turmoil. I did not want an older girl, I wanted a baby. But the thought of helping that little girl all of a sudden filled a small portion of my broken heart with a reason to go on.

I called my husband, and he immediately asked my same question. "What about the baby? Can we get a baby? We don't want anyone older; we want a baby."

After talking for several minutes, we decided that we could not leave this little girl in the Marshall Islands to become the toy of an evil man. We felt God was asking us personally to help him save one of his little ones. So we agreed that I would call and tell them yes, on the grounds that we also received the little baby girl that we had asked for.

I made that call, and they agreed whole-heartedly and said, as a matter of fact, there was a little baby that was going to be available in a couple of months and did we want her. Of course we did!

You see what I mean by God knowing us better than ourselves. We had been so convinced that there was no one for us except a baby girl. But our hearts were prepared for our little Emily, for that is the name we picked for her right from the start, naming her after our first little Vietnamese girl. Interestingly enough, our Emily from the Marshall Islands was eight, which was the exact age that our first little Emily would have been if we had been able to keep her. It is wonderful how the holes in our hearts are filled in beautiful ways.

But we did not have her yet. We just knew that we wanted her and we wanted a little baby too.

We quickly sold our home and busied ourselves getting ready for the move to Albuquerque, New Mexico. We were hoping to hear any day that it was time to go to the Marshall Islands and pick our girls up. We filled our minds and hearts with plans, house hunting, and getting acquainted with the new area. Always hoping that if we kept ourselves busy enough, we wouldn't have time to remember, time to feel, time to hurt and to cry all over again.

Sundays were the hardest of all. I have always loved going to church with my family. It is a time of refreshment and renewing of relationships. During the week, life can get crazy. There's disciplining, working, running here and there, dealing with financial crises, laundry, and all that comes with just living each day, but Sunday is my time to reflect on the wonderful parts of my life. My husband and children were always on the top of that list. And sitting in church with my family around me was one of the best parts. I would gather my children and hold them, squeeze them, stroke their hair, play with their hands, and literally just pour out my love to them as I feasted on the words of Christ being shared. Somehow it was as if my love could be magnified and shared in a way that didn't happen on normal days. It would feel as though God, my husband, and I were truly in a partnership, raising these children together, raising them to someday return to him.

So Sunday had always been a special day, and now it was just a day of agonizing pain, a day to endure and plead for faith enough to face the rest of the week with my empty arms that ached and my heart that never stopped weeping. It was not only my heart that struggled on that day but the entire family. There was a little girl who sat right in front of us every Sunday. She was about the age that our little Rebekah would have been. She even wore a dress, every week, just like a dress that Rebekah had worn when we had her. All of us would watch that little girl. We could hardly take our eyes off of every move she made. We would all go home talking about how wonderful it would be if our little Rebekah was really there with us.

I'm afraid that many times during this time our faith and trust that God really did have a plan and really was in control waivered. I just couldn't see through the pain and the sorrow. The situation with the Marshall Islands did not help matters either. For at the same time that we were desperately trying to do the long walk with the four little ones, we started on another long walk for these two little ones.

Shortly after arriving in New Mexico, we received a call.

"This is the adoption agency, and we need to inform you that there are complications with your baby's paperwork, and it is going to take some time to resolve the issue. Would you like to come and get your other little girl while you are waiting?"

No! We want our baby! Couldn't anybody understand that it was my little baby girl that I was looking for? It had now been thirteen years that we had been waiting to find her. Was she really there? Had all the feelings in my heart been truly from heaven or were they just made up by a woman who desperately wanted something that she could not have? Was I the one bringing all this pain to our family because I could not accept things the way they were? I know that God is not to blame for all the hardships in this world, but I am afraid that when my heart was at its lowest, I wondered if he'd forgotten me in this new land that I lived in. And more importantly, if God loved those children, why didn't he keep them in a safe and loving place, a place that needed them as badly as they need us?

These were the questions that ravaged my heart as I set up a home for our family in Albuquerque. These were the questions that filled my thoughts as I walked the streets at all hours of the night and filled my dreams with nightmares. These are the questions that filled every conversation between Brian and I as we desperately held on to the threads of our faith.

Unfortunately, life doesn't stop when hard times come to let you try and figure it all out. Life just keeps moving along, and you face each day with as much courage as you can muster. I knew that I was not on my own because I was still able to get up every morning and look forward with renewed hope that all would be well someday.

After much prayer as a family, we felt that the time was not right yet to go and get Emily. We really felt that there would be a baby girl for us there, and we needed to wait until she was ready.

Against all odds, I still believed in the promise concerning the four little ones. So we got busy remodeling the home we had purchased in order for it to hold six more children. Sarah and I painted, wallpapered, made bedding and curtains, hung fun pictures, and made a home. Brian and my sons, Andrew, Blaine, and Ammon, knocked out the walls I told them, made a bigger laundry room, and made a big table for us all to eat at. Then they turned the garage into the most beautiful master bedroom suite you have ever seen. The one thing that Brian and I insisted on during all our married life, no matter what else was going on, was sweetheart time. So I had asked for a place to retreat to when we needed our space and when we just needed to know that we were still married. They created for us a true place of peace and beauty.

The interesting thing about this was that my husband and sons had never had any training in building or carpentry. They just had this wife and mother who kept asking for things, and so they would get down to business and figure out how to do it. Again, a miracle! My husband was a teacher, and teaching is a great job, but it does not pay well. Brian and our sons had, by this time, remodeled completely three homes, built us beautiful furniture, and were basically becoming professional at what they were doing. Now to have them do that alone would have been miracle enough, but adoptions are extremely expensive. We have paid over $300,000 for our sixteen official adoptions, and my husband and sons' ability to work hard and learn on their own, to build and remodel, has fortunately paid for many of those costs.

We worked all day, and then I walked the streets all night praying; praying for a light at the end of this endless tunnel. I would walk around our circle at two in the morning, and then I would stop and sit on an old fire hydrant. That hydrant has more water in it than the city realizes, for my tears fell freely there as I pled with God for understanding. Every night I would go home with renewed faith. God was very kind, for he never stopped telling me that all would be well. You'd think after the fiftieth time of being with me at that hydrant he would just throw his arms in the air and say, "Enough! I have told you over and over!" But no, he just kept whispering peace to my heart and hope to my soul.

Near the end of the summer, Brian and I went away for a week of seminars with his work. It was a great respite for the first few days. He actually went to class, and I stayed back in our room and oil painted and prayed. Oil painting was a new thing that I was attempting to do. My mother is a professional painter, but I had never really tried it before all this started in my life. Brian also is a wonderful artist. But I found that being able to express myself with color on a canvas was refreshing to my soul, and I was beginning to feel alive again. Things were looking up. We had the promise of our little Emily and our little baby. Life was looking better.

Near the end of the week, we received a phone call that made me even more grateful for those first few days of peace.

"This is the adoption agency, and we need to inform you that there is a problem with the adoptions. Emicko's stepfather has said he is not going to wait any longer. If Emicko is not gone in the next few weeks, he is having her move in with him. Is there any way that you can go get her right now? Also, we know that you wanted a baby, but she is no longer available, and there are no others available either. We need your decision tonight."

Phone calls that ruin the tender peace that you fight so hard to maintain. What to do with this information? My mind would hardly take it in. It's not that we didn't want to go and get Emily right that minute; we just simply did not have the funds. The adoption costs were going to be about $35,000 for two, if we were able to pick them up at the same time. We just simply could not go twice. And it was the baby we wanted, remember?

Not this little girl whose presence never left my side for even a minute.

And so, in the confusion of losing once again our little baby, we called and said, "No, we do not want Emicko after all. You will have to find someone else to take her. We are waiting for our baby." They then informed us that there was no one else who would take an eight-year-old. We were her only hope.

I don't have to save the world, do I? It's not my job! We have children to take care of, and this is just too much to ask. We don't want an eight-year-old anyway. She'll be way too hard to raise. We really only wanted a baby girl, so we could just forget it and let someone else take care of the problem. The problem of a little girl's heart being forever crushed by abuse and neglect, the problem that I would know forever that I could have done something and didn't, the problem of the tears that would be shed by this little one that I could have helped God to forever dry. The problem was that by now I felt I knew this little girl, and she was not just simply a name on a piece of paper, but in my heart, she truly was mine.

Oh, what had we done? It was midnight, and Brian and I were out walking, talking, and praying, and trying to put everything together in our hearts so that we could bypass our will and do God's. We held hands and one last time prayed together that our hearts would be made soft and pliable in God's hands, that we might be able to go and do his will.

After that prayer, there was no question in our minds of what we needed to do and do it quickly. We almost ran back to our room, and in spite of the time of night, we called back and said, "Yes, please let us adopt this little girl. We will do whatever it takes to bring her home. Please, let us have her." I could not help but add, "But please, will you do everything in your power to get us a baby girl at the same time, for I know there is one there for us." They said they would, and we hung up, realizing that the peace we now had was worth whatever sacrifice we would have to make in order to truly do his will in this situation.

Brian and I believe that there are specific children who need to come into our home. We have never believed that they were randomly brought in. Instead, we have felt that each child is specifically suited to what we as parents can give them to help them in their journey through this life. Having said that, it does make you wonder why we did not just sit back and trust heaven a bit more. But no, I had to put every ounce of energy into pleading that our baby would be there when we got to Majuro, Marshall Islands.

The time was soon at hand that we were to leave to pick up our Emily. It was September of 1999. We still had not heard word of a baby, but I just kept telling the agency that they would find one, for I knew our baby was there. They just kept telling me that they would try.

Our daughters, Annie Laurie and Katie, had saved up a great deal of money for school but decided it was more important to be with their mom and dad on this journey. After thirteen years of trying, we were going to finally adopt our first child. Sarah said she would stay home and take care of the boys and the home. We were excited and yet dreadfully disappointed all at the same time. This just simply was not what we thought it was going to look like. But we were being obedient to the whisperings that we had felt, and that was all that we could do.

I have definitely been accused of having stubborn faith before, and this was one of those times when this showed itself. We packed a bag for our little eight-year-old. We put in toys and gifts, clothes, and special food and hoped she would love it all. But we also packed a suitcase for our little baby girl. We put diapers, bottles, formula, wet wipes, clothes, blankets, everything that you need for a tiny baby, for I knew she was there waiting for us to come. I did not know how that would happen; I just knew it would.

My poor husband has had to have the patience of Job with me, as I have taken him on one crazy ride after another. But he has always had so much faith in me. He said that if I knew that a baby was coming, then he would just support me with his whole heart and add his prayers of faith to mine. So did our daughters and those we left behind at home. So off we went, believing with all our hearts that our prayers would be answered.

I believe that when you gather together with that kind of faith, God has greater power to answer those prayers. Now, I say answer, not give us what we want. What we wanted was for everything to fit into a nice little package that we had prepared and we could go merrily on our way with not a care in the world. God's package looked just a little different.

We were going to a third world country and were told that we needed to bring everything with us, as there was no way of getting things over there. You should have seen our suitcases. They were loaded with food that we could eat in our hotel room. We brought tons of rice and canned chicken and were ready to eat like kings. We weighed each suitcase carefully, so it was not over the limit. We wanted no glitches on this perfectly planned trip.

We were also told that ladies only wear skirts or dresses and men wore slacks. That my girls with long hair must always keep it up and it would be hot enough that there was the possibility of melting before we were able to return home. So, with that encouragement, we got in the car (it was cheaper than flying and money rules) and headed for Los Angeles, which was our first stop. We were to then catch a flight to Honolulu, where we would spend the night.

At the airport in Los Angeles, we just kept feeling like we needed to call the agency one more time before we headed off over the ocean. Thank goodness for sweet whisperings. We called, and they informed us that they had been frantically trying to get hold of us as they had found a baby for us; a little girl that had just been born. We were ecstatic. We could hardly believe that it was all going to work out. They also told us that we were going to meet about nine other couples in Hawaii who were also coming to adopt babies. I assumed they must be boys they were adopting, as we had been on the top of the waiting list for over one year for our little girl. But we were fine with whatever because we finally had our baby.

The excitement between the four of us was at a feverish pitch as we flew over Hawaii. I don't think any of us got very much sleep that night, as we were too excited about the next morning.

As we boarded the plane, we just kept looking at each other and grinning, and the girls and I would break into giggles.

On the plane, we started meeting the other couples. They were all great people, and we were excited for them. We asked each one who they were coming to adopt. To our bewilderment, each one said they were there to adopt a little baby girl. In fact, one of the couples was there adopting the very baby that we had originally been going to adopt and had been told we could not.

Our excitement and joy began to diminish as we struggled with this news. We wanted to be happy for each one of them. I didn't want to resent their joy at receiving a child, but I just did not understand. How could there be nine couples there to receive little baby girls, and we didn't know about ours until the very last minute? Why was the little one that we had planned on for so many months and then had been told we could not have being given to someone else? Always so many questions, and there never seemed to be any answers.

My husband and I sat on that plane and wept together as we struggled with the feelings that once again our hearts were being toyed with. So, where was our miracle? After all of our prayers, suffering, sacrifice, and supposed answers, what was happening to our miracle? What were we doing wrong that we did not warrant the blessings that others were receiving? You might say what crazy questions to be asking, but when your heart is being wrenched, your thinking goes crazy, and for a few moments, I was just too weary to hold on to my faith.

But we quickly rallied ourselves and decided just to be grateful for the gift of knowing that we did have a baby and we also had a little eight-year-old that needed us.

We flew over that tiny island and marveled at the beauty of the water. I had never seen a blue so real and alive. It seemed to glow. The island was so small I could not even imagine where that plane would land. But I guess they have been doing it for a while, and we arrived safely in Majuro, the main Island of the Marshall Islands. The island is shaped kind of like an hour glass with a thirty mile strip between the two larger areas. The strip was so narrow that you could throw a stone either way and hit ocean.

The end of the island, where we were going to be staying, was wall-to-wall houses, or shacks, and rock. There was hardly a tree, and there were also big government buildings that you knew at one time were very fancy for this little island. But now everything we saw was run down. The French-style homes, which had originally been all bright tropical colors, were faded and falling apart.

The other end was a tropical jungle with huts scattered all over. The ocean was a beautiful turquoise and warm, and the sand was soft and white. It was beautiful, and yet the poverty was appalling.

As we got off the plane, the smell of the islands hit us. The air was thick with humidity, and our clothes stuck to us immediately. We stood in line outside the main and only building, waiting to show them our passports and to claim our luggage, and I remembered the statement that we might melt before returning home, and I believed them. The airport was primitive, and so were the people. There were people everywhere lining the fences with their children all around them. We looked around wondering who they had come to greet. We found out later that they met every plane. It was the most exciting entertainment on the island.

We finally got through their form of customs. We were

scared that they would find something wrong and take us away or make us leave without getting our children. It was all so new. At that time, we had traveled to foreign places such as Europe, Jerusalem, and Egypt. But we had always had others there to take care of us. This time, there was no one, and it was very intimidating. We did not know their language, and they did not know ours.

We found our luggage and headed for the beat-up van that everyone else was heading for. We were hoping it would take us all to our hotel. We were told that we would be contacted that afternoon and given our children that evening.

The incredible wait was almost over. We all went to our room and waited, anxious to meet our little girl and to hold our little baby for the first time. Was this the little one that Father had promised?

And there we sat and sat. We saw others bringing their babies back to their rooms, and we sat. We went to the dining room and saw others there with their little baby girls, and we went back to our room empty-handed. Finally, later that night we received a call. We all waited in anticipation to hear what Brian had been told. Where do we go? How long? Five minutes? Please no more. I couldn't wait another minute. My husband hung up the phone and turned to us with a troubled look on his face.

"The mother of the little baby would like to meet us in our hotel."

Okay, we could do this. She could meet us and then surely she would be thrilled to give her baby to such wonderful people who wanted to help her little girl. Isn't that why we were here? We didn't want to just take anybody's baby, but we had been told there was a great need and that this mother had no resources to take care of her little one.

We all sat in our little room and tried to converse with a young woman who spoke no English, and we spoke no Marshallese. It was awkward, to say the least. She left, and they said we could have the baby in the morning.

We slept fitfully, not accustomed to the humidity and still wondering what was in store for us. The next morning, we saw the other couples with their babies. Every single one of them had received their baby the night before. We wondered what in the world was going on, and yet we could not get a hold of our coordinator there on Majuro. We prayed with all of our hearts that God's will would be done with our family and that we would be willing to accept it.

Faith is an interesting thing. So often when you have faith you get caught up in praying for things to be done your way. You see the picture how you think God has it planned, and so you pray for what you see. Well, I saw a baby, and this baby had been offered, and so I was pretty adamant in my prayers that I would do his will, since his will was obviously to give us this particular little girl. We don't always see the picture clearly, and I am so grateful that he is a forgiving God. He has forgiven me over and over for my weakness in thinking I am asking and bending to his will when, really, I am demanding and so busy counseling him how it should be done that I miss the real picture. This was one of those times.

Around eleven that next morning, we finally received a call. We had all been sitting huddled around the phone, not daring to leave for fear of missing our call. This was it!

"I sorry, mother said not give baby to you. Papa try force her but she keep baby. Your girl come three in front. Bye."

I burst into tears. We had come so far, and I just knew there was a baby, but once again, it was out of our control, and some-one said no. All I could say was, "Father, where are you? Do you know where I am, and do you care about my heart?"

All four of us sat and wept and wondered. It wasn't that we wanted her to give up her child. If she wanted her baby, I defi-nitely did not want to take her away. That is not why we were there. But I knew there were many who could not take care of their babies and were excited to give them a better chance at life. Look how many couples were there with babies that we were supposed to have been in line for first. So, what was going on?

It was three, and it was time for our little Emily to come. We tried so hard to put our hearts into this meeting. Annie Laurie and Katie were so good. They did everything in their power to be positive and to be filled with smiles and faith. They have always been such a strength to me. I love those girls so much.

There was an upper walkway on the hotel that overlooked the circular drive in front of the hotel. We stood on that walkway watching for our little girl. A car pulled up, and a very large man got out. He was Marshallese, and we assumed he was our coordinator. He then went around to the side door and opened it. He pulled out the tiniest little girl and told her to stay. He looked at us, pointed at her, and got back in the car and drove off. Our little Emily had arrived.

I ran downstairs and threw my arms around her and tried to tell her I was so glad to see her. She, of course, did not understand a word I said. I found out later that she had no clue that I was adopting her. She had no clue she was leaving her home. They had just told her a lady from America was here to see her. I cannot imagine what emotions must have been going through her mind and heart. I must say, that little girl is a beautiful young woman today who loves us, and we love her with all our hearts. We could not have had a more wonderful daughter if we had turned in a recipe for the perfect child. The day we received her into our arms was a blessed day indeed.

She was a beautiful little girl, but so emaciated and covered with open sores that my heart cried out in pain for her. We found out that she had been raised eating off the local garbage dump. She used the ocean and the rocks as her toilet. She was filthy, and her hair hung in ragged pieces. They told us later that they had to cut it right before she came to us because it was so tangled they could not comb it out. I held her anyway, wanting her first moments with us to be happy ones.

But that came to a crashing halt as I looked down at the front of my blouse and saw hundreds of tiny black things all over me. I was covered in lice. Oh my goodness, what do we do now? We rushed her inside and immediately started pulling off her flea infested clothes. I look back and can't help but wonder what in the world she thought of these crazy Americans who said hello, gave her a hug, and then started to strip off her clothes and throw her into this big white thing that held water; hot water at that. And that wasn't the end of it.

We cleaned her all off, scrubbed her hair, and got her out to get her dressed. During all of this, Emily just smiled the cutest smile I had ever seen. She had teeth going every which way in her mouth, and the sores all over her body were pussy and infected, but oh, she was adorable. I held her close again as I got her dressed. I looked down at the front of me and once again I was covered with black crawling lice. I gasped, and we tossed her back in the tub and scrubbed again. Katie then informed us that she had heard of a sure fire remedy to get rid of lice. You cover their heads in mayonnaise and then put a plastic bag over their heads for about an hour and it kills all of them, including the unhatched eggs. Well, I was ready to try anything. So my husband ran to the store in hopes of finding some mayonnaise, and I entertained our new little daughter without holding her too close.

As soon as they got back, we slathered that mayonnaise all over her head and then proceeded to put a plastic bag over the top of that. Now remember that not only is this our first few hours with her, but she also has no English to understand what we are doing to her. We just stripped her down, lathered her hair, got her dressed, stripped her down again, lathered her hair again, got her dressed again, and then smeared this white, gooey stuff on her head and put a bag on it and made her sit that way for an hour. I still laugh over the comedy of it all.

And our little Emily just smiled through it all. It wasn't until a few hours later that she folded and started what came to be known as the Emily howl. It wasn't crying, it wasn't whimpering, she would just simply howl for an hour at a time. It didn't happen very often, but I just think that every once in a while the whole business of being in a new place, having new caretakers, seeing new things, and having so much expected was just more than her little spirit could handle.

That first time she did her howling, we all panicked. We had never done this before. When you adopted a child, weren't they supposed to just immediately fall in love with you and everything was perfect? We had so much to learn.

The rest of that day, we took turns rejoicing in our new little one and weeping at the loss of the other one.

We prayed that night. My husband and I prayed with all the faith and power that we could muster that somehow, before we left for home, we would receive our little baby and we would be able to adopt her. Somehow I knew it would happen. I just knew it!

The next morning, we spent the day getting passport pictures, going to court to fill out some paperwork, and getting acquainted with our new daughter. We took her swimming in the salt water filled pool, and she swam like a fish. My husband spent hours on our little back patio playing ball with her. It was so cute because she had never played ball before, and we had to teach her everything. We had to teach her how to use a toilet, wash her hands, eat correctly, and basically just be an eight-year-old. We also spent a great deal of time taking care of the sores all over her body. She never cried or even winced as my girls scrubbed them out. She just smiled her beautiful smile. (She still smiles all the time.)

It was a stressful time for all of us on the island who were adopting children, as the government was closing all adoptions down after our court session. We were to be the last adoption performed for some time in the Marshall Islands. So we were all very anxious to get them finalized.

It was added stress on our part as we kept seeing everyone with their little babies, and we would dissolve into tears every time we did or get angry and have to work through that emotion too. I must say that we were definitely a mess switching from excitement, to anger, to repenting for anger, then to hope, a bit of fear, and just ceaseless praying. It couldn't have been worse, could it?

Another sleepless and prayerful night and we woke up to our day in court. A day that should have found us rejoicing, instead we were miserable. It wasn't going to happen. All our prayers, all our faithfulness over the years, our obedience to every whispering was all for naught. We had felt so sure that we would be given a baby, and now it was too late. We headed for court.

We entered that courtroom, and there were all those couples who sat with their babies; all nine of them with their nine baby girls—all names that were after us on the waiting list. And close by was the little baby that we had been told we could have and then told was not up for adoption anymore sitting on someone else's lap, being held by someone else's arms, going home to someone else's family. I ached. I looked at my husband and saw confusion and pain in his eyes. I looked at my girls and saw such a desire to support, but there too was pain and confusion. I looked down at our little Emily and loved her, but the confusion in my heart was so great that I could hardly bear it. I wanted to run and cry and ask more questions of *why. Why?* Was there something wrong with us that we could never *qualify* to actually be able to keep a baby? Was this all some big joke, and I just wasn't getting it? *Father, just teach me what I need to do in order to have the blessing. Oh, Father, Why?*

One by one we went to the front of the courtroom and went through the adoption process. We were one of the last ones to go through the process. I tried so hard to look happy, but I was grateful that no one there, except my family, knew me well enough to know what was really going on inside.

Emily was ours. After thirteen years of trying, we had finally been successful in adopting a child. She was a beautiful child who, even with all the confusion in our hearts, we felt grateful to have been blessed with. We left the courtroom and went outside to meet her birthparents and the stepfather. I did my best to be friendly to him, but I admit it was very hard knowing what I knew about him.

As we were taking pictures, a young woman came up to me with a baby in her arms. She motioned for me to take the baby. I did so, wondering what was going on. She then, in broken English, asked if I would please take her baby daughter and adopt her as my own.

"Yes! Yes!" I stammered, not quite knowing how to act. I called Brian over and told him what was happening. He started to weep and held out his arms to hold that little girl. She was about five months old and beautiful. Oh, yes, I would take her and love her and be the best mother ever to her.

I called the coordinator over and told him what was going on, and he was thrilled for us. He said that he would have to find the girl's father, as she was not married, and he would have to give his permission before we could go forward with the adoption. I pled with him to hurry and find him as soon as possible. We did not even know for sure if we would be able to have one more adoption, as we had been told that no more would be allowed. But, oh, we would certainly try. Heavenly Father would certainly take care of those little details.

I put that little one back into the mother's arms and told her I would see her soon. We left and went back to the hotel room where we started the waiting game all over again. We huddled around the phone willing it to ring. A few hours later, it did, and we were told that the father had been found and to meet the coordinator out front in ten minutes. We were out there in three.

We drove down the road about half a mile and pulled over onto the dirt where a man was sitting in a car. We stood by as our coordinator talked with him and asked if we could adopt his granddaughter. As we watched, we noticed that he was drunk but didn't think much of it. The conversation ended, and he told us that he would let us know soon what his decision would be.

We went back to the hotel and prayed and waited some more. Late that night, we received a call from our coordinator.

"So sorry, the father lose face when you saw him drunk. He so shamed he no can give you baby. So sorry, we try find you baby tomorrow."

Tomorrow? It was almost time for us to leave the Marshall Islands. Tomorrow? Who was going to give us a baby tomorrow? What were they going to do, knock on doors until they found a baby? That isn't what we wanted. We wanted our baby, the one that God had for us here in the Marshall Islands, the one that he sent us here to bring home. Where was she, and how were we ever going to find her. That night, I lost all hope. For the first time, I gave up believing that God had a baby for us in the Marshall Islands.

We all cried ourselves to sleep, including Emily, as she howled out her own world of confusion. This time that should have been so joyous was once again just another world of pain. Could it get worse? It had!

katurah

—Annie Laurie

The next morning, we woke up bleary eyed and just wanting to get out of there as fast as we could. It was Thursday, and the plan was that Brian would leave on Saturday, but the girls and I would be there until the following Monday. I tried to look faithful for my girls, but inside I had given up. As we were getting ready for the day ahead, we heard the phone ringing. I almost did not answer it because I could not bear any more bad news. I finally reached for the receiver and said hello.

My window into heaven was just about to open.

"We found baby. Baby girl. You must come now to get. Find car, ten minutes."

You have never seen two people move with as much speed as we did. We had ten minutes to find a car and be ready to go wherever it was that we were going. I started knocking on hotel doors until I finally found someone who would let us borrow their car for the day. We paid them a heavy price for it, but we didn't care. We were going to get our baby. We were out front in fifteen minutes, but we were on island time, so we were fine.

We drove to the other end of the island. We drove along the long, skinny strip of land until we reached the jungle side of the island. It was beautiful. Trees laden with exotic fruit were everywhere. Beautiful brown-skinned women and girls were sitting outside of their huts combing and grooming each other's hair. We found out later that this is a big part of their culture, as it keeps them free from lice. I saw young men cutting open coconuts with sharp machetes, and I saw poverty—crushing poverty. We had thought we were coming to see an island paradise, and on the surface, that is what was there on this side of the island. But underneath it all was the ever present, ever suffocating poverty.

It was raining by now, and we pulled up beside a tiny little hut that was not tall enough to stand up in. The air was heavy with the smell of overripe breadfruit that lay everywhere, smashed into the ground. There were electrical cords running along the ground that gave minimal sources of light here and there in that little complex of huts. There were no fancy homes or fancy cars. There were no bathrooms or kitchens. Just little huts with no furniture and mats to sit and to sleep on. This is where my baby was going to come from? It was a place that I could not even imagine living in for one day. The heat itself was unbearable, even with the rain that was a steady downpour.

We did not have much time to look around as we sat in the car wondering what was going to happen. Within just a few minutes, a beautiful woman walked out of the hut, silently put a child into my arms and got into the backseat of the car.

I just sat there not knowing what to say or do. I tried to say thank you, but she just stared at me. Was she the mother? Why was she giving me her baby? Could I take another woman's baby? We drove to another area of the jungle where there was a building with livestock and some huge gardens. A man was standing outside. As we pulled up, not a word was spoken. He just quietly got into the car by the young woman. We started the long trip back to the other side of the island.

It was a very silent trip, but I didn't care. There was so much to think about. So many questions swirling around in my head. All I wanted to do was look at my little girl, but the questions just kept coming. Was this my little girl that I felt I would someday come? Did I finally hold her in my arms? Was it okay to take this child home and make her mine?

We found out that she was two months old that very day, and she was beautiful. Surely I had my little girl! The only thing we had to do now was convince the judge to hold one more court session and allow us to adopt this little miracle from God.

When we arrived at the hotel, once again our coordinator disappeared, and there we stood with a young Marshallese couple who knew no English and a new little baby. What were we supposed to do?

We provided them the hotel room next to us and showed them in. I didn't think about it until years later that they probably did not even know how to use the bathroom.

Why would this young couple be willing to let us have their baby? So many children die every year in the Marshall Islands because of the poverty and living conditions. This family had three children die. They wanted better for their children, and they knew that if they could get them to America, they would have a new and better life. We have a great deal of honor and respect for those who sacrifice in order for their children to have what they cannot provide for them.

Because of this, we now find ourselves with a beautiful little girl that was loved enough by her parents to want her to have a better life with our family.

So, there we sat again, huddled by the phone, waiting for word of whether or not we would be able to adopt our new little girl. Only this time the pain had disappeared and joy and excitement had taken its place. We knelt and said a prayer of thanksgiving, but also once more petitioning God for his swift intervention with the courts.

I gave that little baby her first bath. I dressed her in the clothes that I had packed with such faith and fed her the formula that I had brought with hope in my heart. My heart was full.

A short time later, we received another call letting us know that the judge had said if we were there first thing in the morning, he would perform one last adoption before the courts closed on adoptions for good. God really was in heaven, and he really was in charge. We prayed our thanks again and began the process of paperwork to get our Katurah out of the country.

• • • • • • • • • • • • • • • • • • • •

—*Brian*

When I first met the young parents of this little baby girl, I couldn't help but wonder why they were doing this. How could they do this? Would we ever understand their motives? There was also this little half-starved eight-year-old that would have made a normal five-year-old look big. What choice did we have but to take her home to a safe place, with a safe and protective daddy; a daddy who would protect and honor her virtue. I made a silent irrevocable vow to myself and to heaven that I would become the best man I could and raise these little girls with as much love as any child has ever known or felt. I promised that

I would cherish and protect them from harm and any and all unnecessary suffering that was even remotely within my ability to do so.

After our court appearance with the American judge, where he performed the adoption for our little Katurah, we began the routine process for taking legally adopted children home to the U.S.

Up to now, I had not been the one who did the work, the searching, and the fighting. I was too emotionally depleted and skeptical from our painful experience of losing the four little ones. I was not against adopting children, nor was my heart hard. My heart just wasn't in it. I kind of felt like this was Annie Laurie's journey. In retrospect, I now realize that I had grown protective of *my* feelings; I was nursing *my* hurts and disappointments, and in that self-centered process, I had grown cowardly. I wish I could say that the battle that was about to be fought was because of my vow to heaven to watch over both little girls, or because it was the right thing to do, the manly or fatherly thing to do, but no, I can't say that. I fought the fight because of my love for Annie Laurie, because she so desperately felt that these children were ours. So, maybe after all, doing it for the love of a woman is not so bad.

I, along with several other American fathers, went to pick up the passports for our newly adopted children. When we arrived at the government building, a couple of the other newly adoptive parents met us at the entrance and with great anxiety told us that the government refused to give them the passport that had been paid for, approved, and printed. The documents were completed and waiting to be dispensed, but we also were told that the passports for the newly adopted children by the Americans were to be withheld. No more explanation was given, other than the passports were probably not going to be available for a very long time, if at all.

What recourse did we have? Someone suggested going to the police. What good would that do? They were part of the government that did not want us to adopt these children. The cynical part of me wonders why after all of the money had been paid to the government for fees, processing, and countless other things, then why was it decided that we were not qualified to be the parents of these precious Marshallese children? Someone suggested that we contact the American Embassy.

We called the embassy, and in the usual bureaucratic way, they said that there was nothing they could do. I remember pushing a bit and telling them that we really needed their help. I explained that the children from these families were indeed legally adopted, and we were being deprived of our legal rights. The person at the embassy finally agreed to see us if we came immediately, because they were getting ready to leave for the day, as it was the beginning of a three-day weekend. For crying out loud, it was only 11:00 a.m. By that time, I and the other parents were pretty desperate and would not take no for an answer.

We piled into a small car and sped off toward the embassy. We did not have to wait long before receiving an audience with embassy personnel. They explained that this was a Marshallese matter and they had no control, which was true. It probably would have ended there but not without a fight from me. My spirit is not a diplomatic or political one. I had once belonged to the First of the Eighth Cavalry in the First Cavalry Division. My spirit is a fighting spirit, so I did what came naturally, I fought. I did not do it gently or with kindness, which is what Annie Laurie would have wanted, but she wasn't there, so I just went into combat.

"Look, as far as I'm concerned there *is* something you can do. If you're not willing to stand up and help us, at least make a call to INS or customs in Honolulu and explain the situation so we can get back to American soil with our children." I then asked if they had the telephone number of a particular U.S. senator. That caused an almost perceptible raise of the eyebrow.

Thank goodness there was another man next to me who had

the skill of genuinely smiling in times of trouble. Without this softening effect, I probably would have been escorted out, but no, the official began writing a letter for us on embassy letterhead and then made a call to Honolulu customs, or INS, or whomever is in charge of letting people through the borders of this wonderful nation. The embassy person reminded us, once again in her bureaucratic official tone, that the letter was not an official document and it would not guarantee anything. We thanked her and headed off to our only other ally—the American judge.

The judge met with us and listened quietly as we explained the situation. He was not surprised by the workings of the Marshallese government. I guess this was not the first time that they'd pulled the rug out from under adoptive parents. We asked if we'd done anything illegal or wrong, and he simply said no, but explained, "That's just the way it is."

He had an idea and told us all to take the birth certificates of all the children and find a place with a copy machine. He then told us to find a notary public and added that it would be difficult because it was so late. It was only about two in the afternoon. I remember thinking to myself, *How can it be late?* He continued, instructing us to get a passport photo of the children and make a copy of the birth certificate with the child's photo on it.

"Bring it back as soon as possible. Also, you've got to get off of the island as soon as you possibly can."

As soon as we possibly can? The possibilities were pretty slim. As I remember, there were only a few flights a week going to Hawaii, and the next flight was that night around 8:00 p.m. Annie Laurie and the girls had tickets for the next Monday, but this was Friday. We were counseled strongly to stay out of sight and get off the island on the next available flight.

We raced out of his office and followed the directions to the letter. The whole process took about three hours, and we returned to the judge's office later that afternoon with birth certificates in hand. He reminded us that these documents would not take the place of a Marshallese passport; they were not legal documents and really meant nothing. He simply put official embossed stamps on the certificates and said, "This only shows that you have legally adopted the children." He intimated that these might take the place of the documents which the government passport agency had withheld, for airline boarding purposes only. He was very clear that this paper was not illegal; it just had no legal value. Well, at least we had something in hand from another official source, but the problem still was not solved. In order to board the plane, a passport was required. Before leaving, the judge reminded us again to get off the island as soon as possible.

We needed another miracle! We needed four seats on the next flight out that very night. I figured I could stay and come home the next day, but I wanted my family out of this country; now! We also learned that very day that the government was closing its borders to all Americans connected with adoptions on Monday. Somehow I had to get this part of my family on the plane. The need for heaven's intervention increased.

I picked up Annie Laurie and the girls at the hotel and went to the airline office downtown. I remember we had to kind of run-trot as the office would be closing at 6:00 p.m., and it was just after five. We arrived breathlessly around five thirty and took a number from a broken and rusted dispensing machine.

We requested a flight change for four people. With no cheerful greeting and without looking up, a woman said there was a two hundred dollar change fee for each ticket and she could not guarantee that we would even get on the flight. "You'll have to fly on standby status. You will be added to that list, and there are eight people ahead of you on the list."

I asked what the probability would be to get a seat. She looked at me and said, "The flight comes from Guam, and it's always full. I don't remember a time when there has been any space available for standbys. In fact, I don't think there have been any standby seats for about six years."

Not a lot of hope- or faith-inspiring encouragement. "You'll just have to take your chances if you want to change your tickets," she continued.

I then asked, "What if we can't get on, can we have our original reserved seats back?"

She dryly answered, "There are no guarantees, and you'll have to pay the change fee again." This would mean another thousand dollars. So this risk could potentially cost us an extra two thousand dollars that we simply did not have. What it boiled down to was this: If we didn't take the chance, the girls might not make it off the island. We went ahead and bought the standby tickets and left the office, once again running and trotting.

We hastily packed our suitcases, got a rental car, and headed out. There was only one major road on the island that went from end to end, about thirty-eight or so miles. The speed limit was thirty-five miles per hour, with no passing lanes. Talk about a gut-wrenching, sweaty-palm drive! The airport was not anything like the airports we're used to in America. It consisted of an open air pavilion with some kind of covering to partly keep the rain out, and a passenger gate, which served for departures and arrivals. The place was packed when we arrived. It was like the whole island had come out for the arriving flight from Guam.

While we were standing there trying to look invisible, Katurah's biological aunt showed up to say good-bye. She walked right up and demanded to hold the baby. At the time, we had no idea who this woman was, but she was so persistent and seemed to know our situation, so we reluctantly handed her Katurah. I figured I could outrun and overpower her if necessary. She must have held our new little Katurah for thirty minutes. I was her shadow the entire time. She warmed up to us and spoke in slow broken English. I now realize she was just bidding this little niece farewell. She thanked us for taking Katurah to America, smiled, and thanked us again. She then disappeared into the thronging airport crowd.

Finally, the plane landed and with great anticipation we watched as the passengers from Guam filed off the plane. Most were greeted by smiling loved ones, and everyone seemed so enthralled by their arrival.

Our eyes and attention were glued to the airline agents who were preparing for the new passengers that would soon board the plane to Honolulu.

The time finally came, and they began to call out the names of all the passengers that had reserved seats. Our fate would soon be announced. "Please God, let there be some open seats," I pleaded quietly. Everything but our focus upon the gate agent faded. It was like there was no sound other than her voice. Every pause in her speech caused us to lean forward with great anticipation mixed with anxious impatience. Could it be that this time would be different than the other times over the past several years? Could there actually be available seats?

After a few moments of paper shuffling, which seemed to go on for hours, the agent, in a very businesslike manner and with no emotion whatsoever, announced that there were twelve open seats. Annie Laurie and our girls were numbers nine, ten, eleven, and twelve; they were the last to board. The first step of getting my family home had been accomplished. I knew that God was in this, and I could not stop the praises of gratitude from spilling out of my heart and the tears of gratitude from pouring out of my eyes. They were on their way, and I would follow them the next day.

. . . .

—*Annie Laurie*

We were finally on our way home. As we boarded the plane, our long walk was almost over. It had been a hard one but was worth every step. As I held that little Katurah in my arms and snuggled Emily next to me, the plane took off. I looked at my two older girls in the seats in front of me, and I began to weep. Then my older girls began to weep also, and we knew that we had done it. We had gone and done what we had been asked to do, and in spite of all the opposition that was thrown in our way, we had accomplished his will. We had put ourselves in the way, and he had worked a mighty miracle. The tears of joy just kept flowing as I went over in my mind all the little miracles that had been performed in order to give us our big miracle of this little baby finally being in my arms and my sweet Emily by my side.

I still get goose bumps all over me as I think of the magnitude of God's hand in our lives that week. He took us from a place of believing to a place of knowing; a place of pain and longing to a place of absolute joy. Interestingly enough, of all those families there adopting children, the girls and I were the first ones to leave that island in safety. We were the first ones to bring our little ones back to American soil. And we actually brought the youngest baby home with us too. God is kind, and he knows what he is doing if we will just allow him to do it! He did not want us to have any of those other little girls; he wanted us to have our Emily and our Katurah. And that's what he made happen.

But the journey was not yet finished. We had to still get these girls through American customs without passports. We prayed nonstop as we flew back over that ocean and began our descent to the Oahu airport. What lay ahead? Would they turn us back, or would we be allowed entrance back into our own country?

I can't tell you what happened. I don't quite understand it myself, but we went through customs with flying colors. Maybe it was the fact that it was two in the morning, or maybe we just looked so tired they didn't want to hassle us, or…I don't think so. What happened was that God was holding our hand, and he led us right through those men and whispered to their hearts that everything was okay. Because it was! We had made it!

I wanted to get down on the ground and kiss the floor in my gratitude. As I walked through the rest of customs, getting our luggage and having it checked, I realized I was holding on to those four daughters as if our lives depended on my ability to hold them close. I looked in their eyes, and I knew I had to get control of myself and speak peace and comfort to them. I dug deep and drew on the power that God gives mothers in times of stress and smiled and let them know that everything was finally okay! We could breathe again!

Well, everything was okay except that it was 2:00 a.m., we had no car, and Brian was coming in at two that next afternoon, and I did not want to pay a fortune for only a half night's sleep in some hotel. So what were we to do? I look back and think that I was just crazy, but when you don't have money and you just spent $35,000 that you don't have, you do crazy things. We found this little circular couch that we kind of fit on, and we all curled around the tree in the center of the couch and tried to sleep right there in the airport. It was by no means what I would call comfortable, but Emily fell straight to sleep and so did Katie and my Annie Laurie. Katurah woke up immediately, of course, and I soothed her for the next three hours. I was desperate for sleep myself, having been up the last several nights weeping and praying, but somehow I managed to keep her in my arms as my head nodded, and I almost fell off the couch as I rocked myself into a stupor. Finally it was 6:00 a.m. and we could go get a rental car, eat breakfast, and find a hotel. I figured we could ask them to give us early check-in and we would take a little nap while we waited for Brian to arrive.

After renting a car, we took off in downtown Honolulu trying to find a restaurant. We found a place that had a breakfast buffet and went inside. I have absolutely no idea what was served. I sat down on that bench at the table, everything became hazy, and I slowly fell over and went to sleep. The girls must have taken care of the little ones, but I knew nothing except the blissful world of dreams. My Annie Laurie woke me up sometime later saying that everyone was staring at me. I looked around and greeted the stares with a sleepy smile. I didn't care. I usually am very conscious of what impression I am making, but that morning I just wanted sleep. They hauled me off the bench and out to the car, and we started our search for a hotel that would let us in early.

We finally found one, and I can still remember the blissful joy of lying down prone for the first time in days, it seemed, and fading away once again to that wonderful world of dreams. The only problem was that in my dreams there was a baby crying. Katurah was ready for some attention. I remember thinking, *And I asked for this baby?* But I had asked and miraculously I had been given. I loved every minute of caring for her.

We met Brian at the airport that afternoon and found out that he had definitely had an eventful trip home. Babies had been crying everywhere, and parents didn't know what to do, so he was walking and rocking and consoling all the way home. But everyone made it through customs, and what a sweet reunion that was right there at the airport with all of us on American soil.

Brian left later that day as had been previously scheduled, but our tickets did not get us back to Los Angeles for another couple of days. Once there, we drove home to Albuquerque, arriving in the middle of the night. I took those little ones into that wonderful room that my husband and sons had built for me and laid Katurah in the middle of the floor with Emily beside her. We then called the children in to see their new sisters. They formed a circle around our new baby, and one of them grabbed

Emily and held her close in their arms and we cried, we prayed, and we rejoiced. We were home, and we were a family. The long walk with all of its gifts was finally over.

● ●

Blaine—our twenty-five-year-old son

This experience was a very significant turning point for me. I will always remember the way that that moment changed my life forever.

While my parents were in the Marshall Islands, my brothers and I stayed home with Sarah. I remember the thoughts that were racing through my mind as my parents would call to keep us abreast of how things were going. This was unlike any other experience that we had previously gone through.

I had tried to be kind and gentle with each of the different children that had come and gone, but I had kept a part of my heart locked up, and there was a small part of me that didn't consider these kids to be my *real* siblings. Looking back, I can see how that withholding on my part influenced my behavior and sometimes was manifested by a greater lack of patience or frustration when someone got into my personal belongings or when taking care of them interfered with my *important* teenage plans. This time, the kids that my parents were bringing home were going to be my siblings legally, and there wouldn't be any more wondering or going back.

I struggled with my feelings as I realized that these two new little girls were going to be just as real children to my parents as I was. Not only were these little girls going to be my parents' children, but they were going to be my own little sisters also. I didn't know if I was ready to open up my heart all the way to them. I was still very tender because of all the children that we had lost. The time for my parents' return was approaching, and I was no closer to finding peace than before.

As I walked into my parents' room to meet them for the first time, I made a decision that forever after changed me. Those new little sisters were going to be just that in my heart, really and truly my little sisters. I remember seeing Emily for the first time and saying to myself, "This is my new little sister and that is that."

I walked over to her and gave her a big hug, telling her that I loved her and that I was so glad that she was in our family. I tried to get a moment with Katurah, but as can be expected, it was a losing battle with my sisters and mother, who all wanted to be holding her.

I think that Emily must have felt my love for her from the beginning, because she and I shared a special bond from that day on. As the years passed, our relationship changed and deepened, and she always held a special place in my heart. I am sure no brother could care for a sister more than I did, and still do, for my little Emily.

After making the decision with Emily and Katurah to love and accept them, I never had to make that decision again. God blessed me to open my heart to the rest of the children that were brought into our home.

our faith tested

—Annie Laurie

One week after arriving home from the Marshall Islands, we took our son, Andrew, to Utah, where he was leaving us to do missionary work in Brazil for two years.

Before heading back to New Mexico, we decided to just place a quick call into DCFS to see how the four little ones were doing. We had not heard anything since that terrible night six months before when we had taken them back to a very hard situation and left them there. We were shocked to hear the news.

"I'm sorry, it has been so busy that I was only able to visit with them once right after they went back home. I was then given some other families, so I don't know how they are doing."

"Would you please check and let us know as soon as possible?" I could not believe what I was hearing. They had promised me that they would keep a close watch on those children. What if something terrible had happened? The next day, we received another phone call.

"I am so sorry. I found out that no one has been following the family. They thought that since the kids went back home that everything was okay. But I have heard some rumors that things are not okay. The parents are separated, and things are not going well. The mother has been on drugs again, and we don't know about the father. They are with the father right now and ... I am so sorry!"

I'm sorry? *I'm sorry?* Well, sorry just isn't enough! What was happening to my children (for they were still my children)? I had never given up the belief that they were mine and that some day we would have our miracle and they would come home.

I had to know! Brian and I talked about it, and we decided that I would stay there in Utah with Emily and Katurah. I would stay until I could find out what was going on in their lives. I was sure they needed me, and I was going to be there. Brian and the boys left to go back to New Mexico, Sarah went to stay with some friends, and Katurah, Emily, and I stayed at my dad and mom's home so I could be close to DCFS and my children.

This is when people really began to think that I was crazy at best, but there were a few who thought I was truly obsessed with these four children. I had some members of my family who I was very close to look me in the eye and tell me that they had prayed about this and they knew that these kids were not meant to be mine. Well-meaning family and friends would say that I had done my part and to now just leave it alone; I had other children to take care of.

I did! I know I did! But I could not find any kind of peace with those kinds of thoughts. I do not blame anyone, for they were desperately trying to help me get through a very hard situation the best they knew how. I can't help but think I may have done the same to someone else because my heart would have so ached for them and I would have just wanted it to all be over for them. They were right. I did have other children who were already in my home. But these four were my children too. I had been told that. How could I turn my back and walk away just because I had *other* children? My other children were safe. If anyone needed me, these four lost and lonely children needed me. I could not get their faces out of my mind and their whispers out of my heart. They were in every thought, every dream, and every prayer. I couldn't walk away. You might as well have asked me to cut off my right arm as to give up my dream, my quest, my mother's love for these children.

They were mine, I knew it, and I knew that God knew it. My job was to be there to do whatever he needed me to do as he worked his miracles and worked out all the details. Always details! I never can figure out the details, although I sure try hard enough. I always have the big picture and the end of the story in front of me, but the details escape me, so I leave them to God.

For the next six weeks, I stayed at my parent's home and every day I called DCFS.

"Where are they? Are they all right? Can I see them? Please let me just see them? What is happening to them? Is anyone taking care of them? Are they happy? *Does anybody care?*"

Questions, always questions, and so few answers. The voices kept coming, "Go home. Leave well enough alone. They are not your responsibility!" I couldn't help but ask the question, "Then whose responsibility are they if not mine? Who is going to care enough to make sure these four children have a chance at life? A happy life!" I cared, and I was not going home. So, I continued to call.

My husband was such a support. I would call him, going crazy with fear and frustration, wondering if I should just give up. He always told me to stay, stay and do what I knew I had to do. So I did.

Three weeks had passed, and we finally got word. What we had heard as rumors was indeed true. The parents were separated. The mom had been in trouble with drugs again, and they were living with the father. Other than that, they knew nothing but would do an investigation. I prayed some more and wept until I thought my eyes would never be the same again. How can there be this many tears, this much pain, this much loneliness? And what, dear God, were my little ones feeling?

• •

—Brian—our fifteen-year-old son

I want to tell you about how God answers prayer. But first, I'll tell you why I prayed in the first place.

The Richardson's had been our foster parents for almost two years. During the time that we were with them, they taught us that there was someone so powerful and loving that he was listening to each and every one of us here on earth. They taught us that we can pray to God for help. So, during that time, I learned that there was never a place or time that I could not pray. I also learned that there is strength in numbers.

When we were given back to our biological parents, I would gather my two sisters and my brother into the bathroom to pray. We had to go into the bathroom because it was the most private. Sometimes we would pray in us boys' room, but then we would get caught. We would get in big trouble, but as the mastermind behind the plan, I would be the one that would get in the most trouble. It wasn't that we were praying that made them mad, it was that we were praying for our parents to come back and find us.

I was always the one that would be punished. They would beat me with a belt or lock me in a closet with a gag on my mouth. They would scream at us that we were their children and we would always stay that way.

I still remember the feeling of peace that came every time we prayed together, even when I got in trouble.

I can now say that God answers prayers, even the prayer of a five-year-old who needed his real family.

* *

Clarissa—our thirteen-year-old daughter

I remember when I was four years old, my brothers and sister and I going around our apartment neighborhood and knocking on doors. We would ask every woman if she would be our mother. We would tell them that we were hungry and had no food to eat. Some would give us crackers or snacks, but no one would be our mother.

I clearly remember the night that I woke up to my brother, Brian, shaking me and saying, through crying eyes, "They're gone! They left us all alone!"

It didn't take me long to fully wake up. I gathered clothes for my baby sister, diapers, and clean underwear for all of us. I knew where to go—my brother's friend's house. His mommy was so nice. She had told us that if we needed anything to just come over.

I knocked on her door, and when she opened it, she asked, "What are you doing out here in the middle of the night?"

I said, with my eyes starting to water, "We are scared because Daddy is at work, and we don't know where Mommy is."

She let us in and fed us lots of food. She turned on the nightlight in the guestroom, and we were soon fast asleep.

I woke up to a scream. The scream came from outside. It

sounded a lot like my mommy's scream. I quietly opened the door to the balcony. The lady stood outside, and she was calmly saying, "They're up here. Just come up and get them."

I know that my biological parents could not properly take care of us. I believe they were tools to bring me to the wonderful family that I have now. I love my real family so much.

I am grateful God let me grow during this hard time. I am still growing from this today as I face each day's challenges. I hope more people will understand that there are children who need help and that they are praying for that help.

· ·

—Annie Laurie

Hearing the stories of my children makes me incredibly grateful that God is aware of us all and that he had the children in his arms while I could not have them in mine.

It was a few days before Thanksgiving, and we had been in Utah for five weeks, hoping that somehow we would be able to take these children home with us. I had asked to please talk to the father, and they said that they would try to arrange it. One morning, I received a call, and I recognized the voice. The father had called.

"Would you like to spend the day with the kids? They have missed you and would love it. When is a good time for you?"

Oh, heart be still or you will surely explode! My prayer was being answered. I would be able to see them and know firsthand how they were doing. I would be able to touch them and hold them. I would hear their voices and know they were real.

"Yes, a thousand times yes. Please, yes!"

I wanted my husband and children to all be there too. I could not leave them out, as they had put as much into this as I had—almost. So, we set the visit up for the day before Thanksgiving, which was the next day. I called Brian, and he got in the car immediately and traveled six hundred miles to be there. We were going to all be together again.

I need to share my little Emily's heart. Here she was in a new family, a new world. She was learning English fast but still had so many things to understand. She had been in America about seven weeks and did not know these four children except from things we said and pictures we showed her. But that sweet little girl pled, didn't just pray, but pled every night that God would bring her four brothers and sisters home. I don't know how much she understood, but I know God understood and heard those pleadings.

It was hard because here I had two brand new children who needed me, and many times I was emotionally somewhere else. I tried to fulfill their needs, but my heart was in such turmoil over my four little ones that my two little girls did not get all that they should have. But you can't go back. I was doing everything that I knew how to do to balance everything, and I just asked God every day if he would please just make up the difference for me and for my family. I know he heard my prayers just as he heard Emily's.

Brian and the children had arrived the night before, and now it was the big day. The day that we were to once again hold those four little ones in our arms. Would they remember us? Would they still love us? Would they let us hold them? Questions, always questions, until sometimes I thought my brain would go crazy if I didn't somehow get answers to those questions.

I don't know if I even have the words to describe that day. Every emotion was there and raw to the touch. It seemed like we all just soaked in every breath that was breathed by them, absorbed every word that was spoken and put it on the recording that was being held in our hearts, and found intense joy in every handhold, hug, kiss, and passing touch that came our way.

Every minute was filled with exquisite happiness and unbelievable sorrow. Why couldn't this day last a lifetime instead of mere hours?

We filled that day with all the things we loved to do most with those children. We played on the school playground. We dressed them up in new clothes and did their hair. We took a family visit to Home Depot. We sang and played dress up. We watched and watched every move and every expression, memorizing them and placing them in a safe place in our hearts.

My questions were answered. They did remember us, but they asked over and over why we left. They put their arms around us and begged to be able to stay with us. They did love us, but their hearts were confused, and we did not have the words to bring them peace.

When it came time to take them back to their father, we all knelt in prayer once again and petitioned God in their behalf. We pled for peace in everyone's hearts, and we said good-bye one more time. We had been told by DCFS that we were to leave the situation alone, as we would never be able to get these children, and to just get on with life.

Had this been the right thing? What had I done to these little ones, for they were the ones who had to go back into that horrific situation? Had I made that even more difficult for them to bear? Had I crushed, once again, my own children's hearts beyond repair?

I'm afraid it didn't matter whether it was right or wrong, it was just something that I had to do. I had to know and now that I knew, I had no choice but to send them back and continue to try and live each day. I had to face the hurt and pain in my children's hearts. I had to now go home and be a mom to those in my care and keeping. I knew more than ever that God would bring those four home, but he had a plan, and as hard as I tried, I could not figure it out or change it.

I went home to New Mexico and picked up the pieces of our life and prayed for understanding.

. . . .

It was shortly after Christmas that God worked another miracle in my life. I was given the gift of joy. My parents had shared with me their thoughts on finding joy in life no matter what the circumstances, and I had been praying and studying that principle. As I did so, a great truth came into my heart. Either I believed in God's mighty power and trusted that he truly was involved in my life, or I didn't. Which was it? For I had not been acting like I believed in him. I had been going around droopy, sad, and totally miserable. Oh, I had faith all right. But that faith didn't translate into my everyday living very well.

What this meant for me was that if I trusted God, then I needed to show that in my countenance. I needed to start finding joy in his journey for me and my family. He could have at any time brought these children home, but he had not chosen to do that yet. Did I trust him? Did I believe that his way or my way was the best? Was I going to allow him to work his plan and be cheerful about it, or was I going to whine and cry because it wasn't done my way?

This was one of those life-changing moments for me that has helped me through many hard times, when I simply could not understand the plan. If I wanted God to run my life, and if I really believed he could do it better than I could, and if I really meant the words "thy will be done," then I had some changing to do. But I could not do it by myself. It was at this time that my prayers changed. Instead of pleading to bring those children home, I started pleading for the strength to joy in his plan, in his timing, and in his understanding of what we all needed.

I cannot explain how profoundly my life changed at that moment, as I let truth fill my soul. I had a mighty change of heart. Even though I have still been weak many times, I have never again felt quite as alone or quite as empty. God is amazing! He is a wonderful tutor, if we will just allow him to be. I thank him every day for his patience with me.

I was finally ready to get down to the business of being Katurah and Emily's mom. Now, lest you feel concern, I was taking care of them and I loved them. I was just so involved in my inner turmoil that I was not all I should have been with them.

Emily was learning quickly and was starting to communicate with us. I'll never forget the moment she first shared feelings in her heart with us. It was at 12:15 a.m. on January 1, 2000. We had just brought in the New Year in our family's traditional way. We bang lids for about ten minutes, set off fireworks, and yelled, "Happy New Year." But after that comes the real celebration of the new year—as our whole family, my parents, brothers, sisters, cousins, and all of our children—wherever they are in the world, at the same time, sing a hymn of praise, and then we have a family prayer to bring in the New Year. It was after that celebration that my Emily was sitting on my lap. She looked up at me and started talking in her broken English. She simply said, without any lead up to her statement, "Daddy hit face many times. Hurt me bad." Then she collapsed in my arms and sobbed.

I sat there holding that beautiful little girl in my arms and felt my tears join hers.

* *

Emily—our seventeen-year-old daughter (Emily's challenge is autism)

My birth mother's name is Catalina. I remember that she was very good to me but often did not know how to take care of me or protect me. She tried with everything she had, but her life was so hard. I lived in fear and danger. My father drank so much that he really could not take care of us. My mom and dad divorced. This was hard because they both loved me, and I love them.

Mom married a very mean man who began to beat her. He would just hit her over and over again for no reason. I remember watching and feeling like my heart was breaking. I now have a daddy that believes that any man who hits women is not really a man. Sometimes, my stepdad would hit me and my little brother, Junior. Catalina would jump in the way and take the hits for us. My brave mother would stand there and take it even when not recovered from being hit before.

My heart would break a lot. This happened lots. It was like a big, black cloud would just surround us or a big, black thing that would just hunt you forever and that would not leave. My mother started to talk to people about letting me be adopted to a family that would take care of me. She decided to send me to my father's home so I could be safe. He could not take very good care of me because he drank so much. But he did not hurt me.

My father is a good man. He was always kind, gentle, and loving. I lived with him before I got adopted. He would drink like crazy, even though it was so hard on him. He would come home drunk and just sit and cry in front of me and say he was sorry for drinking. He would always promise to do better, and I knew he meant it, he just could not. Joba, my father, was a good man, and I love him.

My mother was and is a good woman. She took care of me as best she could. She loved me so much that she let me go to my wonderful family. I am so grateful for my new life. I am safe, and I am loved. My new parents love me with all of their hearts. One of the greatest gifts my mother gave me was a new family. The other great gift is that she also gave birth to me. I am so thankful to her.

* *

—Annie Laurie

Why had God chosen me to be this little girl's mother? Could I possibly be qualified enough to help her heart heal, to raise her the way God wanted her raised? Would I be able to make up for all those years of pain and give her the life of joy that she deserved? Her skin was not the same as mine, and her race was not the same. Did that matter? I knew in that moment that God would be the one to qualify me, for he was the one who had given me the role of being her mother and our family the role of being her family. I knew he had the power to take us and mold us into something wonderful if we would just allow him. That molding would prove to be painful, many times, but the miracles and gifts that came with that molding, and continue to come, are worth every pressing, pushing, shaping, and stretching that we endured.

All I could do that night was rock her and sing to her of my love and God's love. I told her over and over that she was safe and that I would always be there for her. She seemed to be at peace.

I must share an experience that happened about three years after this when Emily was eleven. We had just brought another little baby girl into our home, and we all loved her immediately. Emily spent many hours out of every day at my side helping me take care of her. Emily had a natural gift for mothering right from the start. As I was holding my new little one, and Emily was, as usual, right there beside me, I looked over at her and a tear was running down her cheek. Nothing bad had happened, so I was surprised and quickly asked her what was wrong. She looked into my eyes with the deep emotion she was feeling overflowing and simply said, "Why didn't God let me come out of your tummy so I could be your baby too?"

What could I do or say to answer such a question? I quietly put down my new little baby and drew Emily into my arms. I held her snuggled up next to my breast, as you would hold a tiny baby. I rubbed her cheek, played with her fingers, and kissed her all over her face. I dried her tears and said, "God has the power to bless us with the gift of anything our hearts desire that is right. Let's ask him to give us the gift of loving each other just as if you were born to me out of my tummy." It was one of those wonderful moments when two hearts join together in supplication to a loving Father and you know immediately that your prayer has been heard. I don't know how to describe the feeling that came and bound us together that day, but we have never been the same. I love my Emily, and she loves me with a special love that was born that very day as I snuggled my baby, my Emily, in my arms and felt the power and gift of God moving upon us and taking away all the hurt and missing of the years apart and just leaving us with the joy of a lifetime together.

I must go back to that time of being a new mother to children that were adopted; children who I did not give birth to and who I was learning to love as if they had been born from my body. This does not always happen over night or as soon as that baby is placed in your arms, no matter how much you have wanted them.

I was now in a place of peace and joy about God's journey with our four little ones. I finally trusted that he was working things out in the perfect way, whether or not I could see that perfect way. You would think that after receiving that knowledge I would just be peaceful and get on with life, but no, my heart was troubled. I went to God over and over with my concern.

I had been looking for sixteen years for my little girl. Eight of those years for the little girl that I felt had been promised to me after giving my little one to another. I had now been given Katurah, and surely she was the gift God had promised. I knew my little girl was coming, I knew he would bring her, and I knew I would know her when she came. The problem was, every time I looked at Katurah and tried to have her be that little girl, I just felt confusion. This was not my little girl that I was waiting for. But with these feelings came guilt and self denial. I was crazy for certain this time. I had my baby and I should just love her and be done with it, right? Right!

No, not right. Sometimes I could hardly hold her because of the confusion that I felt at the battle that was going on inside of me. I dared not tell anyone, especially God, because you are just supposed to love your babies. She was a miracle, for goodness sake, and I needed to just stop being whatever it was that I was being, but, unfortunately, I had no clue what that was.

Finally, one day shortly after the holiday season was over and things were settling back down to normal, I could take it no longer. I fell to my knees in the quiet of my room. I looked at that beautiful baby beside me, and I poured out my heart. I shared my concerns, my guilt, and my desire to be forgiven for my utter failure at being a mother of adopted children. How could I be anything but a failure if I could not love completely those who were put in my care? What was wrong with me? Everyone had been right. I simply was not good enough or qualified enough to be a mother of adopted children.

Miracles! That is what this book is about. That is why we have felt so pressed to share our story, because miracles still happen. They can happen daily if we are willing to receive them. I had another miracle that day as I knelt in the middle of my room, wrapped in despair, and pled with God to forgive this worthless soul.

He opened my eyes. The blind saw! There, lying beside me, was my daughter in every sense of the word. I knew in that moment that she was indeed not my little girl that I was waiting for, but she was indeed part of the multiplying of my motherhood, and she was mine. My little girl would come, but until that time I had been given a remarkable gift to hold to my heart and to whisper peace to my soul. Katurah was my daughter, and all the confusion left, and I had so much love for my Katurah that I thought I could not hold it. It has been that way ever since. I love all my children, I have no favorites, but Katurah has a special place because she was given to me to bind up my broken heart, and she did just that.

It is interesting how much she is like her older sister Katie. For Katurah too came with a peaceful, healing heart. Everyone who is around her feels her spirit and comments on it. She is the peacemaker in our home. Everyone loves her and would never think of arguing with her or being cross with her, for she radiates peace and love.

I was finally able to feel the peace and the joy of being a new mother, and I loved it. Every day was filled with light as I watched my children all fall in love with each other. My older boys' hearts became soft as they tenderly took care of Emily's needs in a world that was so new. We laughed and kept calling each other to come look as Katurah would be doing something cute. We would all leave whatever we were doing and run to wherever she was, for she delighted us.

I loved having older daughters to share all this with, as I had never had a sister. I only had three brothers. My older daughters became more like sisters as we shared the joy of new motherhood. This was a peaceful time. It was a breath of fresh air in a world that had been smothering us. It was a time of regrouping and filling ourselves back up for whatever the future would hold. We now had eight children: five of our own, Sarah, and our two from the Marshall Islands.

Were we finished? How could we be? There were at least five more who, even though we were in a time of peace, were written on my heart and could not be erased. My four little ones and my little girl had not yet come home.

the return

—*Annie Laurie*

The next couple of months were peaceful ones for our family. We had put the four little ones in God's hands and were finding a great deal of joy in our Emily and Katurah. Brian was enjoying his new job as coordinator of religious studies in the New Mexico area, and our boys were adjusting to our new life. Even though Blaine was only fifteen, he and Sarah were attending the college in Santa Fe and having a great time together. Ammon was homeschooling and working toward his own graduation. Everything seemed to finally be back in place, and life was good.

Then one night in March, I had a dream. It was one of the clearest dreams that I have ever had, and I woke up from it in a cold sweat, weeping. I spent the rest of the night pondering on my dream and praying that I might have understanding.

This was my dream: I was not in the dream. I was just watching all that was taking place. I saw a gathering of people at a party. I recognized the people as the family of our four little ones. They were laughing and seemed to be enjoying themselves. I then saw my four little children join the party. Their father turned to them and told them to go get in the truck, as it was time to go. They did as they were told and got into the cab of the truck. The party disappeared, and I saw that the truck with the children in it was next to the precipice of a high mountain. I was in back of the truck and could see the children's faces as they knelt on the bench seat looking out the back window. All of a sudden, the truck began to move forward. There was no adult in the truck, and as the children realized that it was moving, they began to scream. I watched as that truck began to gather speed as it headed for the edge of that precipice. All of a sudden, those children's faces changed. They looked right at me, and with terror written all over them, they screamed for me to save them. I could not move, and I watched in horror as the truck with my four children went over the side of the mountain to fall to their death.

I awoke feeling as if I could not breathe because of the silent scream that was raging inside of me. I lay there in horror as the image of their faces and their screams for help rang in my ears. What did this mean? Was this a chance dream or were my children crying out to me to do something to save them? By morning, I knew that I had been given a message, and I prayed nonstop for the next few days for some way to please help them.

It was at this point that I received a phone call that once again changed the direction of our lives.

"Hi, this is the father of the four little children that you fostered. My wife and I are getting a divorce. We are not living with each other, and I do not want her to have these children. We are going to court again in three days, and if the judge says that we cannot have them, are you still interested in having these children?"

Immediately, the memory of the dream that I had a few days previously came forcefully to my mind. Here was my answer. They did need me, and they needed me now.

"Absolutely we want them. We would love to have them! Where do we go and when do we need to be there?" I replied with tears streaming down my cheeks and my heart in every word I spoke.

He quickly responded with, "Oh, I don't want you to come now. I was just wondering. I will call you if I need you." And he hung up.

I sat there in stunned silence. Wait for a call? There was no way that I was going to just sit there and wait for a call. My children needed me, and I was going to be there for them. I started packing right that moment, even as I was calling to tell Brian to please come home now and that we needed to leave. As usual, Sarah stepped up to the plate and took over the running of the home, and in less than two hours, we were on the road heading back to Utah and to our children.

I have to admit that Brian and I were definitely in agreement that we were to go, but we did disagree on one matter. He wanted to take our small car, as it was so much better on gas. I couldn't do it! I told him that we had to bring our Suburban, as it was big enough to bring these children home, and they were coming home with us. He tried to remind me of the impossibility of this, but I knew that this was it. It was finally God's timing, and I was going to show every ounce of faith I had by bringing that big car to take them home in. My good husband put his doubts aside and once again trusted my heart.

We arrived in Utah in the wee hours of the morning and checked into a hotel. We slept for the few hours that remained in the night and awoke early, anxious to move things forward. We didn't know exactly what to do or who to talk to as we had been told by DCFS to just let it go. I was a little nervous to call them, as I did not want to offend anyone at this critical time. Nevertheless, we had to do something.

We went to the office of the state appointed children's attorney. We asked for an appointment and were told that he was busy but would be able to see us later. We didn't even dare leave, so we waited in the parking lot, hoping to see him later that day. The day ended and there was no appointment. Another day closer to court, and we were no closer to knowing what to do.

We went home that night and called the children's father. I don't think he was very pleased that we were in town. We let him know that we were there just as a support to them in whatever way they needed us to be. We also let him know that we were not there to hurt them. I could feel his heart softening, and we told him that we would be praying for them and hung up.

Brian and I just sat there wondering what we were doing and wondering if we had made a mistake and were crazy to be here. But we had come this far, and we were not going to turn back yet.

The next day, we were back at the office of the children's attorney, hoping for an appointment. This time, we were able to see him.

He was very surprised to see us, as it had been eleven months since we had lost the children. He told us what was going on with the family. Evidently, the parents were getting a divorce. They had been living apart for some time. At first, the children had been with their father, but they were now with their maternal grandpa. This good man wanted to adopt them, but we knew this was not the ideal situation for these already confused and disturbed children. His wife had already died from drug and alcohol use, and he had three other adult daughters who struggled with drug abuse and a young boy. We had met him before, several times, and liked him very much, but we were very concerned about what would happen if these children were raised in this home, still so close to all the craziness with their parents.

The attorney said that he would love to see these children in our home but that there was no way the court would allow that, as we did not live in Utah anymore. But we were welcome to come to court and see what happened.

That night, we called the mother and asked if we could please visit with her. She agreed to see us. We went to her home, and it was uncomfortable to say the least. Her family would walk through the room glaring at us and would not speak more than a few curt words to our polite questions. Now, I understand that totally. To them, we were the enemy. We always had been. In their eyes, we were the ones that were trying to take the children. I just don't think that they could comprehend or accept that it was their lifestyle that was the enemy. It was not even DCFS. It was their own decision's that had been and were being made that was turning their lives upside down. DCFS had given them every opportunity to prove themselves a healthy and safe place for these children to belong to. I feel DCFS tried so hard to do this that it was detrimental to the children in many ways. But they had to. The parents and family had the right to try and clean up their lives and get themselves in a place where they could take proper care of these little ones. They had been given chance after chance. They simply were not equipped with the ability to do so. My heart goes out to them even today as I think about how much they would have liked things to be different, but they were just not able to make it happen.

Brian and I shed many tears with the mother that night as we talked and prayed together. After a great deal of talking and sharing our hearts with each other, she informed us that she would indeed like us to have the children if the judge would not allow her to keep them. We were ecstatic, and yet we knew the vulnerability of that decision. We prayed together again that she would be able to hold on to that decision in her heart. We left exhilarated and scared to death.

We had done all that we knew to do, and the rest was up to God. We went to our hotel room and knelt together and quietly put it in his hands.

The next morning was court. This was the day that would decide where those children were to go. We showed up early at the courthouse and asked if we could meet with the attorneys that were running the case. They agreed, and we went up to a special conference room to talk with the parents' attorney and to the children's attorney. We presented our case and why we felt the children should come to us. They laughed at us. They told us to just get in our car and go home, that we had no business being there and no judge was going to give children to us just because we had once been the foster parents. They also told us that that very morning the mother had called and said she definitely wanted the children to go to her father. Case closed, just go home!

They walked out, and we just looked at each other. It was true! What were we doing there? No one had asked us to come. No one wanted us there. We were fooling ourselves, and we had just better get in the car and go home.

We walked out of that courthouse and went to our car and sat there in unbelief and incredible sorrow. We had tried, but it must just not be God's will to have these children in our home. Isn't that what everyone kept telling us? Why were we still fighting? Why had we left our children behind, children that we already had, to fight a dream that had no possible happy ending? It had been almost three years of grinding pain and turmoil. It was time to throw in the towel, to give up and accept what life was trying to tell us. Just go home!

Brian went to start the car, and as he did, we looked at each other, and we both knew we had to offer one more prayer before we could put that car in reverse and drive away. We held hands and prayed with all the strength and power we could muster. It was a simple prayer. We told God what we had found out and asked him what we should do. Did he want us to go home?

We ended the prayer and turned to each other to see what the other had felt. I no longer remember who shared their impressions first. I just know that as we shared with each other what answer we had received, we had both been given the same picture in our minds. We saw God parting the Red Sea for the Israelites to cross on dry ground. We both heard in our mind the words, "Today you will see the Red Sea parted!"

Again it was one of those experiences that you know what you know, and you know that God knows that you know. You have no choice but to follow the promptings and let him work out the rest.

We went back in that courthouse holding our heads high amongst the daggers that were being sent our way by those in the family who were there in the waiting room. They did not want us there, and no one would speak to us. A few minutes later, it was announced that the session for the four little ones would begin.

We walked in after everyone else had entered and sat quietly in the very back of the room. I had never been in a courtroom before. I was overwhelmed. The father and his family and friends were on one side, and the mother and her family and friends were on the other side. We looked up at the stand, and I have to admit that it was a very daunting sight to see the judge in his robes ready to pass judgment. He looked like he wanted to just throw all of us out of his courtroom. He had met with these people over and over in the last three years, and I think he was just as weary as we were of the whole thing.

He heard both sides as both the mother and father pled their cases. The mother requested that if she was to lose her rights that her father be allowed to take the children. I actually was very proud of the mother as she stated that she felt that as much as she loved these children, she was not capable of meeting their needs. The father just talked about keeping them himself.

The judge looked down at them and chastised them for not getting their lives in order. He reminded them of how many times they had been in his courtroom and had made promises only to break those promises. He talked about loving children enough to do what was right, and then he sat in silence.

It was at this moment that he looked out over the audience and saw us sitting on the back row. He pointed to us and asked who we were and why were we there. We stood, and I must admit that I was trembling from head to foot. Were we in trouble for showing up? Would we be kicked out of his courtroom? We attempted to answer him with a calm voice.

"We are the foster parents. We had these children in our home for almost two years before they were sent back to live with their parents. We were transferred out of state to New Mexico with our job, and so the children went back home."

He looked at us with confusion and said, "Why are you here?"

We answered with all the feeling that was overflowing in our hearts. "We love them, and we had to be here to see what would happen to them!"

He then looked at the mother and father and said, "This is what love is. To drive all the way from New Mexico to see to the future of these children is what love is all about."

He then looked at all of us and said with a voice that broached no argument, "I want this courtroom cleared. I have many other cases to see this day, but all of you will remain in the courthouse. You will bring to me your plan on behalf of these children by the end of the day; a plan that all will agree to. Now, clear the court!"

The waiting room was full of people, but for us, no one existed except for the attorneys and the other family—all the family. For some reason, whereas before it was mother against father, it was now them against us. We were the threat once again. We did not know why until later. The attorneys kept pulling different members of the family out to talk with them. They would come back and glare at us some more. Hour after hour this went on. No one would talk to us. We kept wondering if we should just leave, but the words of the judge were clear that we all were to stay in the courthouse.

Finally, near the end of the day, the children's attorney called Brian and I to a corner of the waiting room and asked us one simple question.

"If you were to be given the children today, would you have a car big enough to take them home?"

Oh, the miracle of the whisperings of the spirit. "Yes!" my husband replied as he held me close and gave me a special squeeze. "Yes, we have our suburban here with us, and we have plenty of room."

He walked off, and we wondered.

The waiting room was empty now except for our group. We sat waiting. We still had no idea what all the discussion was leading to, and we were going crazy. Our prayers had not stopped ascending to heaven all day. It was now after six, and they came to call us in to see the judge. Only instead of having all of us come in, they had only the parents and the attorneys enter the courtroom.

Fifteen minutes later, the doors opened and the mother stepped out. She looked over to Brian and me and said words that I will never forget.

"You won! They are yours!"

I did not stop to even take it in, I just ran over and threw my arms around that mother and wept. For as happy as I was, I knew her sadness was as great. She quietly told me to come and get them that evening, she would have them ready. The family turned away and walked out.

The attorney who had been so adamant that we had no place being there pulled us aside. He looked at us. There were tears in his eyes, and he simply said, "Do you believe in God?" We replied that we believed in him with all of our hearts. He then said these words that were a direct answer to our prayer as we sat in the car and heard the words, "Today you will see the Red Sea parted."

He said, "Never in all my years of working in the court system have I seen what I saw today. There was no possible way for you to be awarded these children. Nothing like it has ever happened. But today, in that courtroom, God worked a miracle. I would not believe it if I had not seen it with my own eyes. God must really want these children in your home." And he turned and walked away.

God had worked his mighty miracle. We had put our faith in his hands, and he had taken an impossible sea that needed to be crossed and he had parted it. I am still in awe today as I tell this story again. Who were we that we should have a miracle of this magnitude take place in our lives? The answer to that is simple, really. We are his children, and we had enough faith to put ourselves in the way. And when you do that, his love can pour out upon you, and he can take you on a journey, a journey that for us had been the longest and hardest walk that we had ever taken and yet, in his mercy, he had turned it into an incredible gift. There would be more long walks, many of them, before our gathering was complete, but for now, the battle was over. It was a fight that had been worth fighting, and we were in a place of wondrous gratitude.

We went that night to pick up the children and put our smiles in place as we faced this challenging moment. We were all trying to be happy for the children's sake. That was the last gift that those parents could give those children, their support of what was happening in their lives. I admire them for that.

We pulled away from their home, and I just stared and stared at the children. They were ours. No, they were not yet legally adopted, but the court had given us custody and guardianship, and nothing could take them away. What an incredible feeling that was. We gloried in every breath of each moment. God had made true his promise of almost three years ago when he said as I walked through the door that first night, "These children will be yours forever."

We soon headed back to New Mexico, to the place that had witnessed my tears, my anguish, and my quiet acceptance of God's timing. We were going home!

That summer of 2000, the adoptions were finalized for those four children. I remember that day and how it was so anti-climatic. There was no courtroom, no big party, just a call from our attorney telling us that he had received word that the adoptions had been finalized a few days before. Congratulations! Isn't that how it is? You work and struggle and give your very life's blood to accomplish your heart's desire, and then it is almost as if nothing ever really happened and life just goes on. It's amazing!

But something had happened. I now had six little ones, two teenagers, two young women, and a husband to care for and to try and create and mold into a family. And those were only the ones that lived with us. My Annie Laurie and her new husband, David, needed us, and so did our son, Andrew, in Brazil. We had the names of brother, sister, mother, and father, but those names had to become real. They had to be relationships, friends, and somehow they all had to grow to love one another with all their hearts.

· ·

Andrew—our twenty-eight-year-old son, one of the twins

Seventeen years old—the age where the world revolves around you and connections with family are often placed second at best. That was the age I was when I was first introduced to adoption. Four little blondies, as we affectionately called them: Brian,

Clarissa, Rebekah, and Benjamin. On the surface, I did the best my seventeen years of maturity could to be supportive, but it was just that—surface. The ability to connect was more than I was able to do at the time, especially under such unstable circumstances. Many times I felt my parents had no room left in their hearts as they were consumed with the battle for these children. Support was literally all I could do at the time. And then came two more: Emily and little Katurah.

The difference with these two (Emily and Katurah) was that the adoptions were immediate. No questions, no disappointments, they were my sisters. This permanence created more of a bond than with the other four (who were still in the workings), but still, my connection with my new sisters was limited, to say the least. I left for Brazil with two little sisters who I didn't know that well and who I liked but couldn't say that I loved yet. And then I got a letter saying that those four blondies had come home. Now I had six little brothers and sisters that I didn't know very well and certainly did not know how to love yet.

A few months later, as I was sitting at my desk in my meager apartment in Brazil, I got a letter. The adoption of the four little blondies had been finalized.

I sat back in my chair, tears coming to my eyes, and saw as if for the first time, all the years of uncertainty, disappointment, and hurt that my parents had endured. Gratitude overwhelmed me as I considered the amount of pleading that had taken place for this end, not necessarily my own, but that of my parents, my siblings, extended family, and just as importantly, that of these four little ones. And what was to be my role in this new family?

The oldest of now twelve children, I felt the duty that comes with being the oldest son resting squarely upon my shoulders. I could no longer be indifferent, as I had been, in carrying the responsibility that came with my birth. I had to know that what my parents were doing, and the responsibility it gave me were what heavenly Father wanted. I then felt an immense amount of worry that I would not be able to fulfill this responsibility and, even more, would not be able to love these new (and any additional) brothers and sisters the way an older brother should.

Right then, in that apartment in Brazil, I prayed to understand my role and accept my parents' ability to receive inspiration. In that same moment, an overwhelming amount of understanding and appreciation came over me, and I no longer had any doubt that my parents were doing what was right. I realized, as the oldest son, that I would be blessed with an extra capacity to love and accept and would indeed be given the strength to fulfill my role. As if to prove the truth of this, an immense feeling of love for my new brothers and sisters came over me, and a connection was placed where there had not been one before. From that day, there has never been a question in my mind. This is the calling and purpose for my family.

● ●

—Annie Laurie

In our family, the role of the eldest son is very important. Ever since that moment, Andrew has worked and struggled to prepare himself to fulfill that duty. He does a beautiful job. We are so pleased with him and with all of these children who truly have taken on the titles of sister and brother and made this whole drama play out in a wonderful and awe-inspiring way.

But now, as if all that drama was not enough, we were asked to take a young man of fifteen into our home for the school year. Tosin was from Africa and was with the study abroad program. This added a whole other dimension to our lives.

What a year that was as we faced the reality of what we had been fighting for. There were many hard and overwhelming days. The four little ones had grown up. They were not just cute little babies and toddlers. The eleven months that they had to go back into that horrific situation shattered their hearts but left them with an intensity and a determination to make it together at all costs. The things they had to witness and were exposed to during that time were terrible and will be with them all their lives. Our job was to turn their hearts to God, who would help those terrible experiences turn into wonderful gifts.

That is how I have looked at life, and that is how I looked at their situation. I had to! How else could I live with the fact that my Emily had lived off a garbage dump for eight years with no one to care for her? How could I live with the things that these four had gone through and not feel that God had just abandoned all of us? From my viewpoint, he could have made things so much better for these children if he would have just left them in our home. He is in charge, isn't he?

Well, then, the big question was why did they have to go back? Why did they have to suffer so many hard things during those eleven months? He could so easily have stopped it! So, I spent much time on my knees because these were the same questions that our little ones were asking, and I had to have an answer. My answer was simple. *All these things will give you experience, and if you will allow it, they can bring you some of your greatest gifts.*

It truly was simple, but the application of that teaching was infinitely hard. I, in retrospect, find it very interesting that at this same time, when I had a houseful of struggling children who needed to heal, I too was going through some of the greatest personal struggles I have gone through in my life. I share this with delicacy, as this book is not about my personal struggles with healing. That is another story, but that story was going on at the same time as all of our children's hearts were also healing. It is enough to say that as a four- and five-year-old my life was shattered by abuse from outside my family that was horrific and life changing. I was at this time struggling myself to heal. I was searching for answers, and in a very sweet way, that searching gave me the tools with which to help my own children to also heal.

Isn't it interesting that the very thing in my childhood that I thought was a curse, with God's help, has brought me some of my greatest gifts. The overcoming of the effects of that in my life is what has helped to mold me into who I am today. It has given me my absolute love for, and faith in, my Father in heaven. It has truly given me the experience that I needed in order to help these children overcome their struggles also. I have taught them to turn to God. Instead of raging against a God who would abandon them, they are so grateful for his gift of helping them overcome their situation and of being able to receive the gifts that come with turning your hearts over to God.

So from the very first, that is how I have helped all our children deal with all that they have faced. It has not come over night, but every one of them is grateful, so grateful, for the challenges that they have been given, for it has given them character, self worth, love, an unending desire to serve others, and a faith in God that he will always be there.

* *

Little Brian was now six, and he had become so used to being the sole caretaker of these children that he struggled to allow us to fill that role. He had been responsible to see that they had food, clothes to wear, and he was the one who took care of them when they were hurt or lonely. He was so old for his years. He was fiercely protective and had no idea how to let a mom or dad take care of his needs either. He also struggled to focus his mind on anything. He would sit for hours and just look at the paper in front of him and not be able to accomplish anything. But if I would sit by him, he could breeze through his work. We soon found out that he had ADD.

He has worked to let go of the need to be the one who has to take care of his brother and sisters. Instead, he has turned that into the ability to be a wonderful leader. His fourteen younger brothers and sisters look up to him and want to be like him. He is straight as an arrow in his belief and following of God's word. When people meet him, they know immediately that there is something different about our Brian. He knows God, for in his hour of need, God was with him.

Clarissa was five, and she too was old beyond her years. She was so desperate to be known for herself that she had weird behaviors that would cry out, "Do you see me?" One such behavior was marking her territory. Everywhere she went she would take a marker and just make a mark on the wall, on the furniture, on the bed covers, anywhere that she could to let us know that she had been there. It was interesting that as soon as I understood what she was doing, the behavior stopped. With understanding, she could let go of it.

I have seen that happen over and over. They just needed to be loved and understood. It became my quest to not just stop behaviors but to understand their hearts and why they did what they did and then help them understand why.

She has wisdom and gifts beyond her years. Clarissa is now thirteen and looking at college next year. She can cook, clean house, do the laundry, and take care of her thirteen younger brothers and sisters without batting an eye. She has taken hold of what her journey has given her and turned her experiences into profound gifts from God.

Benjamin was now four and looked like an angel. He acted like one too, and then, all of a sudden, he would go into a rage that would shake the whole family. We soon found out that he was dealing with fetal alcohol syndrome. Because the mother took alcohol while she was pregnant, his brain did not develop fully, and among other things, FAS kids are not able to choose right from wrong. They do not have that processing time that we have that lets them make a choice. They just act on every thought.

All the children were born addicted to meth. They have joint pain and other issues going on in their bodies because of that, but it seemed to hit Rebekah the worst. She was now three and the apple of her daddy's eye. She had addictive behaviors that were showing up already. She could not control them and would seem to go crazy at times with the need to be satisfied. Sugar was one of those addictions. Now I know that many of us are addicted to sugar, but with her, it was crazy. She would beg us all day for something with sugar. She would weep and say she just really needed it. *Please, please, couldn't she just have a little taste?* She too has worked hard to be her own master. Rebekah is our child who has the never-ending imagination. She is always acting, dressing up, getting her siblings to put together some play or dance, and she lives to perform. She truly does delight us.

We also found out later that both Emily and Katurah are autistic. We did not know this at the time or anything about autism. I wish I had. I would have been able to handle things differently. Instead, my patience would not only be thin but often nonexistent as I would ask Emily a question and she would just stare at me. It was as if a wall would go up, and there was nobody home behind the wall. I was confused because she was anything but a belligerent child. She loved to work, to serve, and she was such a happy girl, but when that wall came up, she was gone.

We have always believed in the power of nutrition, and we would find many wonderful answers with a nutritional supplement called Reliv. But I didn't have those answers yet, and life was crazy. I could not have done it without God's help every step of the way.

Even though every day was a challenge, I never got tired of being their mother. Maybe that is one of the reasons that I had to fight so hard for all of our children. The harder you fight for something or someone, the more you love them. We loved these kids, and they loved us back. Slowly we created a family. A family that would be able to blend all the different cultures, skin color, personalities, personal pain, and health issues with love and end up with a beautiful haven of peace that welcomed all who God would choose to bring in.

It all starts - 1978

The Miracle of Jenai' in Vietnam

annie laurie & brian richardson

Katie, Annie Laurie and Andrew

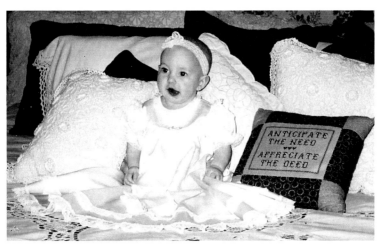

Rebekah – our sweet princess

Our Original Five

Our Little girl comes home
- Julianna Joy

Three for One
Heavenly Special
– Joseph, Jenai', Joshua

The day the cereal won

Katie, Sarah, Annie Laurie

Blaine and his special sister Emily

Annie Laurie's Father, Brothers and Brian
– serving our country

Grandpa with his first two adopted
children, Emily and Katurah

The four little ones come to our family

17 of the 19 adopted children – 2008
(Esther and Sarah missing)

I find my Bethany in Haiti

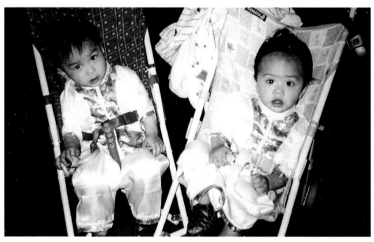

Joseph and Joshua come home

We are growing

Still growing

Emily - Lice and mayonaise

The Orphanage nannies in Haiti

Bethany, Jislene, Kaneasha, Laura,
Fayetta(Grandaughter) In Haiti

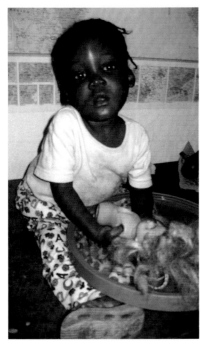

Jislene "not worth saving"

Katurah's goodbye with Biological Mother

Kyrstin and Jislene on the Ranch

Esther and "Cinerella"

Kaneasha and Anson – Haiti Orphanage

All of our adopted children 2008

Our family just keeps growing – 2007
Children, spouses and granchildren

back to the marshall islands

—Annie Laurie

It had been a little over a year since our children had come home. It was a very full year of change and adjustment. Everyone was fitting in to their roles in this growing family. We had enjoyed Tosin, but it was time for him to go back to Africa to his family there. We were still struggling with the Sarah situation, but she was such a support during this time that she was truly binding our hearts to her. Katie had come home after being a nanny in Connecticut for a year, and we loved having her there.

We had also decided to build us a large home to better fit our needs, so every day, Blaine and Ammon worked on the new home, and my husband would go there at night and in the early morning hours to get it done as quickly as possible. It took a full year to build it, and we were able to move in that summer of 2001. It was beautiful! Once again, the men of my family had created a place of peace for their wife and mother.

I had also started teaching in our home again. So we had about twenty kids who came three days a week to be homeschooled.

It was at this time that I started to feel those urgings in my heart that there were more children. Where were they and how was I supposed to find them?

While we had been in the Marshall Islands adopting Emily and Katurah, our hearts had been drawn to the people. Someday we would love to go back and somehow help them better their lives. As we had visited with Katurah's family, they had mentioned that she had two biological sisters. One of them was two years older than Katurah, and the other was one year older. Her father had mentioned that someday he would love it if they too could come to America. They are the ones that other members of the family had taken as their own, but this father wanted more for them.

These two little girls started coming to my mind and heart. The thought of them would not leave me. So I called The Marshall Islands and talked to the father. I asked him if he was still interested in having us bring his two other girls to America to raise them as our own. He said yes he was very interested, but he did not know if the aunts who had taken them would allow them to go. He told me that if I would come to the Marshall Islands, he was sure that they would let me take them home.

It was going to be a lot of money, and I could not bring myself to take the chance of going there and not getting them. So, I tried to ignore the feelings. Besides, Brian thought that we were through having children. For some reason, he thought twelve was enough!

I found that I could not ignore the feelings. I tried. I really tried. They just would not go away, and so I approached my husband. He just looked at me like I was crazy and said he did not feel anything. So, I kept trying. Every few days, I would go back to Brian and tell him again what I was feeling. He still felt nothing.

It was the first of September, and I went to him one last time. We were sitting at the kitchen table, and he turned to me and said, "Go! Find the money and go get those girls!" I was shocked. Could he be serious? Did he really think I should go? I still don't know to this day why he said go, but I went!

I booked tickets that very day for Katie and myself. I called my daughter, Annie Laurie, and told her that we were going, and she booked tickets also. She wanted to be there for this wondrous trip. They had gone with us before, and they wanted to go again. I booked tickets for the 15th of September, 2001. I am sure you all remember what happened that fateful day of 9/11/2001. New York was attacked, and all airports were closed.

I must admit that even as I was shedding tears for all the families who had lost so much, I still felt the need to get those girls as soon as it was possible to fly again. The trouble was that by the fifteenth, only a few airports were open. In order for Americans to land in an airport, the airport had to follow all these new guidelines put out by the government for our safety. The main airports in the United States were open and so was Hawaii, but how long would it take for a tiny airport like the Marshall Islands to comply with those regulations? Did we wait or take our chances and go? Brian said, "Go!" So we went.

We arrived in Hawaii and found out that the Marshall Islands airport was indeed still closed but should be open soon. Tough life! We were stranded in Hawaii. We found a hotel in Laie, where I had lived as a young girl, and had a great time. In just a few days, the flights were opened, and we took off for our second time to that beautiful island.

Nobody was there to meet us this time, as no one knew that we were coming. We just walked off that plane and figured we could take care of anything that came our way. We hired a man with a beat-up, old van to get us to the hotel and checked into our room. It was still unbearably hot and muggy. Nothing had changed since the last time we were there; except the bugs were worse. You know the two-inch roaches that skitter so fast you can't catch them? Our room was full of them. We assigned Katie (I'm sorry, but she was the youngest) the job of catching them. She couldn't bring herself to do it, so she would take the glasses that they provided and chase them down and put the glass on top of them. Annie Laurie and I would be jumping from one bed to the next screaming as we tried to get away from the terrible monsters. By the time we left our hotel, you had to be very careful where you stepped because there were glasses and roaches everywhere. I can't imagine what the maid thought!

Here we were at the hotel, and the place we needed to get to was thirty-five miles away down a very long strip of road. We had to find a car. You must remember this is not really a modern city. In fact, far from it. We went to the information desk and asked where we could find a car. They told us the rental place was about two miles away, and we were more than welcome to walk there. When we arrived, they told us they had one car that was available. We said we would take it sight unseen. It was a nice enough car, it ran, barely. But we were not the only ones who wanted a ride. It was full of roaches. Only these were just the one-inch kind, so they could hide much easier. Remember that we had to wear dresses over there. Every time I would open the car door, I would see bugs skitter into the interior depths under my seat. The whole time I would be driving, I could just feel them crawling up my legs and ... Now, I really don't think they actually crawled up my leg because they were as scared of me as I was of them, but it sure felt like it. But, hey, we lived through it, and I am sure we are better people today because of it.

We had no idea how to find this family. We had come all this way and had no clue where to go except that we knew they lived somewhere in Laura. Laura was the part of the island that was jungle and very lush. There were little houses and huts strewn all over. It was also located at the other end of the island.

The three of us prayed together and decided that we would go to one of the churches in Laura on Sunday and see if anyone knew the family. It was a long shot, but the best one we had.

Sunday morning we set out bright and early, as we had no idea what time church was. We arrived in Laura and found a building that said they had services at ten. We were a bit early, so we drove around to see what Laura was like. We had been here before. This is where we had picked up our sweet little Katurah two years previous. I wish I had paid more attention so I could find their home again, but I had no idea where to look.

We walked into church that morning, and I'm afraid we were a little obvious, being the only white people there. I did not want to ask about the family until after church, so we just sat quietly and tried to sing when they sang. There is nothing like hearing the islanders sing praises to their God. They sing with their whole hearts and in a very singsong fashion. All the notes were connected to each other as they slurred from one tone to the next. It was more like a droning sound that was more musical than melodic singing, and I loved it. I tried to sing along, and they heard me sing, so they had me go up and sing a solo for them. They then asked me to testify of God to them. They had someone there who could translate brokenly. It was a wonderful experience.

But, you know, God really likes his miracles! As I was up there singing, I looked on the very back row, and there sat Katurah's biological mother. I couldn't believe my eyes. We had been directed straight into their lives. She smiled at us, and I am sure she was wondering what in the world we were doing there on the other side of the world.

After the church services ended, we went back to see them, and I threw my arms around her, as that was the only way I knew how to communicate with her. We spoke no Marshallese, and they spoke very little English. However, there is another language that speaks louder than the spoken word. Her family—Katurah's biological grandmother and the aunts—were there, and they let us know through sign language that they wanted us to come back to their home.

We left the car where it was and followed them down one of the paths and through beautiful tropical wildlife, past many other little huts, until we arrived at their home. There it was; the hut that we had parked beside in the rain two years ago. I couldn't believe I was back. Memories flooded, and feelings of gratitude welled up inside of me until I was once again in tears. Fortunately, no one could tell as the tears just mixed with the sweat that continually dripped off of me. It was a poignant moment for the three of us. We had no idea what was still ahead, but we knew that we were supposed to be there.

We spent the day sitting and trying to understand each other the best we could through hand motions and their limited English. Mostly we laughed a lot as we tried to communicate. They were warm and friendly, and we fell in love with the family. There was a young girl of fifteen who knew a bit of English, but she was too shy to do much translating. After a few hours, we told them we must leave but we would come back tomorrow. As we pulled away, I wondered how we were going to be able to communicate why we were there. There would somehow have to be yet another miracle.

We went back to our roach-infested car and drove to our roach-infested hotel room and crashed on the bed. What an emotionally exhausting day it had been. We were worn out and went straight to sleep.

We arose the next morning determined that this was the day to talk about the girls. We arrived in Laura mid-morning and joined the family in the very hut that Katurah had been born in. Their home area had more than one hut. They had a hut where the men slept, a hut where the women slept, and a hut for cooking. Then they had the hut that we were in for visiting and for older married children to use if they desired. Things went a little easier this time because they knew us a little better, and the daughter, who was fifteen, decided she would help a little more with translation. She had studied a little bit of English in her school, but it was very meager.

We sat there talking, or really mostly laughing as we tried to talk, and the grandmother turned to me and said, "My name is Cinerila." I asked her to say it again so I could pronounce it clearly. Everyone started to laugh. I didn't get it. She said it again. They were all laughing so I laughed too, just to join the crowd. I tried to say her name, and they just laughed harder. I was extremely uncomfortable at this point, and so I figured I must be saying something wrong. You know how it is when you are learning a new language; you mispronounce words all the time. Well, I decided I would try to change the subject by doing some other irrelevant hand motions. It worked until I tried to get her attention, and so I said her name, Cinerila. Everyone burst out laughing, and I just sat there. All of a sudden, I got it. She had jokingly told me her name was Cinderella, thinking I would laugh at the joke, and instead, the joke was on me. That broke the ice between us all completely, and we had a great time together.

Later that day, I was able to meet with the father of the two girls and ask him what he wanted to do. He said that he really wanted his girls to come home with me, and he wanted his wife and baby daughter to come also. We had told them that we would love to sponsor them in America, but he told us he couldn't come at that time. He had been caught growing and selling marijuana to the boats that came to port. There are no jails on the island. They are just grounded to the island. He was not allowed to leave for three years. But he really wanted his wife and children to go to America. I told him I would do my part by getting passports and tickets, but he would have to talk to the aunts. He said that he would.

We decided that we would get the paperwork started the next day. If you remember, all adoption proceedings had been cancelled on the island. So we figured we would just take them to America and do it there. That was perfectly legal, especially since we were bringing the mother anyway. It was a very hot day with seven people and a baby piled into our tiny car. Thank goodness I was the driver and not a passenger.

We got all the paperwork started, tickets purchased, and took everybody back home. They told us to come back the next day and they would have a surprise for us.

We went back to our bug-infested room and didn't even care, we were so tired. We were excited about the surprise we were going to get the next day.

We headed back out to Laura that next morning. They greeted us with hugs and then took us down to the beach. The people in the Marshall Islands live on some of the most beautiful beaches you have ever seen. But they hardly swim at all. The ocean is not a source of recreation; it is a source of food. They are also not exactly islands but atolls. An atoll is a huge coral reef that is partially covered by water, and it gives the appearance of hundreds of little islands sticking out of the water, so as you travel from one island to the next, the water is not very deep. We were about to get our first up close and personal lesson on exactly what that looks like.

They motioned to us to get in a tiny boat that was on the beach. We looked around wondering if this was okay and realized a good number of the villagers had come out to watch the white ladies take off in a boat. Now, you have to picture this. The beach is lined with natives that we have never seen before. I am in charge of the safety and welfare of my two daughters, and here we are being loaded onto a tiny dingy that barely has room for us, and then as we sit, two half naked young men get in the boat carrying two huge machetes. I am all of a sudden thrown into a state of panic. For all we know, they could be taking us away to kill us for coming to their peaceful village. I looked at my daughters and could see they were thinking the same thing that I was. We were terrified. Fortunately, you know the rest of the story, as I am still alive today to write this book, but I didn't know that at the time. It is crazy how your thoughts can get so carried away. I was thinking headhunter, cannibals, etc., and instead, we had a wonderful time.

As we started out across that vast expanse of clear blue water, we could see in the far distance a speck that looked like it might be land. The whole way across to the other island, the water was never more than about twelve feet deep and so clear you could see all the way to the bottom. We saw beautiful coral, colorful fish, and even a WWII plane that had gone down. It was incredible. As we landed, I was struck with the beauty and peace that was there. It was very primitive with the only real building being a school for the children who lived on all those little neighboring islands.

We waded in the water that was the temperature of a warm bath. They brought with them those machetes that we were so scared of. The younger of the two men scrambled up a nearby coconut tree, and in no time at all, there were two coconuts at our feet. They then used their machetes to provide us all with fresh coconut milk. It was truly a surprising and wonderful day. We arrived back in Laura safe and sound and loving these people and this beautiful place even more.

The next few days, we visited several times with the aunts, but they had not decided what they were going to do. The girls and I spent a great deal of time praying. We had felt so strongly that we were supposed to come; certainly we would go home with children. We had spent so much money that we simply did not have that surely God would not have asked us to come here and waste all of that either. But who knows the mind of God. He always has a plan, we just have to step into that plan and follow through with however he wants it to look.

I have to share one more experience that we had with the ladies while we visited, as it had a great bearing on the future. The only place that you will find a proper bathroom in the Marshall Islands is in a government building or your hotel room. Well, we really tried to be strategic with our personal needs because of this, but after you drive for one hour, visit for three to four hours, and then drive an hour back, sometimes you just can't plan these things.

There I was in the little hut visiting with the women, and I had to go. The Marshall Islands is not the cleanest place there is, and the water is absolutely off limits or you will get the bug. Somehow I had contracted the bug, and my innards were not reacting very well. I could not wait until I got home to take care of business. I asked if there was a bathroom close by. They all looked at me with pride and said that yes, several families had come together and built a bathroom. I was excited!

They took me off a little way, pointed to a three-foot high, cement wall, and walked off. I went around the wall wondering what I would see and realized it only had three sides. Inside that three-foot, three-sided wall there was a fifty gallon barrel full of rainwater and a toilet set right on the ground. I looked around hoping someone could tell me what to do, but they had disappeared. I remembered Katurah's parents coming to the hotel and not knowing how to use the toilets there, and now I was in the same situation. Well, I couldn't wait any longer, so I did what I had to do, hoping no one would come around that wall. I mean, about ten families shared that toilet, anyone could have come. I then just stood there and wondered what I was supposed to do next. I had no clue, so I just walked away praying no one would know it was me.

I arrived back in the hut and Grandmother (alias Cinerila) walked out. I did not know where she had gone until I saw her return. She looked at me and started to giggle. She said something to the others, and they all looked at me and started to giggle. I wanted to crawl under the woven floor mat and fade away. I don't know if I have ever been redder in my life. I just had to giggle with them.

⁕ ⁕

We found out that the fifteen-year-old girl's name was Esther. She was tiny. I thought she was no more than nine when I first met her. We asked her if she wanted to come and spend a few nights with us in the hotel. I don't think she really wanted to, but her mother made her, as it would give status to them to have their daughter staying in a fancy hotel with the white ladies. It was during one of these nights while we were together that I received one of those whisperings. I just kept feeling over and over that she was to be my daughter. I just ignored it because the possibility was absolutely unheard of. I told my daughters, and they just looked at me. They then told me that each one of them had had similar feelings. They too felt she was going to be in our family. Wow! What do you do with that? Nothing! I did absolutely nothing, for I didn't feel to do anything. It was more like it was just information, not a movement to action.

While we were there, we became acquainted with the two little girls also. They were so very much like my Katurah. My daughters and I were sure that we would be going home with them. We were very excited.

It now was the day before we were supposed to leave. We had tickets, passports, and everything was in order. We were excited to go home. We went out to Laura to visit them again. As we walked up to their living area, the grandmother met us and motioned for us to sit down. She had a very serious look on her face. She then told us that we would not be able to take the girls back to America, as they had changed their minds and could not part with them. You know, that was fine, because I had no desire to take someone's child who really wanted them, but why then were we here? Why had we come all this way just to be told no? We burst into tears right in front of them. She hugged us and cried with us. It was a long ride back to the hotel, as we tried to figure out what we were meant to be doing.

To add insult to injury, when we arrived back at the hotel, we had a message that someone from the American embassy was waiting to see me. I was terrified. We tried to think if we had done anything wrong, but other than going fifty-five on that thirty-five mile per hour stretch of road, we could think of nothing. I went up to the lobby, leaving my girls scared to death thinking that I was going to be hauled off and they would never find me again. I met a lady and a man who said they were some officials from the embassy. They began to thoroughly interrogate me about why I was in the Marshall Islands. I tried to answer their questions, but I was scared to death. They then began to accuse me of stealing children, forcing people to give up their babies. They said I had a business selling babies and I was an embarrassment to the United States. They told me to leave the island immediately and to never come back.

I was in shock. An embarrassment to the United States? Me? Little nobody Annie Laurie and her two sweet daughters an embarrassment? How did I become so important all of a sudden? I asked them for proof, and they said they did not need to show me any proof, for they knew what I was doing. I was stunned and just sat there completely unable to speak. They left me sitting there with one more warning and threat if I went against them. I didn't know what to do. It had not been a very good day, to say the least. First we had come all this way and were now going home empty-handed, and now I was in trouble with my own country.

Needless to say, we laid low until it was time to go to the airport.

The airport! Here we were at the airport. The place we

thought was going to be such a happy ending to our journey across the ocean, and now we walked in silence. Each one of us battling with our own feelings of why; each one of us struggling to remain in control of our ravaged emotions and weary hearts. I just held my two girls and said we must trust and have faith. So, we shed a few tears and then we pulled up our socks, as the English say, and got down to finding joy in God's plan, whatever that was.

It was interesting, but as we talked, none of us felt like we had done the wrong thing. We felt that somehow we had come to do what we felt was right and someday we would understand why. As we made our way home, a wonderful peace came over all three of us, and we looked forward to further understanding but relished the feeling in our hearts of, "Well done, my good and faithful servant."

I have the best husband. Here we had gone on what seemed to be this wild goose chase. We'd spent tons of money and come home empty-handed. There were no words of I told you so or why or anything, just encouragement and support. Brian simply said, "Someday we will know why this was necessary, but in the mean time, we were obedient to the promptings, and we will be blessed for it." Wow! What a husband!

- -

This was not the only time that this kind of experience had occurred during our gathering. I'm sure there are many who have been down the road of adoption and know what this kind of experience feels like. There is no peace in your heart until you find that child, or children, that are still missing from your family. You just have to go for it if there is the slightest whispering that this could possibly be your child. We believe there are many children whose hearts are whispering, pleading to be found, to be loved, and to belong to someone who will care.

Over the years of trying to find our little girl, I had several of these experiences. Two were particularly challenging.

There was a young girl at our church in New Mexico who was also an unwed mother. She had come to live with a friend in our congregation. The young mother respected our family and was seriously considering having us adopt her little one. Once again I knew without a doubt that she was carrying a little girl. We were so excited at the thought of having this little one come into our home.

I still remember how I felt the day that I found out we would not be given the baby. The woman that the young mother was living with at the time came over to our home and informed us that we simply did not deserve to be given a white baby. She said that we only qualified to have biracial or African American children, as we had too many white children already. I couldn't believe it. What a strange world we live in. First it is my skin color and heritage that makes me unqualified, then it is my blood, then drug addicts were more qualified, and now it was because the baby was white that I was not qualified. What? Is there a limit to how many of one color you can have in a family? I wasn't so much sad for us this time as sad for the narrow mindedness of people who think they have it all figured out. Once again, a little girl was given to someone else to love.

This next one just about stopped me from ever trying again. We had the four little ones, and we had Emily and Katurah. I loved being their mother, but still in my heart I knew our little girl was coming. I never stopped looking and asking.

I received a call on Christmas Day 2000.

• •

"I hear that you are still looking for a baby?" said the person on the other end of the line. I had no idea who they were, but they had been told by a friend of ours to call us.

"Yes, I am. Do you know of a baby?" I said with the first seeds of excitement being planted in my heart.

"Yes, I do. My daughter just had a baby, and she wants to put it up for adoption. But you would have to come right now if you are interested. We live in Virginia. How soon can you get here?"

It was Christmas Day! How soon could I get there? We lived in New Mexico. My first thought was, *Do you know how much a ticket is going to cost me at this short notice during Christmas?* But my next thought was, *I will do whatever it takes to find our girl!*

I told her I would need five minutes to talk to my husband and I would call her right back. Brian didn't even need the five minutes, he just said, "Go. Whatever it costs, just go and get her." We prayed and felt it was right to go, so I went, once again.

A few hours later, I left for Virginia. I arrived at their home the next morning. I knocked on the door of people that I had never met and asked to see their new baby. I was welcomed into the home, and a baby was placed into my arms, a beautiful little girl with lots of dark hair. She was wonderful. I fell in love with her immediately. Then they informed me that they were so sorry but that while I was on my way there, the mother had changed her mind and was going to keep the baby. They were sorry for the inconvenience! I looked down at the baby in my arms, and I couldn't even weep. I felt so abandoned that I could hardly breathe. I walked out of that house, got in my car, and drove and drove and drove. And then the tears came. Tears of confusion, anger, fear that I had done something wrong in God's eyes, loneliness, and despair. All I wanted was our daughter! What was I doing so wrong that God would not bring her to us?

I finally began to drive with a purpose as I headed to Maryland to see my brother and his family. I couldn't go home for several days, as it would cost too much to change my airline ticket. But on that ride, I prayed with my whole soul. I had to know where I stood with God. Was I really in his watch care or was I wandering in a wilderness of my own making. Was there really a little girl for us, or had I just been fooling myself? I needed to know.

By the end of that long drive, I knew where I stood. Yes, there was a little girl, and yes, I was in his watch care, but I simply had to walk the journey his way, and sometimes, like this time, I would not understand that journey. The journey I was on was not just a journey to find our little girl. It was also a journey for God to find his little girl. Me! Was I truly going to be his? My job was to trust him and be obedient to his call. If I wanted a fullness of what he had for me, then I must learn to be obedient to his whisperings, whether or not I understood why. By the end of that ride, I had once again promised to go, be, do, and say whatever God wanted and needed me to be.

I believe that many times we are asked to do things just because it is an opportunity to show our true selves to God. It is easy to be obedient to a whispering that has a happy ending. But it is refining to be obedient to a whispering that seems to make no sense at all.

I went home once again with empty arms, but not an empty heart. I knew that this journey to find our little girl was more than just that. It was a journey of gathering. But the gathering was not only a gathering of children, it was a gathering of gifts. As a family, we were learning such things as understanding hearts, greater faith, determination, patience, etc.; all things that we would need in order to face the challenges that lay ahead on this amazing journey. As for me, my gift of motherhood was truly being multiplied. How grateful I was for this gathering process.

daddy send mommy to find me

—Annie Laurie

Shortly after returning from the Marshall Islands, Andrew came home from his time in Brazil. It was a wonderful experience for him; one of great growth and service.

It was not long after he arrived home that I started to receive those whisperings again. I know; you are probably really grateful you don't live in our home. I think there were many times that my family wished I didn't live in their home either. But when those whisperings would come, it didn't matter what was going on in our lives, I had to listen, and I had to find out where the children were. So, the whisperings came, and I started asking questions. Where were my children?

I called an agency that I felt good about, and the first thing she said was, "Have you ever thought of going to Vietnam?" No, that had never entered my mind, but it intrigued me. The feeling would not go away, so I approached my husband.

• •

—*Brian*

How can you be serious? More children! I did not take this new bit of information graciously. The truth is, I threw a fit. I was so concerned about our financial status that this thought overshadowed all other thoughts and feelings. I believe it would be safe to say that I was constantly in a state of panic, and the mere hint of more children sent me into my emotional stratosphere. This happened in November of 2001, when Annie Laurie made this announcement. We already had twelve children, for crying out loud. "How could there possibly be more?" I bemoaned. Twelve children—just hearing the number overwhelmed me, but Annie Laurie was firm and unwavering.

"Yes, there are more children that are ours, and would you please find out for yourself that this is true?" Annie Laurie calmly answered. She was anything but calm on the inside, but the only thing that surfaced was the firm determination that this was the right course, and it was my job to find and accept this truth.

I am not afraid of my wife or afraid to stand up to her. The bare truth is that she had been right about the majority of the things in our then twenty-two years of marriage. There is, however, something that I was very afraid of. It simply was this: to go against the right thing.

It still bugged me that she was so very sure of her impressions, so I decided to find out for myself. I think that I was more intent upon finding out that she was wrong and had been misled by her motherly feelings than I was about learning the truth.

Now I don't know how others seek truth, but for me, after weighing the facts, counting the pros and cons, it usually boils down to just one thing—prayer. I felt that I was ready to get an answer from heaven. However, the answer I was seeking was actually an agreement from God that I was right; that there were no more children to gather. Hadn't we done enough for mankind? After raising five biological children, adopting six more, and bringing Sarah into our home, we were broke, emotionally stressed to our limits, and it was foolishness to bring anymore children into our family, right?

So my prayer began more or less like this: Here are the facts, dear God, and I am sure that you agree with me, right?

No answer, nothing! No thoughts, insights, feelings ... nothing. I repeated my prideful and self-centered prayer. Still nothing.

After an hour or so of struggling, pleading, whining, and letting God know that I did not want this to happen. No impressions surfaced. No feelings came.

The tone of my pleadings changed from my fears and what I wanted and why to a question directed toward God. "What do *you* want?" Was I ready to really know what God wanted? Wow, this was a big risk. What if I got an answer I didn't like? If I didn't ask, I'd never know. So, I swallowed hard and asked—straightforward; still nothing. The desire to know grew and increased until I really wanted to know. I really needed an answer. I began to think about the little children in the Marshall Islands. I began to wonder how many other little children across the globe whisper in their hearts every night as they fall asleep, "Do I have a mommy somewhere? Is there a daddy for me? Is there a safe place to live? Is there a home where there's more than one bowl of rice a day? Is there a home where I could belong—a family somewhere?" Concern for children, any and all children, began to rise in my heart. Where was this coming from? As I pondered about the many little children that certainly must exist around the world, my thoughts went back to the commercials I had seen on TV; little kids with swollen bellies and big, empty eyes staring at me. But why were they my responsibility? I had done my part. Why did Annie Laurie feel she needed to save all the children in the world?

All of a sudden, a perfect quiet came over me, then a feeling of peace. Then it came. It came as clearly as I have heard anyone speak. In my mind, I heard a tiny girl's voice plainly say: "Daddy, please send Mommy to come and find me!" I heard the voice only once, but I remember it clearly, and it replays instantly upon demand in my mind. "Daddy, please send Mommy to come, and find me!"

Now I knew what Annie Laurie knew. With heaven's help, nothing could stop us or weaken our resolve, or so I thought at that moment. I had the idea that if you're doing right things, then everything would be easy. I thought that miracles came out of the sky when God decided it was your turn. I was about to learn, once again, that miracles must be worked for and sought after and sometimes struggled through.

I immediately shared with Annie Laurie this marvelous experience. Her only response was one that could have struck me as an all-knowing response, with the tone of "I told you so." But that's not how she said it. It was so simply put, with such innocence and subtle joy. She simply and quietly said: "I knew it!"

"How did you know, why were you so sure?" I asked. Annie Laurie began to explain slowly and with such conviction that there was no room for skepticism or doubt in any degree.

"I know there are more children, I have felt it. I have seen our daughter! I had a dream a couple of months ago, and I saw a beautiful little girl.

"But Brian, you have got to understand," she continued, while looking into my eyes and down into my heart. "You must understand that I believe there is more than one!" This statement had the same effect on me that a thundering herd of buffalo would have had on a single prairie dog mound, or something akin to that.

I really can't remember if she had told me this clearly before that moment or not. Annie Laurie claims that she hinted about the possibility of more children. I just don't buy the hinting version. When it came to gathering these special little souls, her hints were about as subtle as a cruise missile launched, traveling at supersonic speed, and right on target. I'm telling you that this woman was, and continues to be, undeterred in the cause of right! I did not fight her on the number of children, at least not for the present. The experience of the voice was still fresh, and I chose to place the announcement of more than one child to the side. I put all of my energy into the message from our little daughter that called so clearly to me from another place, with the plea to send her mommy to find her. I knew we had to find this little girl, but where does a desperate search like this begin? We figured that our little soon-to-be daughter was on planet earth, but the next step was going to have to involve yet another miracle.

Annie Laurie found an adoption agency that she felt was the right one. The director suggested that she seriously look at adopting children from Vietnam. Annie Laurie declined, but the director persisted until finally she began to seriously consider this option.

We were informed that an American woman of Vietnamese descent had set up several well-run orphanages in Vietnam. She also had very strong connections with many other government-run orphanages as well. Annie Laurie pressed forward and obediently filled out all of the paperwork, which included a home study, questions about financial situation, medical exams, living conditions, and religious affiliation.

Everything looked good, even though we already had twelve children, nine of which were still at home, and we were certain there would be no problems. This was not to be the case; we were thrown a curve ball that we just weren't expecting. In addition to not expecting what was thrown at us, we simply could not believe the response we received.

We had been rejected several years earlier in an attempt to adopt three wonderful and very needy Vietnamese children. We were told that we were not qualified parents because we were not Vietnamese. This time we were rejected by the owner of the foreign orphanages not because of our race or ethnic background, but this time because of our religious denomination.

I don't know, maybe it was just our turn to see and feel discrimination up close and personal. So many other people in our country face discrimination every day of their lives, so why not us? It still did not feel good, just, or fair. I was ready to pull out and wash my hands of such a shallow and unfair situation, but for Annie Laurie, quitting was not an option.

Annie Laurie announced that she was going to drive to Colorado, where this orphanage director lived. She wanted to meet her personally and let the director feel of her spirit before she decided whether or not we would be allowed to adopt children. She wanted to know what I thought. Well, by this time, I had at least figured out when to stand in her way and ask questions and when to step aside, wave, and blow her a farewell kiss. This was a farewell kiss situation.

Annie Laurie traveled to Colorado, and after a brief meeting, the director agreed wholeheartedly that we would be allowed to adopt, and she would do all in her power to make it happen.

After months of waiting, news about the adoptions finally came. Annie Laurie received a phone call while she was in Utah. She was attending classes to become an emotional release therapist. I was in Albuquerque teaching, finishing our home, and being a daddy. Annie Laurie called and gave me the news and informed me that we had one hour to respond. She told me the conversation had gone something like this, "You have been approved to adopt children from Vietnam." Wow, we were finally deemed qualified, acceptable, fit, and able to be the parents of *children*—whoa, wait a minute! They continued, "There are two little boys ready for adoption, one thirteen months and one seven months old, and the government has decided that you will be given the privilege of adopting them."

I realize some of you are wondering, "What's the problem with that?" especially if our hearts were right. The problem really did not lie with our willingness to bring little boys into our lives; it was far deeper than that. In fact, the dismay and disappointment was founded on two facts. First and foremost, Annie Laurie had been searching for a specific little girl for many years. Secondly, I clearly and distinctly heard and felt a little girl's voice.

Something was changing inside of me. I was, for the first time in this gathering process, actively involved in searching. This now had become my journey as well as Annie Laurie's. I heard the whispered pleadings of a tiny child, a little girl, and I would not rest until we found her.

After briefly talking on the phone, we felt impressed to just go forward. In fact this impression was so strong and clear that it overrode the feelings of uncertainty and confusion that were to come.

Annie Laurie called the head of the adoption agency. At first she tried to bargain with the agency, but apparently their hands were tied. We half offered, half pled.

"Well, what if we don't want little boys at this time?"

Answer: "Then you get nothing."

We tried again. "Okay, if we adopt these little boys, are we still eligible to adopt a little girl later?"

Answer: "No, you're lucky to be offered two children, especially boys."

We couldn't believe what we were hearing. Should we go forward? Was this an omen that what we were doing was wrong or at least headed in the wrong direction?

How can I explain to you with words what this did to Annie Laurie? Her search for her little girl had been going on for a very long time. And she had recently seen a little girl in a dream that was so real. The dream was one of those nighttime realities that almost refused to fade and surrender to daytime reality as one awakens. I did not handle her heartbreak very well. Her hurt and dismay, however, went far beyond that of disappointing news or an unfortunate setback. She had been searching for almost ten years for the daughter that was promised. All she could think of was, "Is this my little girl that I am meant to find?" There were also other pressing reasons why she sought relentlessly for children. There were, and still are, so many children who are orphans, and so many of them are hungry and in danger all of the time. They are lonely and live without being loved and cherished. We are ordinary people, but ordinary people can at least make some difference and lessen the suffering of so many little souls whose hearts whisper and plead for something better.

Our only answer that we could be sure of was to just go forward, stay the course, and run the race with patience, and that is just what we set about to do. We paid the agency fees, dossier fees, country fees, airline tickets, facilitator fees—on and on it went. The outflow of money continued throughout the trip. After all was said and done, the costs totaled to over $40,000 for these two Vietnamese adoptions. Once again, I am so grateful that I could not see into the future. If I could, I probably would have put a screeching halt to the spending of money that I simply did not have. It was like water flowing through a hole in a dike. Only this time the hole could not be stopped by a person's thumb. Oh no, this money leak would require a plug the size of a semi-truck to hold back the rushing waters of debt. I would have stopped the whole process if I had known that we would literally lose just about everything of significant financial worth before the gathering of children was over.

But in spite of all this, it was time to go and pick up our two boys.

We boarded the plane in Salt Lake City and changed airlines in Los Angeles, where we boarded the flight to Taiwan. We really had not spoken to each other so far on the trip. In fact, there were no conversations, no excitement, just the strong impression to go forward and get the job done. What was wrong with us? There were two little boys who needed a home desperately. One had been left on the orphanage guard's bed and the other little boy had been given to another orphanage by a young unwed mother. So why no joy? Annie Laurie turned to me about an hour into the flight and simply asked with tears covering her face, "What are we doing? We should be going to adopt a little girl."

So which voice or impression do you follow at times like this; the voice of a little girl asking me to send Mommy to find her? Did this little girl even exist? And what about these precious little boys? Weren't they as important as a little girl that I had heard in my mind and that my wife had seen in a dream? Did we imagine the voice and the image in a dream? What were we doing?

As we continued our conversation-less flight, the impression to just go forward permeated our thoughts.

It seemed that we flew forever to Taiwan and on to North Vietnam. After landing and seeing what seemed to be utter chaos compared to an American airport, I wondered how all of this was going to come together. How will we ever find our Vietnamese contacts?

It seemed that there were guards in military uniforms everywhere with machine guns slung over their shoulders. There were no smiles or expressions of "we hope you enjoy your stay." There were plenty of expressionless, down-to-business faces as we went through customs. Upon exiting the customs area, the sounds and smells of this beautiful, but very poor, country were thrust upon us. The humidity was almost suffocating compared to the New Mexico climate. Gratitude for our country washed over me again and again during that visit.

All of a sudden, something brought me out of my inner thoughts. It was a sign with one word upon it: Richardson. There he was, a good man that I would never forget. He introduced himself as Uncle No Problem. This is for real. That is how he asked us to address him, for his job was to make sure that everything truly was no problem. He had everything arranged. He introduced us to our driver as he loaded our luggage into the van. Uncle pulled me aside and said, "Be careful what you say about the government or even your own country. Sometimes the drivers are government agents." Uncle then told us that we were headed to meet our first little boy.

I was absolutely shocked by what I saw next. As we wound through the twisted and crowded streets of Hanoi and headed toward the countryside, I was overcome by the sheer number of people on bicycles. I actually saw a little family of four on one bicycle. The father was peddling while standing. The mother was sitting on the seat, holding a baby nestled in her arms, and a little toddler sat perched on the handlebars in front of his dad. They looked happy and actually grateful that they had transportation. There we were, in a van, the only four-wheeled vehicle I could see, immersed in an ocean of bicycles and pedestrians, all on the same road.

As we traveled for over an hour, we found that our grief was somewhat swallowed up in the wonder of it all. We saw people working the rice paddies, using water buffalos to plow and to haul carts with heavy wooden wheels. The people looked at us, as I'm sure we looked at them, with curiosity and amazement.

We tried to make small talk with Uncle and ask questions about our soon-to-be sons. Even though our hearts were confused about why boys and not the little girl, we were beginning to be more and more excited about meeting our two little boys.

After witnessing the extreme poverty in this beautiful country, I was grateful for the life and opportunities that would soon belong to our Joseph and Joshua.

As the van traveled forward at about fifty kilometers per hour, we silently watched the seemingly endless rice paddies and many shades of green in this beautiful country. Then it came, something familiar but definitely out of place in the remote countryside in North Vietnam. It was the ringing of a telephone.

Uncle No Problem quickly retrieved his cell phone and began conversing in Vietnamese so fast that it caused me to wonder how anyone could possibly understand the words being spoken. The cell conversation was paused as he briefly spoke to the driver. Whatever he said resulted in the van slowing and coming to a stop along the side of a vast and beautiful rice paddy. Uncle then asked me if we wanted a close-up view of this rice paddy. Annie Laurie and I got out of the van and followed Uncle about ten yards away. He handed the cell phone to Annie Laurie while explaining that the head of the orphanages was calling from America.

"Hello, Annie Laurie. Are you excited about seeing your two little boys?"

Annie Laurie answered with a hesitant, "Yes."

"Would you mind waiting a day or so before seeing them? There's a little baby girl that became available while you were in flight today. Because you were on your way to Vietnam today, you can have her if you would like. If you had not arrived in the country today, she would have been assigned to someone else."

There it was—our miracle! It was wrapped in plain brown paper, no ribbons or glossy wrapping paper. There were no trumpets and no organ music playing Handel's Hallelujah chorus. But interestingly enough, it happened to be Mother's Day. What an amazing gift to be given to a woman who was doing everything in her power to truly be a mother to God's little children on earth. This miracle came so quietly, but in my mind, I heard something akin to, "For, unto us a child is given." We had witnessed a miracle. Every time I recall and remember this event, my belief in coincidences weakens and my conviction in the workings of heaven, which we call miracles, deepens and strengthens.

Uncle then explained that we would change directions very soon and at the next crossroads turn due north and head for the Quong Ninh province. We arrived late that afternoon, and it became clear, very quickly, that they were expecting us. The experiences in which I was about to be immersed changed me forever and prepared me for the continuing journey of gathering children—not just in Vietnam.

We entered the orphanage, which consisted of a small courtyard surrounded in a U–shaped configuration by several two-story buildings. I was surprised at the touch of French provincial architecture that seemed quite common in many of the buildings. Even though the courtyard had a clean and orderly appearance, everything looked like it was a couple hundred years old. Decay was openly visible in the foundations, and the stucco walls were chipped and cracked everywhere. In the middle of the courtyard stood the orphanage director alongside of his group of assistants, smiling the brightest smiles I think I've ever seen.

They greeted us, and we returned the greeting through Uncle. He then told us that we would now get to see our little girl. I don't remember anything else about the buildings or the people, other than seeing a small, middle-aged woman bring in a little baby. While only about three days old, this precious little girl had been left on the doorstep of the orphanage in a basket a couple of months earlier.

The infant was bundled in a soft blanket. In addition, she had a coat, hat, and gloves on. The temperature had to have been at least 90 degrees Fahrenheit, with 80 percent humidity. But there she was with a little pixie-like face. She was so very tiny, with clear and dainty features. The nanny gently placed this little miracle baby in Annie Laurie's arms. I do not have the words to describe this scene as it really felt. This little meeting of a mother and a two-month-old baby girl will never make the history books. But this obscure meeting was forever written in my heart and certainly observed by heaven. The moment was so sacred that I hardly dared to breathe as I stood by and watched this marvelous scene unfold. Annie Laurie was holding our new little daughter. She had been unwilling to let anything or anyone stop her, and as a result of her tenacity, dedication, and faith in God, she had brought me to see, and soon to hold, this precious little girl to whom the whispering voice belonged.

It was my turn to hold this little one, and oh how I ached to do so. I had been a father for over twenty years, and yet I felt awkward and incapable of correctly holding one so small. What if I dropped her or tipped her upside down? What if she took one look at me and just screamed? I was almost frozen as Annie Laurie handed her to me. She simply said in her sweet and sure way, "Here's your little daughter." Wow, the power of those words. I relaxed just enough to hold this little miracle without dropping or hurting her. I really can't remember if she was even awake.

"Here's your little daughter." In retrospect, with other similar memories, those same words were spoken to me before when I met little Annie Laurie, Katie, Emily, Katurah, Clarissa, and Rebekah. I would also hear the same words again many years later, but that is for another chapter. Perhaps, even after the writing of this book, I will hear those words again and again as the gathering journey continues.

After meeting, seeing, touching, and holding our new little daughter, Jenai', we were informed that we would not be able to take her with us. The government required at least two months from the first time you meet the child until you can take them home. Uncle stood in proxy for us concerning the two little boys, which was a miracle in itself, but now it became apparent that we were going to have to leave our little girl behind. As we began to make plans for the return trip, we had to accept the fact that I could not come back to Vietnam because I was completely out of vacation and adoption leave time. It became so very clear that I would have to send my wife back to Vietnam. I remembered the tiny voice: "Daddy, send Mommy to come and find me." In essence, I would have to send Mommy to go and find her. I am learning that the workings of heaven do not operate on coincidences.

We were taken on a tour of the orphanage. The people were so proud of their operation. As we walked through the different sections, I noticed one little girl in particular, she must have been about six years old. She was always three to four steps away, constantly looking at us with a shy and determined smile. She wasn't just looking *at* us; she was looking right into our eyes. I believe she was looking for something. Looking isn't the right word. I believe searching would describe it better. As the tour proceeded, she began to walk closer and closer until she was standing hand in hand with Annie Laurie. Things changed a bit with this new posture. This time when I would look over at her, she would look away quickly with a hint of embarrassment, but the smile persisted.

We were taken to their schoolroom, where we were asked to sit down on some of the most bent-up and rusty chairs imaginable. In America, these chairs would've been greeted by a city dump long before. We sat quietly for a few minutes, and then older children between the ages of about eleven to fifteen filed in. They positioned themselves in front of us and picked up some obviously handcrafted musical instruments that I had not noticed until that moment. Our little passenger was allowed to sit between us and enjoy the interesting and sweet mini-concert that was being presented. I don't remember much about what those children and teenagers played, but I do recall clearly their faces filled with absolute joy. How could they be so happy? They were so very poor. They lacked all of the things so many of us think we need to make us happy. Here I was worrying about every penny that went out to gather these wonderful little souls from a life of poverty, want, and even worse. We were told that the children in these orphanages are required to make it on their own when they turn fifteen years of age. Even though they were being schooled and taught skills, the streets anywhere in the world are not a nice or safe place, especially for young teenage girls.

We went from there to see the children's sleeping quarters. The rooms were filled with bunk-style beds where thin woven mats replaced mattresses. There were really no personal possessions, but I was impressed with the extreme cleanliness from wall to wall and in every corner.

The next part of the tour was the kitchen and dining area. The kitchen consisted of a small room, about five feet wide by eight feet long. The only way to cook food was an oven-stove made with softball sized rocks with mud as mortar. One large battered pot, which held about three gallons, contained boiling water with a little bit of rice and some kind of greens in it. I guess the evening meal would be a sort of rice-vegetable soup.

Throughout the tour, this little girl with sparkling eyes now walked between us still holding Annie Laurie's hand. Sometimes she would work up enough courage to hold onto my pant leg as she shyly looked up at me and grinned.

Annie Laurie briefly paused and asked if I would be willing to adopt this little hitchhiker. Before the wonder of the miracle of Jenai' had even worn off, before we even had the chance to meet our two new little sons, she was back into the gathering posture. I was feeling like we had finally come to an end, that the searching and gathering was complete. I did not understand, or more correctly, I did not want to understand the deep persistent feelings that fueled the gathering quest that burned within Annie Laurie's innermost parts. I reluctantly told her that I would be willing to at least ask about the feasibility of adopting this curiously, persistent little six-year-old. That was the least I could do, especially with the ever strengthening, ever growing feelings within me of the gathering.

I still remember the way many children from around the world have looked at me. They look right into your eyes, not at your eyes, but into them. I truly believe that they were doing all they could to convey the whisperings of their hearts: "Isn't there something you can do to help me?" "Will you take me home?" "Please take me home with you." I began to experience the desperate needs of children in a different way. I would never again just feel sorry for orphaned children; I now knew there was something I could do about it. It would require sacrifice, and I wondered if I would be willing to make the necessary sacrifice in order to allow the change to deepen and solidify?

It was time to leave our little Jenai' behind. I thought this would be a very difficult moment, but it wasn't because I had an unexpected peace that all would go as planned, and Annie Laurie would return in a couple of months in order to bring her home. I would do everything in my power to send Mommy to go and find and bring our little Jenai' home. This peace was soon crowded out by a sight that still haunts me to this very moment.

I can see her clearly, and my heart still aches and my mind still wonders. As the van pulled out of the court yard through the big wrought iron gate, I turned and looked back. There she was, racing toward the van, and then she suddenly stopped and stood still. She simply held up her little hand in a waving posture but never moved her wrist or arm. She just stood there, perfectly still, holding that little hand in the air, only this time there was no smile, no sparkly eyes. We never saw her again.

• •

The next morning, we left to pick up our two little boys. Our hearts were much more prepared to take them into our hearts and to love them. We were at peace about our little girl, our Jenai'.

We traveled all day heading for the orphanage near Hanoi, which had been Joshua's home during his first nine months of life. I don't remember where the orphanage was, but I do remember that the name of the orphanage was The Center for Miserable Children. In fact, in Joshua's adoption decree, he is referred to as a miserable child from the Center for Miserable Children.

Many orphans in Vietnam have a caretaker assigned to them until they're adopted or until they enter their teen years. Joshua had not one caretaker but five or six. An older woman lived with Joshua in a small little room in the Center for Miserable Children, and she would go home on the weekends to be with her husband. There were three to four young women who would take him on the weekends. They would hold, love, cuddle, and feed Joshua whenever given the opportunity.

They must have been expecting our arrival, because as we entered the small and scantly furnished apartment, they were all standing there trying to smile. We were supposed to arrive the day before, but due to the sudden change of plans with the trip to meet Jenai', we were delayed. They were very kind and willing to let us hold this new little nine-month-old stranger. As the older woman gently put Joshua into Annie Laurie's arms, you could feel the connection they, Joshua and his surrogate mother, shared. She was less than five feet tall and had gray hair and bright, dark eyes. Her teeth protruded so far out of her mouth that she could not close her lips. To the world, she would have had no beauty, but to Joshua and to us, she was such a beautiful person. She stood right next to Annie Laurie as she held Joshua in her arms. It was almost as if she and Annie Laurie were connected with giant rubber bands, heart to heart. The moment Annie Laurie made a move that vaguely suggested that this sweet and devoted woman could take Joshua back, she leaned forward and held out her arms.

As I watched this scene unfolding, I could see that she and Annie Laurie were communicating without words in a way that I believe only women can do. Two women who wanted this little boy stood there with aching hearts and Joshua in between. Annie Laurie understood what Joshua's departure would do to this little woman, and she was aching for her. At this awkward moment, Annie Laurie threw her arms around her new Vietnamese sister, and they both held each other tightly as they wept, with Joshua squished in between. I could kind of sense that while in that embrace, with their hearts close together physically, there was great love, compassion, and a reassurance communicated. I also prayed that healing would be among the energy transmitted to the older and smaller women's heart. God really does minister to all of us through each other when we take or make the opportunity.

When it came time for me to hold Joshua, he just screamed and wanted to go to anyone else besides me. It took Joshua several months before he began to bond with me and trust me. Maybe he could sense my hesitancy.

After about two hours visiting with the caretaker, surrogate parents, and the other young ladies that loved little Joshua so much, we loaded ourselves into the van and once again drove away while looking at those left behind. The older couple stood there in each other's arms, each supporting the other with their frail bodies. The young women stood on each side of the couple, all embracing, all weeping, all wondering what would become of their little beloved boy, our new little Joshua. I often wish I could have spoken with them. I would have listened to their concerns about this little boy and then perhaps could have promised them that I would continue where they were being compelled to leave off.

● ●

—Annie Laurie

Those who have adopted children know that there is a bonding that occurs with your adopted child. There is no rhyme or reason to when this happens. It can happen quickly, or it can take a very long time. A mother who carries her child in her womb has nine months to bond, but an adoptive mother does not have that time, so the bonding comes in a different way. I have bonded differently with each of our children as they have come into our home. Emily's bonding was when we shared that sweet moment as we felt the miracle of the years sliding away and she became my baby in my tummy. For Katurah, it was when I accepted her for the gift that she is. Well, for Joshua, it was the very first moment that I saw him. Never before or since have I been able to experience that bonding so quickly. He was so completely mine from that first look into his eyes. He is a momma's boy through and through. The connection between us has always been incredible. He is such a gentle boy and yet so full of fun. He laughs at everything and makes everyone else laugh with him. I believe that I was given this as part of the gift of just being obedient. Father knew we had struggled, and now he made that struggling the gift of a lifetime.

* *

—*Brian*

We headed back to a city just outside of Hanoi. We were soon going to meet a little fifteen-month-old boy, who we would name Joseph. As an infant, he appeared mysteriously in a woven basket on the bed in the guardhouse of the orphanage of Vietre'.

The only word that comes to mind in describing Joseph is scruffy. He had bright, determined eyes and hair that stuck up in almost every direction. This was one of the wiggliest kids I'd come in contact with. In fact, everybody who meets Joseph likes him immediately; he just exudes friendliness.

The guards seemed to think he belonged in some way to them. After all, he had been abandoned in their little quarters. At age thirteen months, they were putting him on the handle bars of a rickety motor scooter and giving him rides around the inside courtyard of the decaying and aging orphanage buildings. We also found out later from Uncle that one of the guards would give Joseph rides on the open streets. It makes me smile every time I picture a little thirteen-month-old boy, with scruffy dark hair, intensely dark eyes, and a huge smile perched on the handle bars of a dangerously dilapidated motor scooter on the bicycle-choked narrow streets of an inner city near Hanoi.

During those first few days with Joseph and Joshua, I wondered about the rightness of taking them away from good and caring people that loved them. Sure they lived in poverty by our standards, but what's so bad about that if they would be happy. Their needs were being met, so why take them away?

The harsh reality is this: it would not have lasted. With the scanty resources of the orphanages and the prejudices toward orphans, their lives would have become increasingly hard. As much as they were loved as infants and toddlers, another infant would quite quickly take their place, and their lives of harsh survival, both physically and emotionally, would begin. I do not believe that our lifestyle is the only way to happiness. But I do believe and understand that having a family, safety, stability, almost endless opportunities for education, and occupational training is a great blessing that only comes in a free and blessed country. Is America the only place on earth that provides all of this? No. But here's the bottom line: we had a family and a home that would provide for these children for the long run. They would never be looked at as another mouth which consumed the precious and rare commodity of food. They would have a mommy that would always be there; a dad that would try every day to lead the way to manhood. Would they have survived the streets in their teen years? I don't know. Would their lives have been happy if they had stayed in their native country? Would they have what they have now? Not even close. Annie Laurie and I have seen the grinding effects of poverty. We have seen kids on the streets. We have witnessed the aching pleading in older children's eyes for a family, a mom and a dad, and someone who'll take them home.

The journey home was fairly uneventful. We had the formal adoption proceedings in Hanoi and then a ten-day wait in a five-star hotel in Saigon, where we began to truly experience the wonder and excitement of raising two little boys. What a journey we had ahead of us. I'm not referring to the flight home but the adventurous journey of raising our two new sons—Joshua and Joseph. They were into everything they could possible get into and were already egging each other on as they crawled everywhere together. Buddies from the start! We loved it. We soon began our trip home with our two new little sons and with the promise of returning for our little daughter.

* *

Sending Mommy to return and bring Jenai' home was not guaranteed or easy. We have learned that miracles take work and tenacity, and the road to their completion is often filled with obstacles.

The waiting time passed, and the agency called in early August with the wonderful news that it was time to go back and get our little girl. They informed us that only Annie Laurie would have to go and would be required to stay in the country for about two weeks. They also told us that another ten to twelve thousand dollars would be required on top of all the flight and living expenses. We were shocked! We thought that our payment of $40,000 would cover all fees for our little girl as well as the boys. I realize that twelve thousand dollars may not seem an overwhelming amount to some, but to us, it might as well have been twelve million.

We were out of money, and I had nowhere else to go. With a home that was barely finished, no home equity loans were available, and we had no rich relatives. We didn't know any wealthy movie stars with big hearts, and I did not know what Oprah

Winfrey's telephone number was. I had taken all I could from our 401K, and we were already eating rice and beans three times a week. What could I do? All I could see was a dead end.

After the miracle that had given us our little girl, would she now never come home? Well, I went into default mode, one of discouragement and anger. I wasn't openly angry at God, just questioning. But I guess those questions were really expressions of anger. I asked: "Why did you bring us so far on this gathering journey and now, because of money, drop us?"

The agency told Annie Laurie that she had five minutes to give them an answer, they weren't being hard, they simply needed to call Vietnam and give them the green light.

What happened next haunts me to this day. I simply told Annie Laurie, "No, we simply don't have the money." That was the truth. We didn't have the money, and no possibilities within the time frame to get it. I was racked with pain and anger. *How could God allow this to happen?* I thought. What else could I do? After the miracles that had been shed from above, I actually said *no.* This was not, as Winston Churchill coined, "my finest hour." I gave up. I quit because of money, or the lack of it.

Annie Laurie did something far more faithful, practical, and effective. She called the director of the orphanages. They were very compassionate and concerned, but this was a business, and they had expenses just like we did. I remember her pleading on the phone, with tears streaming down her cheeks. I remember her sobbing out, "Please, don't take my little girl away from me." The director listened and promised she would see what she could do. She would call us back when she could.

Money! It was always there, always the obstacle, always in short supply. Why was it that the adoptions and children's lives were so tightly chained to money, of which we had very little? I used to think that was a valid question and practical way of looking at it. Annie Laurie, however, had, and still has, a completely different view of the financial supply channels.

● ●

—*Annie Laurie*

I knew with every part of me that this was not the end. I knew God had a plan and I just had to find out what it was. I knew that even though Brian said no, and I certainly understood why, the answer was yes. Knowing this, I had no choice but to put things once again in God's hands. I went quietly to my room. I told the children to please let me have some quiet time for a few minutes, and I shut the door. This was going to be between me and my Father in heaven.

I knelt down and began to pray with all my heart. It was not a long drawn out prayer, as I had only a few moments to make a decision that would change lives forever. It was just simply laying my heart on the altar and letting God decide what he would do with that offering. I sat there in silence waiting upon the whisperings of the spirit, and it was then that I heard the words as clear as could be.

"My sweet daughter, go forward and do not worry about the money. Bring your little one home!"

Such a simple statement, but the message and power behind it was profound. There was no question in my heart what I must do. I would go forward, and I would bring my little girl home. I would let God work out the details.

As I went to open my door, the phone rang. I squared my shoulders and picked up the receiver. Before I could say anything more than hello, the director excitedly said she had news. In those few moments, she had been able to get hold of her committee, and the very group of people who originally had said we were not qualified to have children because of our religion now said that they would drop the agency fees as well as help pay for some of the international fees. There was a fund that they could fall back on to help.

I could not speak.

She then said, "Annie Laurie, are you okay? You are going to get your little girl!"

I started once again to weep. Only this time the tears were tears of absolute joy and gratitude. God had kept his word and he had parted the Red Sea once again for our family, and we were going to have our Jenai'.

I was driven to the same little orphanage in the very most northern regions of Vietnam, and there I had our precious Jenai' placed in my arms once again. She was mine. The little girl that I had seen in a dream and the one who had asked her daddy to send Mommy to find her. We had done our part, and God had done his.

The rest of the trip was a blur of holding and loving our baby. I felt no need to sightsee or shop or any of the other things that families usually do while waiting for all the paperwork to be completed. I just held my little Jenai' and wondered at the majesty of a God that could find this little one in a remote orphanage, on an island, in the most northern regions of a country that for years had been torn apart by war and bring me to find her. It just filled me once again with the knowledge that truly no sparrow can fall without God knowing.

It was during this time of waiting and loving our little Jenai' that the questions in my heart returned. Was this the little girl whose whispers I had been hearing for so many years? Was this the little girl that had started this whole journey of gathering, or was she to be one of the many blessings of that journey? Was our gathering journey over? The answers came with sweet clarity. This little girl was indeed our precious daughter, a daughter that would bless our lives in so many ways, but...the little girl that I had been promised at the start of this wondrous journey, and who was never far from my heart or my thoughts, was still to come. What an incredible blessing that my search for one would, in the end, bring so many.

We finished all the legal work and then we waited for permission to leave. Everything went smoothly. There was only one odd occurrence that took place as I was waiting to go home.

Here I was half way around the world in the process of bringing my little Jenai' home, and I start having this strange impression. I kept trying to ignore it, but the whispering just got louder and more pressing.

"There are five more children waiting to come home."

"Oh, please!" I cry back to the voice that keeps whispering in my mind. *"Please, just let me get home and find peace in raising these children."* And more importantly, *"Please, don't make me be the one to have to bring this news to my husband. He will surely think fifteen is enough! Can't you give him the whispering this time?"*

But that was not his plan. So, even as I was enjoying the start of a new life in our family, we were being prepared for the next step. I knew from having gone through this same thing many times that Brian would indeed listen to the whisperings. It would just take him a little longer. I have respected and admired that so much in him, for he has allowed God to humble him and mold him when every part of him is screaming, *I can't do this!* What courage that takes! I knew I would soon be looking forward with anticipation to where those children would be found and how God would bring them to us.

But first, I had to get my Jenai' home to her daddy and then somehow let him know that another journey was about to start.

* *

—*Brian*

I drove through the night to reach Los Angeles International Airport. I remember so clearly meeting them at the gate; they were so beautiful. Annie Laurie had courageously traveled to Vietnam without me to find and bring our little miracle girl home. In the stroller in front of my beautiful and powerful wife was our little Jenai', whose name means the one who loves people. It almost seemed anti-climactic after all of the struggles and battles to respond to the faint whisperings of this little girl's heart. She was so tiny and beautiful, and she was ours; a gift straight from heaven. Never was there such a bright and happy girl. She reminds us of Tigger from the Winnie the Pooh stories. She never stops bouncing. Each day is a day of complete joy and of living life to the fullest. It was such a bright day when she came to be a part of our family, and the brightness continues.

Not only has Jenai' brought us great joy, but she also brought us our two boys, Joseph and Joshua. They follow me around everywhere; they want to be like me and be with me. There's a great country song where the little boy says he wants to be like his dad, eat all his food, and grow as tall as he is. They'll probably never be as tall as I am, physically speaking. But I believe the day will come when they will be so tall that I will stand on the shoulders of their lives. I live that song every day, and I love it. They are a delight!

• •

So, there you have it; a three for one heavenly special that has blessed our lives so abundantly. What about the money I was so worried about before? Debt is a reality, but we just pray every day that our cars last just a few more years.

bring them in

—Annie Laurie

Life never slows down much. Two days after returning from bringing Jenai' home, our Katie left to go to England to stay with my parents for four months. Three weeks later, I took my son Ammon, who was almost eighteen, over to England to take part in a special training course that my parents were involved in teaching. I have to admit that he could have flown by himself, but I really wanted to see my parents. They had asked me to come over for a much needed break after all that had gone on. Brian would not let me say no!

It had been a very hard few years, and he knew how healing it was for me to wander around England's countryside for a few days. (I also think that he wanted a break from hearing his wife tell him over and over that there were more children coming, poor guy!)

Blaine had left for Uruguay the week after Joseph and Joshua had arrived in America. He was excited to be able to spend a couple of years serving the people in that country. So our family was growing and expanding in many ways. Our children were doing well and were using the experiences in their lives that had stretched them to bless the lives of others.

While I was in England, I felt even stronger that eventually there would be five more children who needed to come into our family. I knew I needed the support of my husband. So after refilling my emotional bucket that had become very empty with the healing countryside of England, I went home to ask about our five missing children, once again.

• •

—*Brian*

Five more? How could there possibly be five more? When Annie Laurie brought Jenai' home, the total number of children came to fifteen. There were only nine left at home, and that seemed like a workable number of children. I was ready to see if I could put our finances back in order and begin life. I was nervous but ready and willing to continue being the father that each child needed. Would I ever have time to date and court my young wife of over twenty years? Would I have the ability to be there for our older children and the grandchildren that were already starting to come? I was willing to buckle down and try, but it was not going to be easy.

I don't remember how or when Annie Laurie seriously

approached me about more children, but I do remember that the subject always caused tension. Sometimes it felt as if I did not have a voice with Annie Laurie. Sometimes it seemed that she was obsessed with adopting more and more children no matter what the cost financially and emotionally. Our life revolved around raising children, building a family, finishing our new large home, figuring out ways to pay off debt, avoiding the subject of getting more children, and Annie Laurie's poor health. Our marriage suffered during that time; it was really hard. Why didn't we quit? Our goals seemed to be at such cross purposes. The answer is simple and has served us for almost thirty years now. We believe in the institution of marriage. We also agreed to love, teach, guide, and provide a strong and stable life for our children. Marriage and life was hard, but if life wasn't so hard, it would be easy; and who's ever heard of an easy life?

Well, I was set, no more adoptions, no more children, and that was all there was to it. No more! We were stretched to our limits. Annie Laurie did not fight me; however, she very sweetly kept bringing it up. We would go out on a date, and even with all of the pacts and promises she'd made with herself, she would end up talking about her feelings. It took some time, arguments, and silent drives home from many a date, but it gradually got better. Annie Laurie didn't stop sharing her feelings. I just finally got to a point where I could listen to her feelings without my insides being tied into knots. After all, I felt pretty certain that I had received an answer to my prayers, and that answer was pretty comfortable. She could say all she wanted to, but I was certain there were to be no more children.

Things remained status quo for a few months. Annie Laurie would try time and time again to respect my feelings, but those gathering feelings and expressions would just come bubbling up seemingly out of nowhere. I remember a junior high science experiment where we put vinegar in a beaker with baking soda in the bottom. The mixture results in an immediate unstoppable overflowing surge of smelly vinegar foam. Annie Laurie was like that, not the smelly vinegar part, but the unstoppable overflowing surge of feelings. The moment we would begin to share romantic feelings, dreams, or inner emotions, up came the gathering foam. I learned to just let it overflow because I loved her then and I still do.

I felt that we had finally found a comfortable place for our differing beliefs and feelings concerning adopting more children. But then I began to think more and more about Annie Laurie's strong desires to bring more children into our lives and family. I couldn't believe it! All of her bubbling over was wearing through my armor. I couldn't get the thought out of my mind. What was I thinking? We did not have any more money! I was barely keeping up with the children we had, both young and old. I felt I just couldn't handle any more, but the feelings persisted and grew.

My answer came without warning. It was during this time that my mind was almost constantly led to ponder about what my life was really about. This pondering hatched a persistent thought that began to grow and take root in my soul. Could it be that Annie Laurie was right about our specific purpose in life? I believe that everyone has a purpose and it is up to the individual, with heaven's help, to fulfill that purpose. I found I was continually asking myself and God if my purpose was indeed to bring more children into our family.

I was, at the time, hired by our church to teach religion to high school students in Albuquerque, New Mexico. In our classroom, there was a picture of Jesus Christ on the wall. In the picture, the Savior has a slight smile and very searching eyes.

This particular day, I entered the classroom after having said good-bye to the last group of students and began preparation for the next day's lesson. I was searching for music to go along with our course of study. I came upon a CD that highlighted the miraculous rescue of a group of Scandinavian Christian pioneers who were dying of exposure on the high plains of Wyoming in the mid-1800s. As I began other preparations, I was absent-mindedly listening to one song in particular. The words slowly began to get my attention:

> [1]Go bring them in from the plains
>
> Go bring them in from the storm
>
> Like a fire the Spirit's burning
>
> Bring them in and keep them warm
>
> Go bring them in from the plains
>
> Go bring them in from the cold
>
> Wrap your loving arms around them
>
> Bring his peace to their souls

The refrain repeated again, but this time the music had my full attention, and as I consciously listened, I found myself staring at the picture. It was as if he was giving me this message: "Bring them in. Wrap your loving arms around them. Bring his peace and keep them warm." I sat and thought about it for a long time. The CD went on to other songs, but I didn't hear anything; only the repeating of the first song—bring them in, wrap your arms, bring his peace and keep them warm. I chose to listen with more than my ears.

Was I just giving in to Annie Laurie? No, not at all. I began to be filled with a knowledge that there were at least five children still out there. I assumed they were in Vietnam, and I prayed one of them included the little girl in the courtyard waving good-bye.

I don't remember exactly how I told Annie Laurie the news, but I do remember it was pretty romantic. It was my only chance in this lifetime when I, a man, got to break the news that we were not only going to have a child, but God willing, *five!* Think of it! How many men get to break the news to their sweethearts about the coming of a new child? I wasn't trying to be the big hero, I was just so happy that I now felt and knew what she had felt and known for so long.

It wasn't until the thirty-minute drive home to the west side of Albuquerque that the reality questions began to flow.

What are you thinking? You're still broke. Answer: peace.

You still forget what the children's middle names are. How are you going to nurture more little souls? Answer: a feeling of peace.

Okay, so I raise the money to pay for more adoptions, but how do I pay for braces, teenage car insurance, and broken arms and stitches for active little boys. Think of how much shoes will cost, and think of the mountains of food that we'll need for every meal. How will I ever be able to do all this on a limited teacher's salary? Answer: peace.

How will I ever keep up with the emotional demands of so many teenagers in the years to come? Answer: a peaceful feeling and a thought. *Stop thinking about yourself and your limitations. Think about the children, all will come out okay. You'll know what to do. Just stay the course that is set before you!* I am grateful for those clear and undeniable answers of peace. I was going to need every peaceful, spiritual memory I could hold on to.

Bring them in! Bring them in from where? Something must have happened between Vietnam and U.S. international relationships during this time period, because we soon found out that adoptions were closed to U.S. citizens in Vietnam. We never really found out why, all we knew was there was a little girl in Quong Ninh Province whose image remained clearly in our minds and hearts. There were also two other children, a boy and girl in the same orphanage, that had been given hope of adoption by Annie Laurie on her return trip to bring our little Jenai' home. Annie Laurie had even begun the proceedings and paid about $1,500, and we fully anticipated bringing five children into our family from the beautiful country of Vietnam.

So what now? We both had our own answers that we were

to bring five more little children into our home. I was also approaching the age of fifty, and as I remember, we were told that the law set by the Vietnamese government was very clear, an adoptive parent must be under fifty years of age at the time of the adoption. Whether that was really the case or not, I don't remember, but it did have an impact upon our urgency and our devastation when adoptions closed. How were we supposed to bring the children in when it seemed that both governments were standing in our path like a large, unfeeling stone wall without a door or even a crack in it?

Where were these children?

Some of you have seen poverty. Not the poverty on the TV screen that you can see and hear, but the kind that you can smell and are a little afraid to touch because it's dirty and disease ridden. This poverty is covered with flies and open sores, nakedness, starvation, and death. So why this unsettling description of extreme poverty? The next part of the gathering journey was about to take us to the poorest country in the western hemisphere—Haiti. However, before that part of the gathering journey began, it seemed that God had travel plans for Annie Laurie that involved the Pacific Ocean instead of the Atlantic Ocean.

esther joins the family

—Annie Laurie

We both finally knew there were five more, but we had no idea where they would come from. So we just put it back in God's hands and figured he would tell us when the time was right. I had Brian's go ahead, and that was all I needed. I got down to the business of raising the fifteen children that God had already brought to our home.

It just never lasted very long. I mean, getting down to the business of raising children never lasted very long. I would start to get those feelings again. What was my problem? Could I never just be still? Sometimes you have to wonder!

I knew the five children that would eventually be coming into our home were in God's hands. I didn't feel like it would be for a while, so I thought for sure that meant I would be having this wonderful break. I can't tell you how exhausting it was to always be searching and working toward the next gathering of children. But no, it only meant I had a break from looking for the five. God had other plans for the interim.

In November of 2002, my three from Vietnam were home and doing well, the older kids, except Ammon, were all gone from home, the rest of the children were doing great, school in our home was going smoothly, and Brian was doing well in his career. It was a time of peace, right? Absolutely. The only fly in the ointment was that every night I would go to bed and instead of sleeping, Esther, who was then sixteen years old, from the Marshall Islands, would come to my mind.

Not again! I had to go to Brian again? I am still amazed that my husband didn't throw me out. Of course if he had, he would be left with the all the children, so I really ought to write a book on how to keep a husband no matter what. It would be short. "Get as many children in your home as fast as you can, and they'll keep you forever!"

Anyway, all kidding aside, here it was again. "Go back to the Marshall Islands and bring Esther home." What was I thinking? This was an island girl, a teenager at that. How would we bring her into our home and not have things go crazy? How would we parent a young woman with no English, completely different culture, ideas, and life expectations? This was truly my most insane idea so far. I just knew there was no way that Brian would go for it. I put off telling him day after day, but the feelings, those whisperings, just would not quit.

"Brian, I am so sorry to bring this up again, but I think we have another daughter waiting to come into our home."

"Is this one of the five?"

"No, I think I need to go back to the Marshall Islands and bring Esther home. What do you think?"

A pause. "I'd like to pray about it, but I think you should go. How soon can you book the flights?"

Miracles do still happen. I threw my arms around his neck and started to weep. Could there possibly be a more wonderful man in the world? And how did I rate being married to him?

I didn't book flights that same day, as I thought it might be wise to call Esther and her family and see if my feelings were even a possibility. I didn't want to go on another wild goose chase.

They had a phone that served about ten families. You would call, say the name of who you wanted, say the words "ten minutes," and then hang up and hope someone would go get the person you asked for in the next ten minutes. It was a very modern form of communication. Hey, it was definitely better than nothing at all. And it worked. Ten minutes later, I was talking to Esther. Thank goodness she had that little bit of English.

I asked her if she wanted to come to America and live with us. She said, "Yes." I asked her if her parents would be okay with that. She said, "Yes." I then told her to ask her parents and I would call back the next day. She said, "Yes." I hung up wondering if we had communicated at all. I called her back the next day and asked her all the same questions except this time I asked what her parents had said. She said, "Yes." Okay! I knew I was taking a big chance, but I told her I would be there in a week and that I would stay with them if that was okay. Once again her only response was yes.

I booked my flights.

This time I decided to go by myself. Now, my next decision was not made with my husband's blessing. But I felt strongly about it, so he didn't try to stop me. We really didn't have the money for a hotel, but that was not the driving factor behind my decision. I really felt it would be a good idea to actually stay with the family and get to know them and for them to get to know me. I figured if they got to know me they would love and trust me. You know, I'm thinking like an American. I didn't realize the stress this would put on that whole family. So, I bought a little tent and a sleeping bag with an air mattress. I was set to go and live in the jungle. What I didn't realize at the time, but it would soon be made very clear to me, was that I had chosen to go right in the middle of the monsoon season and planned on camping out in the jungle on an island. Great thinking on my part.

Now, you have to understand something about me. I am not one of those women who look good in el natural. I always have my makeup, curling iron, pick, and hairspray with me no matter where I go. I even always have it in the car with me, just in case. It's by far more important than food or a change of clothing, as far as I am concerned. Usually if I went camping and there was no way of getting electricity, the only thing in that list that would change is that curlers would replace the curling iron.

So, here I am packing to go camp out in the Marshall Islands and am really quite excited. I knew firsthand what the toilet facilities would be like and that there would be no bathing for a while and I would be there for two weeks. This was going to be great. I would also be eating food cooked over a fire, and who knows what that would be like. I was ready! Let's go!

We decided we would save some money by having Sarah drive me to Los Angeles to catch the flight. I left about ten at night. Brian had been in a meeting, so he was not there. I pulled over just outside of Albuquerque to call him and say good-bye. I told Sarah to take a little walk so I could talk to him alone. All he did was say hello and I burst into tears. I didn't stop crying again until I pulled into L.A. I drove all night and listened to "Bring Them In" and some other songs on having the faith to do what you know is right and cried.

Those few hours were some of the hardest of my life. I don't exactly know why it hit me so hard, but I was just so weary of leaving my family, of battling against all that seemed to fight me every step of the way, of spending money that we did not have, and of traveling one journey after the other that I just folded.

I wanted desperately to have God tell me I could stay home, that this time I did not have to go. But there was no whispering voice speaking those words to my mind. There was only an even stronger conviction that God would be with me and to go forward. I went.

I arrived in the Marshall Islands once again with no one there to greet me. I didn't know if they were even expecting me. Who knew what Esther understood. I found my way, once again, to the car rental place and, funny enough, was given the same roach-infested car. I threw all my gear in the back and headed for the other end of the island. The jungle end.

I pulled into their little community of family buildings and prayed they would remember me. I don't think there was much chance of them not remembering me as I had made such a wonderful impression the last time (ha ha). And besides, how many white women visit their part of the island?

Esther's mother met me, and this time I actually could pronounce her name. It was Medjio. She hugged me, and I felt at once the rightness of being there. All the worry and despair that I had been feeling melted away in that welcoming embrace. I had a journey to complete, and I knew that God was in that journey. I would just go forward and have faith that he would work his miracles, and I would put myself in the way for whatever he wanted to have happen.I found out that they had built a little lean to on the front of the women's hut to have me sleep in. Unfortunately, my little tent did not fit in it, and I was not about to sleep on the open ground with all the bugs. So I signed to them that I would just put up a tent right by their little hut and would sleep there. I don't think they had ever seen a tent, and they were fascinated by what I was doing. Everyone came to watch and giggle. I sat forever blowing up my air mattress, and then I was set. I had also bought a fan and an extension cord at the one store on the island. They did have electricity for some things. There were only a few sources of electricity on this part of the island, so there were orange extension cords running everywhere on the ground. Here in America, we are so careful not to mix water and electricity, but there it was no big deal. Remember it was the monsoon season, which means there is torrential rain during most of the day, every day, and no one thought twice about those cords running everywhere, and while I was there, we only had one power outage. Pretty great system!

So now I was set up for anything. I had my tent, my sleeping bag with an air mattress, and I could lay there with the fan blowing on me. I was living in style! There were only two problems with my set up. The first problem was that the ants found the extension cord leading into my tent, and I guess they wanted to get in out of the rain. As a result, there was a steady and constant stream of ants entering my tent via that cord. I hope I am not held accountable for the thousands of ants I sent to heaven over those two weeks. They were everywhere. Every time I would enter my tent, I would have a massive kill-the-ants party. I'm afraid it was them or me, as there just wasn't room for both of us.

The second problem was that my tent was not waterproof. Thank goodness for my air mattress, as that is the only reason that even a part of me was dry. There were at least two inches of water in my tent at all times. I baled it out frequently but could not keep up with it. I would wake up soaking every morning. Interestingly enough, I had some of the best nights of sleep I have ever had in my life in that pitiful tent. I slept through everything; just another tender mercy from above.

About the time I finished setting up my little home away from home, Esther arrived home from school. Yes! My translator was here, or so I thought. I want you to know that it was a bit presumptuous of me to call her my translator, as she hardly spoke a word to anyone the whole time I was there. I was pretty much on my own. But she did show me one very important thing as soon as she arrived. The new bathroom!

I did not know the story behind this bathroom until about six months after I arrived back home. But I will let you in on the

secret. When Esther told them the week before that I was coming, I am sure my last experience in their toilet facilities came
forcefully to mind. So the whole area came together to make a
proper bathroom for the white lady, as they called me. They had
dropped what they were doing, which wasn't much, and pooled
their resources and built what to them was a palatial bathroom.

It was located about fifty yards from my tent across the
graveled common area. It was a little hut made with the odds
and ends of plywood and boards. It was approximately five-by-
eight foot total. There was even a door and a roof on it. There
was a little wood step leading up to the door. You walked in,
and the door actually had a little wooden latch on the inside
so you could have some privacy. I walked in, and there was that
fifty-gallon barrel again filled with rainwater. There was a plastic
gallon jug sitting beside it. This time they showed me how to
use it. Next to the barrel there was a toilet. They showed me that
after you used the toilet you would fill the jug with rainwater
and dump it in the toilet and that would act as your flushing
mechanism; it was so easy when you just knew how. Around
the corner of a four-foot high concrete wall was a pipe sticking out above my head. That was the shower. They told me to
tell them when I wanted to shower and they would turn it on.
Later I looked outside to see what that pipe was hooked too. It
was hooked to a green garden hose, which led to another barrel,
which was placed under the edge of a corner of the men's hut's
roof. There was a funneling system on that roof that caught all
the rain and deposited it into the barrel. To turn on the shower,
they unplugged the hose and the water flowed. Ah, what luxury!

I noticed during my time there that children were never
allowed to use the bathroom. They washed in a bowl every night
out on the common area. I don't know where they took care
of their needs. But the bathroom was for the adults. The other
thing I noticed was that every day they would ask me if I had
taken a shower and looked expectantly, waiting for my answer.
At the time, I could not figure out why they were so interested

in my showering habits. But later, when I heard the story behind the bathroom being built, I realized that they had prepared one of the sweetest gifts they could have for the "white lady." They had all sacrificed for me, and they were so excited to see me use their gift and to see my appreciation.

What a sweet lesson this was to me. These people, who have almost nothing, were willing to give all for the comfort of someone they hardly knew and probably will never see again. I truly learned to love these wonderful Marshallese people.

My time there was moving forward, and I needed to get down to the business of getting passports, birth certificates, and all that went with bringing Esther to America. I talked to Medjio, and she said yes she wanted Esther to come and be with me in America, so we went forward. Every day we would make the two-hour roundtrip journey to the other side of the island to visit the government offices. It was more sitting in a muggy, hot car and waiting for people who were running on island time, which can be anywhere from an hour to a couple of days later than what is planned. But that is why I had allowed two weeks. I was somewhat familiar with the ways of this island by now, and it was becoming almost like a second home to me.

Oh, and the thing that was most important to me? My hair and makeup? Ha! That was a thing of the past. When you are sweating, being not rained on but poured on, sleeping in water, and there is no mirror except in your car, it just isn't going to happen. For the first time in my life, I went el natural. When I got home and could actually fix myself up, Esther was shocked that I was so "beautiful!" I had told Father that I would do anything. This seemed to me at the time to be the ultimate sacrifice.

Even as I was going forward with all the paperwork, things started to fall apart. I woke up one morning, and I could tell there was a feeling of uneasiness with everyone. I didn't know why. Without communication, there were so many things going on that I just couldn't quite figure out. I would know something was happening, but it would take forever for me to finally figure out what it was. This was one of those times. I couldn't get answers. It would be like the whole family would shut down. No one would look at me or talk to me, and then time would pass, and they would be all smiles and warm again. I just never knew.

Well, this time I decided that I needed to get away by myself and pray. I walked the hundred yards to the beach. I had brought my own camp chair with me and an umbrella. I took these two things and my scriptures and sat on the beach. I was the only person anywhere in sight, which was not surprising as the rain was coming down at a feverish pitch. I didn't care. I needed to talk to God. I sat there, in the downpour, with an umbrella over my head, and read God's Word. It brought such peace to my soul. I then spent several hours praying and pondering as I looked out at the beautiful, soggy surroundings. I watched crabs scuttling across the sand, and I chased them into their holes. I watched the tide come in, and there was only the sound of the rain and a quiet swishing of the water. There are no waves because of the corral beds. It was amazing. What a place to be able to commune with God. He is so kind. He gave me once again the confirmation that I was on his errand and that he was in this journey.

The memory of our last trip there and going home empty-handed was ever present. I now understood the purpose of that trip. I also knew why my daughters had come with me. Esther would never have had the courage to come home with me if she had not met my two girls and seen that I was nice to them and that they loved me. Discipline in most homes in the Marshalls is very hard and often times abusive, quite abusive. This was the story in Esther's home. The father was an alcoholic and could be very abusive at times for no reason. Esther received the brunt of that abuse many times, so she was quite intimidated when it came to interacting with adults, especially men.

It is an evidence of the rightness of her coming to live with us that she was even willing to take the chance. She told me months later when she could finally communicate with us that she prayed for one year every day that we would come back and get her. She also told us at that time that when I called she didn't even bother asking her parents. She was going! She just figured if I showed up they would say yes. I'm glad I did not know that. I was there acting as if they had already said yes. No wonder there were some uncomfortable times that I didn't understand.

When it wasn't strained, I was having a great time with everyone. I went to the beach one day with Katurah's biological father, who was Esther's brother. He let me know that he wanted me to stay on the beach and watch him as he was going to go get supper for us. I stood there as he walked out into the ocean and then disappeared. He was gone about fifteen minutes, and then I saw him approaching me from the water. In his hand was a net full of fish. He took me to he and his wife's hut that was right there on the beach and invited me in to sit with them. There was not a stitch of furniture, just mats on the floor. I sat and tried to visit. His wife got up to leave and came back a little while later and said dinner was ready. I then went to their eating and cooking hut and had one of the best meals that I have ever had. We ate fish and rice. That fish still had everything on it. Eyes, fins, bones, etc. It was awesome. They use oil to cook everything, but they never change the oil in the pan. They just keep adding to it as the oil runs out. This creates a delicious and tasty seasoning. I ate a lot and could have eaten more. It was so good.

Medjio's cooking and eating hut was bigger, but it had been around longer or something, because the ants were much more prevalent. There were mats on her floor, and every time you would take a step, thousands of ants would scurry out from under your feet. They crawled all over us as we cooked over little propane burners. But those woman could cook. They served me the best fried chicken that I have ever had. They had no utensils, so they ate with their hands. I just dove in and figured when in

Rome, do as the Romans. I was in Laura, so I did as the people of Laura did.

Every morning they would bring a piece of white toast and a slightly cooked egg to my tent. I would eat the toast and throw the egg away. It was just too raw for me. One of Esther's favorite foods was to get three pieces of bread and stack them on top of each other and just eat it that way. To her, that was a sandwich.

They had pigs and chickens running free all over the place. They would raise the pigs and then share them with the whole family; Aunts, uncles, cousins, just everybody. The breadfruit that was everywhere was not in season, but the smell seemed to permeate everything. They were also a very tidy people. After every big storm, they would take big palm tree branches and sweep the ground and pick up all branches and leaves that had been blown everywhere. They were warm and wonderful people, and I loved them.

But then one day everything changed.

Everything was finished. We had all the paperwork, passport, and tickets in hand. Just like the last time we were there. There were still three days before we were to leave, and I was truly enjoying getting to know everybody better. I got up that morning, and Esther came to me crying. In the night, one of the older men of the village had come to claim Esther as his wife. He was one of her father's drinking friends. He came into the hut where the women were sleeping. Then, because he had defiled Esther by coming in and the father had seen it, her father came in and beat her with a broom handle and told her she could not go to America but must marry his friend. She was devastated but did not dare go against her father.

Not again! Not only was I heartbroken for Esther, but I was so angry that once again I had done all of this and was going to go home empty-handed. I am not usually one who ever loses my temper with anyone, especially outside of my family. But this was just more than I could take. I stormed into Medjio's hut and told her that she was not an honest person. They had made promises to me, and they were lying to me. Then I turned around and walked out. I went to my tent and wept. I was beside myself with anger, grief, frustration, and despair. Where was God? Why was he not there to show forth his mighty arm? I was alone, in a tent, in a jungle, in a country where I could not communicate or get hold of my husband, and I had been abandoned by the one who had said to come. I did not understand!

It was pouring rain outside the tent, of course. But I had to get out, I had to move. I took my umbrella and went out under the trees and prayed. I must have stood out there for over an hour. It was there in my hour of need, under a canopy of jungle foliage in the middle of a monsoon, that God stepped forward and gave me one of the sweetest tender mercies I have ever had. He gave me peace! As I stood out there, all I could think to do was sing. I sang the same hymn over and over until God's sweet peace came into my heart.

> 2Be still, my soul: the Lord is on thy side;
>
> With patience bear thy cross of grief or pain.
>
> Leave to thy God to order and provide;
>
> In every change he faithful will remain.
>
> Be still, my soul: Thy best, thy heavenly friend
>
> Through thorny ways leads to a joyful end.

I love Psalms 69:16 where it says: "Hear me, O Lord; for thy loving kindness is good: turn unto me according to the multitude of thy tender mercies." God had truly turned unto me the multitude of his tender mercies. In his loving kindness, he had been my friend, and in my thorny path, he had brought a stillness to my soul. I knew without a doubt that he was on my side and his will would be done.

I went back to Medjio and threw my arms around her, and we wept together. At that point, a beautiful thing happened. I asked her to pray with me. The two of us knelt together, and I began to pray. Here were two women who were the same age, from two completely different walks of life, joined together before God, each of us desiring the same thing for a young girl. The worldly language barrier was great, but the language of the spirit was clear and untainted. It was at that moment, when two hearts joined as one in a pleading prayer to God, that something wonderful happened. In my mind's eye, I saw the two of us standing together as equals. No language, education, monetary, or worldly standards stood between us. We were sisters. Each of us a child of a God who loved us and who also wanted the same thing for a young girl. It was amazing. After the prayer, we held each other and wept and knew that God was real and that Esther was in his hands.

Within hours, everything had turned around. Hearts were softened, and now there was excitement in the air as final preparations were made for our departure.

I gave all that I had brought with me, my tent, chair, food, etc., to the family, and we boarded the plane to go home; home to a family that had once again supported and sacrificed while their mother hearkened to the whisperings and brought home another one of God's children to the safe fold of our home. They welcomed Esther with open arms, and I had the peace that one more child was gathered. Esther has been such a blessing to our family from day one. She brings her sweet smile and sense of humor into every family gathering. She is a hard worker and not afraid to try anything. People are drawn to her and the wonderful spirit that she carries. The long walk to get Esther had been fraught with challenges. But what marvelous gifts we received once again.

a time of change

—Annie Laurie

We were now living in Logan, Utah. I think heaven finally figured I needed a rest. In the four years that we lived in New Mexico, we had remodeled one home and completely built another. I had run a school out of my home for two years. I had also earned my bachelor's and master's degrees in education. We had a foreign exchange student for a year and sent four children on missions to foreign countries. I had earned my certificate to practice emotional release therapy and we had a daughter get married. We had traveled all over the world and had adopted ten children. That was a busy four years, and I was tired. So very tired. I just needed a rest.

I got that rest in 2003. The only thing that happened that year was moving to Utah and sending Ammon on a two-year mission to Korea. My health had really declined, but I was looking forward with hope that I would find answers.

All I can say is that it was a good thing I had a slow year, for 2004 came in with a bang. Andrew was married shortly after the first of the year, and we were excited about his sweet wife, Lyndsey.

But that wasn't busy enough. I had decided that if we were going to live in the house that we were in, we needed to make some changes. We made plans together and talked about what we wanted to do, but the look on Brian's face when he came home one day and the whole main floor was gutted, was a sight to see. He now had about 2,000 square feet to remodel. But not only that, we had plans drawn up to add another 4,000 square feet to the home. The house would total over 8,000 square feet when it was completed. That would be Brian's nonstop project for the next four years. The funny thing is that we have never been able to live in that completed home that was planned with so much excitement. We had to sell it in order to pay off some of our adoption debt. But how grateful I am for the blessing of having the resources to do just that. God works in mysterious ways.

Right after we tore everything apart, our Katie left for a mission to Baton Rouge, Louisiana. This was a hard time for me for several reasons. She had always been such a support and such a help in all that we were doing. I would sorely miss having her by my side as a daughter, friend, and companion.

But the other reason was a place in my heart that held fear. It was at this time that I found out that I still had emotional scars from when I was a youth living in Alabama. It was also around this same time that the whisperings started once again about our five children that we knew were coming. Only we didn't know yet that they were coming from Haiti. But as this whole process began to unfold, I was amazed that at the same time, both my daughter and I were going through experiences that would give us an incredible love for the black people and their cultures.

Over the years that we had been adopting, people had suggested several times that we adopt black children. I had always been very quick to respond with, "Oh no! We will never adopt black children. I would love to, but it just isn't right for our family." I really believed this. But I was about to take a really good look in the mirror, and it would be life changing.

Here we were looking for children again and wondering where God was going to lead us this time. I honestly had no clue. I was just waiting for some kind of guidance from on high. I received a call one day from a friend. She said she had heard about an orphanage in Haiti that was being run by a husband-and-wife team from America.

I still was not interested in adopting black children, but my pat answer of "it just isn't right for our family" was no longer good enough. Why was I so averse to having children from the black culture? Why wouldn't I even entertain the thought? I had always thought that I was such an open person who loved everybody. Come on, I didn't have a prejudiced bone in my body! Did I? But if that was true, then why was I not even willing to look at the possibility of adopting a black child? And what if this was the direction God wanted us to go? It was really starting to look like it was going to be the right thing to do. I was getting just a wee bit nervous.

Many prayers later, the answer came. Two words: Alabama and fear. I had lived for three years in a place that had caused great fear in my heart every day. And now, I was still living out that fear every day. I had lived in Alabama during my junior high school years. The struggle between the blacks and whites at that time was very bitter. In order to have a better understanding of what I was dealing with at this time in our life, I must share some experiences from that time living there as a young girl.

The year we moved to Alabama, I was in seventh grade. I was very innocent and was suddenly thrown into a world where innocence did not exist. It had been long since torn away by racial discrimination and hatred. It was the first year that my particular school had integrated the whites and blacks. We were bused in to their school, and they did not like it. I can understand because I think they were as afraid of change much as we were, but we were on their territory, and I especially was at a disadvantage, as I hadn't lived with all this bitterness and had no idea how to handle it.

Every day was a little bit of hell for me as I entered the doors of my school. I was quickly spotted as an easy target for many of the black boys and girls frustrated attempts at getting back at a society that had treated them cruelly. They only knew to treat others the same, in particular, me! I was physically and sexually molested every day as I walked the halls by young men. After school, I would be kicked and thrown to the ground by the girls who were bigger and tougher than me. I was accused of being a homosexual with one of my teachers, the only kind teacher I had, and witnessed some of the most horrible behaviors right in class. I told my father what was happening only one time. He came to school in his military uniform and complained to the principal. It got worse than ever after that. I didn't tell anyone again. I just got a bit tougher.

So that was it! I was letting fear rule my life. It was time to change. I believe that one of the biggest things that stop people from changing is ignorance. I also believe that with the proper use of knowledge comes power. With power comes the ability to overcome or change anything, especially with God's help. This knowledge about myself caused me to want to change. Obviously, God wanted the change also. If our next five children were going to come from Haiti, then my heart needed to change, and it needed to change completely.

And now my Katie was going to live with and serve the very culture that terrified me. It truly was time to change.

● ● ● ● ● ● ● ● ● ● ● ● ● ● ● ● ● ● ● ●

Katie—our twenty-seven-year-old daughter

When I shared with my family that I would be living in Louisiana for a year and a half as a missionary, I was so excited. But I distinctly remember my mother's face falling, and then I watched as she covered whatever emotion she was feeling with a smile that didn't quite reach her eyes. I didn't connect the dots until sometime later.

At the same time, I was getting everything ready to leave, my parents were also struggling with the decision of whether or not to adopt from Haiti. I found out later that their indecision stemmed from the long-harbored feelings of fear my mother felt toward black people. Here I was going to a place that was very prominently populated with the very people that she was so afraid of. I was soon to find out that my love for the people of Louisiana would become one of the driving forces behind the love I now have for my Haitian brother and sisters.

I arrived in Baton Rouge in February of 2004. We loved to share God's Word with people. We also loved to serve the communities in many different ways. But there were also times of struggle when the memory of my family and the prayers I knew were being said in my behalf at home were the only things that kept me going. That and all that I had been taught by two of the most wonderful people I know, my parents. Their influence in my life and the example they had set became so apparent that I couldn't help but silently praise their names on a daily basis.

People continually ask me what it was like to grow up in my family and what it is like today. I can just imagine what thoughts they have when they hear there are twenty-four children in our family. *Twenty-four!* I can imagine there is a very chaotic picture painted immediately in their mind. One of fighting and arguing, messes everywhere, meals sporadic and on the go! And of course, piles and piles of laundry (well, that one's not so far off). But if the truth be told, it is quite the opposite. It is a place where truth is taught and feelings are shared. There is order and love. Peace and oh so much fun. It is hard to even remember that there are so many people living under one roof.

These are the reasons that remembering my family all the way on the other side of the United States was such a comfort. These are the reasons someone as shy and timid as I was could go out and help God's children. I had been taught the very same things that the children coming into our home are continually being taught today, and not only that, but they are living it every day. My family is actually living their walk with God.

As a result of my time there, I came to love the African American people and their beautiful culture. My parents have since brought into our family five of the most beautiful Haitian children ever. I adore them along with of all my brothers and sisters. I can't imagine our family without them. It has been a hard journey but one definitely worth the walk. I will always be grateful for my parents and their willingness to not only find their own walk with God but then in turn teach us to search for ours.

● ●

—Annie Laurie

Fear is a powerful emotion. But it is an emotion that stops your progress. Faith is the opposite of fear. I didn't need to carry around an emotion that stopped me. I needed the power of my faith to move me forward in the direction God wanted us to go. I admit that change did not come over night. In fact, it took almost three years before it was complete.

So here we were with whisperings, friends running an orphanage, and God working a mighty change. What choice did we have but to step out and embrace the journey before us?

I e-mailed our friends and asked them what we had to do to get started.

More paperwork, another dossier, more people peering into our lives. Only this time, there were even more questions. Why are you still wanting children when you have fifteen? Can you possibly take care of their needs? Aren't you getting too old for this? Are you ever going to stop? I didn't have a lot of answers. I just knew that having children come into our home was a gift. We all worked together, and we had a great home. There were children who needed a great home. I also knew that they were God's children, and he would help us see that they were clothed, fed, loved, disciplined, and taught of his great power. I didn't know how finances would work out, but I knew they would. I did know that we could love them and our children would love them. It just worked in our home.

This adoption was special because Sarah and I decided to do it together. Sarah had always been such a stalwart in this whole adoption process. She had taken care of children, listened to my endless attempts at trying to figure out just what God was saying this time, and she and her husband had also financially stepped in to help. It was an honor to now be a part of helping her bring children into their family. She felt there were three for them, and I was anxious to find our five. By July, all the paperwork was done, and we were ready to go to Haiti to see our children. We planned on being there for ten days.

The director had warned us about what it would be like, but I was still not prepared for the poverty, the heaviness in the very air. My heart ached for these people. We went straight to the orphanage, but just driving down the roads filled me with despair. Was there anything that could ever turn this country around?

When we arrived at the orphanage, I was surprised to see that it was a house with two levels. I don't know what I was expecting, but not a rundown house in the middle of an even more rundown neighborhood. The directors and their family lived on the upper level, and the children lived on the main level with their nannies. As we pulled up, there were several ladies of all ages sitting on the driveway with big metal tubs full of laundry. There were no washing machines, and everything that was worn had to be washed every day, by hand, and then hung out to dry. That was enough to overwhelm anyone.

The director asked us if we wanted to meet our children immediately, and we, of course, said absolutely. This is what I had been waiting for ever since I was in Vietnam, getting my little Jenai'. I couldn't wait. Sarah was pretty excited too. We walked up to the front porch, and there were children everywhere eating a plate of rice with about twenty beans mixed in. They were eating as fast as they could. I didn't know at that time how familiar that particular meal would become to me. But for them, it was indeed familiar, as it is the main staple for children in orphanages. It is the only meal they get in a day, except sometimes they would receive a sugar pudding as a second meal. I was offered a spoonful by one of the little ones. I declined. I could not even imagine eating something that was offered from an orphanage. How much I still had to learn and experience.

As we approached the home, the director had called out seven names, and soon there were children running toward us. As they got closer, they stopped and just stared at us. She explained to them that we were their new mothers coming to visit them. We sorted out the children so we would know which children belonged to each of us. Sarah had only two of hers gathered around her. She had a sibling group of twin boys and their little sister. One of the twins was not there that day. He was with his mother. They looked so good together. You could just tell that it was right.

I looked up, and there were five more children standing there. All of a sudden I felt like I had been kicked in the stomach. These were not my children. I knew it, but what could I do? Not even one time in all the adoptions had I really had a say in who came into my home. But on the other hand, all the children who have come have always felt like they were mine from the first time I saw them. Except, of course, the four little ones, where it took me about an hour to feel that assurance with them. Maybe I was just tired from two days of traveling with no sleep. I was sure I would feel it soon. I was questioning things in my head, trying to make sense of the feeling in my heart and my stomach. But right then, I had to do what anyone would do; take those kids in my arms and act like their mother. I held them close and smiled for the pictures, but the feeling in me kept growing. *These are not my children.*

Let me back up a little bit to a prayer that I had had about a year before this. I am so very grateful for adoption. My life would have been so empty if I had not been able to have more children after the age of twenty-five. I don't want to even imagine! And we had been so blessed in the children that God had put in our home, and we knew that his timing was perfect. But one of the things that troubled my heart incessantly over the last twenty years was that I had no choice or say in the matter of choosing my children. I couldn't say let's get pregnant and have a child, and I couldn't go to an orphanage and choose my child. Man often seemed in control of my destiny as a mother. Now I know that God is ultimately in charge, but when you are going through one heart-wrenching journey of gathering after another, you find yourself having weak moments. This was my weak moment that showed up over and over in each adoption process until I would finally hold my children and know they were mine. So, about a year before this, I had gone to my heavenly Father and pled with him to please enable me to somehow choose my own children the next time. I had forgotten that prayer until this moment of meeting these children whom I knew were not mine. And yet once again, I had no say in the matter. What was I going to do?

We left the orphanage as soon as we could graciously get away. I just wanted to go back to our little hole-in-the-wall room and figure this out. I went to bed that night troubled. Maybe it would all go away the next morning when I saw them again. I felt so guilty. These children needed a home. Why couldn't I just be glad to have found my five little ones? That was the problem. They were not my five little ones.

I awoke the next morning exhausted from a very sleepless night. I dreaded going to the orphanage. What was I going to say to the director? In her mind, she had done me the biggest favor by choosing her favorite children to give to me. But I knew I had to say something.

As soon as we arrived at the orphanage that morning, I pulled her aside and told her we really needed to talk. We went into her room, and I threw myself on her bed. I started to pour out my heart but could hardly speak because of the emotional turmoil I was in. When she was finally able to make some sense of my babblings, she just looked at me and then told me that it was not the adoptive parent's option to choose their children. I just sat quiet and looked at her, praying with all my heart that God would intervene. Sure enough, God was right there, ready with one of his sweet miracles. After a long pause, she looked at me and said, "You tell me who you feel is yours, and I will do my best to make it happen." Yes! I was going to choose my children! Yes!

But, now I had to find them. How do you look at a home full of starving, sick, and lost children and just choose a few? Was there any way that I could do that? I would just put it into God's hands and let him choose. But I would be able to be there for the journey. Little did I know at the time what that journey of choosing my children personally would mean. I thought it would be a matter of pointing and getting, but as with so many of God's journeys for us, he has so much more, so many gifts that he wants to give in the process of completing the experience.

Before our long walk with Haiti would finally be finished, we would be taken to the absolute end of our ability to endure. God would literally have to carry us in order for us to finish the tutoring process. As I walked this journey, I became more and more grateful for the faith-building experiences that we had already gone through. Otherwise our family would never have made it.

So this moment in Haiti that seemed so traumatic was just the tip of the iceberg. Thank goodness I could only see the tip.

I began looking around at the children with different eyes. Which children were mine? How would I know?

There was one little girl who was part of the original group of five I felt my heart drawn to. She was four years old and a quiet little thing with pursed lips. She had been a crack baby. Her mother had lived on the streets of Haiti and nearly starved to death. Her grandfather had taken care of her for a while but was starving himself, so he brought her to the orphanage. This was the second orphanage she had lived in. My heart connected with hers, and I fell in love with her.

Later on that day we went to another orphanage that just had a few children in it. The director had a meeting that she had to go to, so I stayed outside with the children. I sang them songs and did finger plays and was really enjoying myself. During one of the songs, I felt someone at my elbow. I turned around and there stood the sweetest little girl. As I made eye contact with her, I got the warmest feeling in my chest, and the words that came to my mind were, "This is your daughter." The feeling was so strong that I stopped singing and had to sit down. I couldn't believe it. God had let me know.

There was only one problem. She was not in our orphanage. I couldn't wait for the director to come out. When the orphanage director returned from her meeting, I told her what had happened, she just looked at me and said, "She's not available, you can't have her. That orphanage does not do adoptions!" That didn't stop me. I just told her that God wanted her in my home and would she please work something out. By the next morning, that little girl was in our orphanage and available for me to adopt. Yes! Another miracle!

Over the next few days, I couldn't figure anything else out. I didn't feel anything really strong about any of the other children. I wondered if I was supposed to only get two children, but the feelings I had clearly said that there were five but not to worry about it. There was a cute little eighteen-month-old who I thought was so darling. I went back to the director and asked her if I could have that cute little one. I then told her to pick out two that really needed a home. That was all I knew to do at the time. She chose two more of the original five, the eight-year-old girl and another eighteen-month-old baby girl who needed some medical attention for a terrible hernia. I felt content knowing that if there needed to be any changes, somehow it would be taken care of.

We spent the next few days with the children in our hotel room. We had a lot of fun. Sarah's other boy came, and her little family certainly fit her. I was thrilled for her. We fed the kids all the peanut butter and crackers that they could eat. But try and keep eight children who can't speak English happy and well behaved in a tiny, grubby hotel room. It was a little crazy, but we did it. The sleeping arrangements were even more interesting, as we had wall-to-wall children. They were wet every morning, but my cute little four-year-old loved to help me wash the clothes in a bowl and then lay them around to dry. By the time we left to go home, I was exhausted.

One of my favorite things while we were in Haiti was our drive into the mountains. Sarah and I rode in the back of the truck. I loved it! I had always wanted to ride in the back of a truck, and doing so on the streets of Haiti was like a Disneyland ride. You also saw what Haiti and its people were really like. In order to get to the mountain village where we were going, we had to drive through the city of Port au Prince and the outlying cities which were even worse. The streets were thronged with people. The homes were all rubble, and yet they were still living in them. I have never seen so much garbage in my life. I think the streets were actually a few inches higher than they were meant to be because of the packed-down garbage that covered them. There were animals everywhere, and you couldn't tell if people were just sleeping along the side of the road or if they were dead. I didn't see another white person the whole time I was there, and yet I felt safe. The miracle was happening. In my compassion for these people, my fear was slowly being erased and an incredible love had been planted and was ready to bloom into something wonderful.

The mountains were beautiful, but just because there was beauty, it did not take away the poverty. How could people even exist in such circumstances? It made the people in the Marshall Islands seem wealthy.

It was soon time for us to go back to America. I was not sorry to leave. We said good-bye to the children and told them we would be back for them. We boarded the plane and let out a huge sigh of relief. I didn't know how the director could live there with her family. I knew that I could never live in these circumstances. Not ever. Little did I know what the future held for me.

cami

—Annie Laurie

We were finally home again, and it felt so good. When you go to places like Haiti, you come home so much more appreciative of what you have. I had missed my family too, and it was good to be together.

That summer our Blaine had also come home from his time in Uruguay and one month later was married to his sweetheart, Michelle. They had fallen in love before he left, and she was waiting for him to come home. They moved into our basement apartment for the next six months, and it was so fun to have them close.

There were a few complications with our adoption proceedings that seemed to be stopping the progression of our paperwork. We decided that I better go over there and see what I could do to help. So in January of 2005, I went to Haiti by myself for a week. It was a hard week. I became very ill from bad food, but by the time I left, things were worked out and I came home more determined than ever to bring those children home.

I have mentioned several times that our children had some real personal struggles. They were trying to deal with autism, ADD, fetal alcohol syndrome, depression, constant pain in their joints from meth in their bodies while the mom was pregnant, and a myriad of other things that plagued their young lives. I believed in nutrition, so I was desperately looking for ways to help them nutritionally. I just wasn't having much success. At this time we were also really struggling with my health. We were once again looking at the possibility that I wouldn't live to raise the children. It was a dear friend who brought me my answers. She introduced me to a nutritional product called Reliv that changed our lives. Many of those issues that the children were struggling with became manageable and my health started to improve.

I mention this for a few reasons. One is because people are always asking me how I can mother all these children with all the baggage that they bring. I have to answer that it is because we have help dealing with the baggage. You talk about miraculous gifts from God, this was a huge one for us. And then to get their Mom back and know that they weren't going to lose her again anytime soon, was also huge for our family.

It also changed the course that our life was taking. We were in financial ruin with all the adoption costs, and this turned that part of our life around as we embraced the business side. It made it so that eventually Brian was able to quit his job of teaching and be a fulltime dad. With both of us being fulltime parents, there was no end to the children that we would be able to help. That was our dream, to help children, and this also looked like it could help make that dream financially possible.

So our future started to change at this point. We had been afraid to bring more children in to our home, and now that concern was lightened. It gave me a new excitement and determination to get these children in Haiti a home. But it didn't matter how excited I was, nothing seemed to move forward.

We had started a school again in our home that fall, and quite a few families signed up. We had a great year together.

At the end of the school year, I took all the older students on a two-week history camping trip. It was during that camping trip that we found ourselves involved in our next gathering.

The previous fall when I started school, there was a young woman in my class who never smiled. She was seventeen and seemed to be one of the unhappiest people I had ever met. Her name was Cami. As I worked with her that year, I slowly saw her smile come to life. By the end of the year, she was a vital part of our class. She had mentioned a few times during the year that she would love to come live with us and be a part of our family. I would laugh and think nothing of it. Well, during that two-week camping trip, the impression came very strongly that we were to let her move in with us. *Okay,* I thought, *but there is no way that she is going to ever really be a part of our family.* No way. I already had two unofficially adopted daughters, and I didn't need any more.

After much thought and prayer we decided to give it a try. I expected her to come into our home and conform to our way of life. I figured that would be enough to probably chase her away. Cami said that she had always thought that she was a hard worker, but after a few days in our home, she told me that she had no idea what hard work was until she came to live with us. But it didn't scare her off. I used to ask her why she didn't just leave. Her response was always the same.

"I would be willing to do anything to live here and be able to experience the love and the spirit that is in your home."

What a sweet compliment. And she has done just that. She has been with us ever since, except for a few short months when she was a live in nanny for a friend. She is now twenty-one, and we consider her one of our very own. She is truly a blessing in our home. The children love her, and it is her specific job to teach the little ones to read. She has been such a blessing to us, as we are now living on a two-hundred-acre ranch and she grew up around animals. Her family has had some serious struggles that ended in divorce and remarriages. They have respected Cami's desire to stay with us and supported her in that.

So now we had one more that had been brought into our fold. We now had five biological, three unofficially adopted, and nine legally adopted. Our oldest was thirty-two and our youngest was three. We had five more that were hopefully coming soon, and we had seven grandchildren. We were finally getting healthy, and our financial future was looking not quite so desperate. What more could you ask for in life?

That August, Sarah and I spent a month in England and Germany sharing our new Reliv business with friends and family. I came straight home from there and drove to Louisiana to pick up Katie. A few days before I arrived, Hurricane Katrina hit and New Orleans was flooded. We were able to witness a great deal of the destruction caused by that storm. It was a rude awakening of how fragile life really is. I came home and went to work starting another year of teaching school. Sarah and Katie, helped me teach in the school. It looked like it was going to be a good year.

Within a very short time, Katie became engaged to a young man that she met while in Louisiana. He, like Katie, was on a mission there also. They set their wedding date for December. I was so excited to watch her get married and to share those first few months with her. Unfortunately, it wasn't going to happen like I wanted it to. Right before she was to be married, we received a terrifying phone call.

haiti

—Brian

I was serving as the principal of a faculty of about ten teachers and a small student body of 1,200 students. While enjoying lunch with my faculty, a uniformed highway patrol officer entered and asked to speak with a Brian Richardson. I invited him into my office, and he came right to the point.

"Are you in the process of adopting children from Haiti?"

Had we done something illegal? Did Annie Laurie do something that was not in accordance with the law? The thought was silly, but why would an American law enforcement officer be in my office asking about adoptions in Haiti? He said that someone had called inquiring about an Annie Laurie Richardson who was in the process of adopting children from Haiti.

The officer proceeded to explain that this woman had called his dispatcher wondering if they knew of or could find an Annie Laurie Richardson in their jurisdiction. Officially, they could do nothing. But it just so happened that a few weeks earlier we had been invited to speak to a large gathering. We told the story of Jenai and the many other miracles of gathering our precious children. This officer was part of the congregation and remembered our names, and his daughter was a member of our student body. He relayed the message given to him by this inspired woman who was seeking us out. He said that the children Annie Laurie had begun the adoption proceedings for in Haiti had been abandoned. He related that one of the parents who also were in the process of adopting children from this particular orphanage, traveled to Haiti and found the children had been locked in the orphanage with no food for an entire week. The older children, seven and eight year olds, kept the younger ones alive. He provided me with the woman's name and number. I thanked him sincerely, and he left and returned to his duties.

This wonderful man's visit to me is a direct miracle. He just happened to hear the dispatcher's conversation. He just happened to remember us from our speaking engagement. His daughter was a student in one of our classrooms. Coincidence? This good highway patrolman, a father himself, took action when it was not required or part of his duty as one of our valiant law enforcement officers. But this man took it upon himself to do the right thing. God bless him.

* *

—*Annie Laurie*

I was in the middle of teaching my class of students, ages ten to eighteen, when I got an emergency call from my husband. Once again, as I had years ago, I gave my students some work to do and told them I would be back as soon as I could. I went to a quiet place in the house and called him to find out what the emergency was.

He gave me a message that was so jumbled I could not understand it. I just knew there was a problem in Haiti with our children and there was a number that I needed to call. There was something about a policeman that made me scared, but I just couldn't get it straight, and he had to go back to class. So I took the number and called an unknown woman who would hopefully be able to shed further light on the chaos that my husband tried to explain to me.

"There has been a crisis in Haiti at the orphanage. We have been trying to get hold of you for two weeks. My husband went over there because we could not get hold of the director, and we thought maybe something had gone wrong. When he arrived at the orphanage, he did find something wrong, terribly wrong! He found the children abandoned and starving."

Wait! Wait! What was I supposed to do with this information? It was all coming too fast for me to know how to feel. *Help me God to accept this news without falling apart. Please help me stay in a place of knowing that you are there.* So many questions filled my mind that I could not even form one to speak, so I just said, "Please tell me more."

"The nannies had not been paid for a few weeks, so they took everything, bedding, food, clothes, everything, and left the children there. They locked the doors and left them to die. They were almost dead when we found them. There was five gallons of powdered lemonade, and that is what they have survived on.

The older children, who are only seven and eight themselves, sacrificed so the little ones would have something."

I was finally able to squeeze out one question from the swirling thoughts in my head. "Did any of the children die?"

"No, but the situation was so serious that they formed a hospital on sight and flew in doctors from America to save the children."

My mind was reeling, but I had to know about Sarah's and our children.

"What about the children? Where are they?"

"I am sorry, the news isn't good. The orphanage is closed, and the children whose adoptive parents were able to claim them have been sent by the government to other orphanages. You were the only ones that we could not find a phone number for, and I am afraid we do not know where your children are. They could be in orphanages or sent back to families or they could just be on the streets. I am sorry, so sorry."

"What do I do? Have we just lost our children? Do we go over there? Please tell me what to do?"

She softly said, "I don't know. I just don't know if you will be able to find your children. But your only chance is to go to Haiti and go from orphanage to orphanage in hopes that they will be there. I'm just so sorry."

I hung up from that phone call in a state of shock. I didn't know what to do. I had a wedding to prepare. I couldn't leave. *Please, Father, just take care of our children until I can get there.*

⬤ ⬤

The wedding was over, and they were on their honeymoon in Disneyworld. I was so excited for them to come home and to share in Katie's life as a new wife. We had always been close, and this was one of those things we had been talking about sharing for years. But I had children who were lost somewhere.

It was December 17. Do we just leave and miss Christmas with our families? We had no choice. We knew that we needed to go. Two days later, a friend of mine who was also adopting children from this orphanage, and I left for Haiti hoping that somehow we would be home for Christmas. Little did we know that this long walk was going to be the longest I had ever taken. If I had any idea of what lay in store for me and my family, I would never ever have gotten on that plane!

⦁ ⦁

We arrived in Haiti on December 19. This arrival was much different than my other two arrivals. We were met by a man who was holding a sign with our names on it and were told to follow him. We then went through a door leading into another part of the airport while the rest of the passengers went on to the customs area. We were excited and yet nervous. Where were we being taken? We were seated in this little lounge adjacent to a bar that I didn't even know existed in that third world country airport and then left there for what seemed like an eternity. Someone came and took our passports, and we were left again. Were we being taken care of by friend or foe?

Soon, a very tall and overpowering woman came in. She was wreathed in smiles and hugged us. She had no English, and we had no French. I felt like I was in a movie. She motioned us to follow her, and since we didn't know where we were or what we were supposed to do, we followed. She led us to a car that already had our luggage in it and gave us back our passports, and we were told to get in. We did as we were told. I wouldn't have dared not to. We then drove to a part of Port au Prince that I had not been to before. The roads were amazing. I don't know how cars last for more than a month, for they are jolted and jerked beyond description. The holes they fall into are so large, I can't imagine how they ever come out the other side. But we made it. However, not before I was sure that every part of me had been put in a bag and shaken and then put back together willy-nilly.

We ended up at a home that was behind a big wall with a locked gate. In Haiti, every home that is not rubble is behind a big wall and a locked gate. You didn't find a house by what the front looked like but by what the gate looked like. It was the only way that they were safe.

Once we pulled into the driveway, we were surprised at how lovely their small little piece of heaven was. There were beautiful flowers and trees everywhere. The home was big by Haitian standards, having four bedrooms and a large living space. It had a tiny kitchen, but really all the cooking was done in an outside kitchen. It almost looked like a normal home. This is where we would live for the next two weeks. Usually they had water, but not all the time. Usually they had electricity, but again, not all the time. The cooking was done on a propane cooker, but their maid could really put out some wonderful things on that cooker. In those two weeks, I was introduced to eating goat, every part of a goat I might add, and various other dishes that I cannot begin to describe. I found that I actually liked most of it.

We found out the lady's name was Micheline. Her brother, who knew my friend, had asked her to take special care of us and help us get these children home. She was very interested in humanitarian work, so she was excited to be a part of this. She had her daughter, Sandy, come over to translate for us. Sandy spoke very good English, and this made things so much easier. We soon found out that Micheline was a very influential woman in Haiti. She knew the president and many of the high officials. If anyone could find our children, she could. It was close to Christmas, so we were afraid that we would not be able to get much done, but we had not reckoned on the power and influence of Micheline.

We had gone to the government offices several times trying to find out where our children were. They evidently were supposed to have record of where all those children from the closed orphanage had been taken. They were not at all cooperative until we greased the hand of one of the officials. We gave him an early Christmas gift for his kindness. It was the first of many hands that were greased while we were on this journey. I hated supporting this mentality, but I was not about to sacrifice my children at the expense of my American ethics. In Haiti, it was just a way of life.

We started finding out little pieces of information. Some of the news was hopeful, some devastating. One of my baby girls had been taken by her family, and they were sure that she was dead. My other baby girl just disappeared on the streets of Haiti. My other girl, who was nine, was nowhere to be found. We did find her several months later, but I was not able to adopt her. I was amazingly calm about this news. My heart ached, but I know that my heart was being held in a place of safety by a Father's loving hands.

We were finally told that some of the children were in an orphanage up on the mountain side of Port Au Prince. It was run by a man who everyone called Pastor because he also taught a congregation on Sundays. We were desperately hoping that we would be able to talk to him. We had also been told that they had an unclaimed child in another orphanage, and they thought that maybe she was one of ours too. We set up times to be able to visit each one of them.

On Christmas day, we went to the first orphanage where the unknown child was. I had one of the greatest presents imaginable on that Christmas day. I found our Bethany. She was the little three-, now five-, year-old who was a crack baby that I had felt so strongly was ours. They brought us in to a little sitting area, and after waiting for about thirty minutes, a skinny little girl was placed in front of me. It was our Bethany. I just wrapped her in my arms and told her over and over how much I loved her. She had gone through so much and was hardly responsive at all. She just sat in my arms like a limp rag doll. It broke my heart to see her so listless. When I looked in her eyes, they seemed to have no life in them. The hardest part was that I knew I was going to have to leave her again. Would she ever learn to trust me? We were not allowed to take her with us, as we had to prove to the government that she had been ours.

We spent Christmas at the orphanage with little Bethany and the rest of the children. It was a sweet experience to watch those children and to play with them. They all wanted our attention. They would vie for the attention of Americans because that meant gifts or maybe even someone to take you to America if you were really lucky. I just enjoyed holding our little girl. It was so hard to leave her there. When it was time to leave, I walked away and felt like I was abandoning her all over again. I tried to let her know that I would be back very soon. She just stared at me with no emotion, no life, and no hope.

Bethany's full name is Bethany Hope. We gave her that name because that is what we wanted to restore to her—hope. Life had robbed her of all hope and all the brightness of life. She has that back now and is a wonderful young girl. She has some pretty big challenges still to face, but her future is so much brighter than it was that day as she stood there watching her mother leave her one more time. My heart was heavy and yet absolutely excited because I had found one child. I had seven more children to find.

We left and went back to Micheline's home for their Christmas celebration. It was very different, as there was no tree, no gifts, and only one tiny Santa Claus hung on a nail; but they did have family members over for a big dinner. I celebrated with the family, and then I sat in our room and sang Christmas carols and cried because I missed my family so much. My family went without Christmas because they wanted to wait for Mom to come home. Several months later, the tree and all the decorations were finally put away, but the presents still sat there waiting for my return.

A few days later, we went to the orphanage on the hill to see if the rest of our children were there. What a wonderful moment that was when I walked into that orphanage and saw Sarah's twins come running up to me. They literally jumped into my arms and almost knocked me over. They were so glad to see me. They brought me in and showed me that their little sister was there also. I hugged and hugged them.

But at the same time, I was looking around for our other children. As I perused the faces of over a hundred children, a quiet little girl with a shaved head came up to me. It was our five-, now seven-year-old girl that God had said, "She is your daughter." Our name for her was Laura. She had gone through so much in the past few months. She had almost died, and her head had been so covered with sores that they had to bleach it and then shave all of her hair off. I thought she was beautiful. I fell in love with these children all over again. I was so grateful to be there and to let them know that we had not forgotten them.

But I had lost three children in all of that chaos, and I started immediately looking around to see if there were others for me to take home in their place. I remembered my plea to be able to choose my children.

I was holding Laura when I looked over at a tiny little baby. She wasn't moving or smiling or anything. She was sitting, but only because her tummy was so big that it would prop up her body. If she tried to move her head at all, she would topple over. She looked like she was at the most about six months old, and not a healthy six months. I found out she was two years old. I couldn't believe it. I asked about her, as I could feel myself being drawn to her. They said that her mother had died from starvation and she had also been one of the babies that had almost died in the other orphanage. The doctors had declared that she was not worth saving. They said that if by some miracle she lived, she would be crippled the rest of her life. I couldn't help it. My arms were aching to hold her. I sat her on my lap. No response, she could not support herself, just a listless body that still had just a bit of life in it. I fell in love with her. She was mine; I knew it.

Yes! Another one of our children found.

There was the cutest little girl there who kept coming up to me and asking if I would be her mother in America. She was the tiniest little thing. She was the same age as our Bethany. I fell in love with her also. I found out she had a brother who was ten. He was so quiet that he would not say a word to me, but I felt good about taking both of them. I wanted to be that little girl's mother in America. I had our children!

As I left the orphanage that day, I was a very determined woman.

It became obvious that we were not going to be home for the New Year celebration. But actually that was okay, for I could not have made the trip. I became extremely sick with typhus. I lay on my bed for five days with raging fevers, horrific head-aches, and an extremely painful crimson rash that covered much of my body. Every joint in my body screamed in pain, and the sheets touching my skin caused even more excruciating pain. Nothing stayed in, and I would literally crawl to the bathroom when I could not put it off a minute longer. Up to that point I had never experienced anything like it in my life. There was no medication, no doctors, just unending agony of both mind and body. Where was my husband? Where was my family? The heat was unbearable, and there were bugs in my bed, and I cried, but then it became too painful to even cry.

Micheline did finally have a doctor come see us. I put out a most valiant effort to look as well as I could, for I knew that if they put me in a Haitian hospital, I might never come out alive. They were scary places. He soon left saying I certainly would not die, for Americans cannot die while in Haiti. I agreed.

I eventually started feeling a little better. I remember get-ting up to try and eat my first meal in days. I had to leave half way through the meal as I was too weak to hold up my head.

On day six of my sickness, we received word that the director of the orphanage where our children were wanted to meet with us. I had to sit in Micheline's office all day waiting for that afternoon appointment. No soft chairs, no air conditioning, and no privacy. I sat there at a table with my head in my arms and went back and forth between crying and laughing because I was so pitiful. I spent much of the time praying that I would have the strength to stay and carry on the conversation that was needed to convince this Pastor that we needed his help. I had promised to do anything to get these children. As Pastor finally walked into the room, I remember feeling my limbs gain strength. My head came up, and my mind cleared. I knew what I had to say and what I wanted to have happen, and God was right there giving me the strength to do it.

Pastor had brought with him the U.S. liaison, who was the head of the organization that were the sponsors for this particular orphanage.

I found out that all orphanages had American congregations or organizations that were supporting them financially. That is the only way that they were able to keep these orphanages going. I also found out later that that was why the original orphanage that our children were in went under. The director and her family were trying to do this out of their own personal funds. They could not get anyone in America to sponsor them. They ran out of money. The nannies stole everything because they did not get paid and locked the children in the orphanage without telling anyone. The director had moved his family to another home so that their family could have some sane time together, and they were struggling themselves. I know a lot of blame has been placed on many, but even though I had children in that orphanage, the more time I spent in Haiti, and the more I learned how things worked there, my heart goes out to this family who tried so hard to do something good. Instead of sitting at home and doing nothing, they were out trying and giving everything they had to help in the only way they knew how. I am truly sorry for them, for I am sure they feel the failure of their efforts acutely. I didn't understand all of that at the time, but every day in Haiti I would learn things that I could have learned in no other way.

This meeting with Pastor and his sponsor gave us a lot of hope. The sponsor told us he would do everything in his power to get those kids out of Haiti in two weeks. We found out that sponsors really have no say in the matter. But this chance meeting of the sponsor was a miracle in another way. Many times over the next several months, we would be persecuted for who we were and what our beliefs were. But because he had met me personally, he stood behind the decision to let us adopt. Nothing happens by accident.

By the end of our meeting, Pastor agreed to bring Bethany into his orphanage. All our children had to be in the same place, or the government would not let us adopt. He also agreed to let me have the children that I had chosen as my three to replace the ones I had lost. He also agreed to let us come live in the orphanage until our children were adopted. It would cost us seventy dollars a day to live there, but we would be with the children. He also agreed to do everything in his power to help us. This was a great blessing, because the only way to get anything accomplished in Haiti was to get someone influential on your side. We were blessed to have several such people. I went back to Micheline's still so sick I wanted to die, but my heart was light. Things were starting to fall into place, and I was certain I would soon be taking my children and grandchildren home.

• •

—*Brian*

Even though the plan was for Annie Laurie to be in Haiti for a couple of weeks at the most, I had a nagging feeling that her absence would be longer.

I remember our home was decorated for Christmas. We had a Christmas tree with presents for the children beautifully displayed in one of the main rooms of our home. As we approached Christmas Eve and Christmas Day, it was becoming clear to all of us that Annie Laurie was not going to be home for Christmas. Neither would she be home for our traditional New Year's Eve family party. As those special holidays came and went, it seemed that everything was in black and white, no color. Our lives were like a beautiful song where the words are all correct, but the music was all wrong. The children decided to postpone opening their presents until their mom could be there. Surely she could not be gone for more than a month, or so we thought.

When I think back upon that challenging time, I am very grateful to our daughter, Sarah, and her husband, Joseph. I still had to go to work every day. I still had the demanding responsibilities of teaching, working with my wonderful faculty, and the many challenges that come with students. But Joseph and Sarah were always there, supporting our situation and picking up the pieces. I was, for all intents and purposes, a single parent.

My respect for single parents has grown immensely since this experience. Every morning I would awaken feeling hopeful and happy to face the day, and then the realization that Annie Laurie was not home would strike me in the face, like a cold, stiff breeze.

Before work every day I would have to work up to being positive and deal with our children's intense feelings of missing their mother. I felt like I was wading through two feet of wet concrete emotionally, but I still had to be a strong and soft dad. Intellectually the children understood why Mommy was gone, but their little hearts were aching. They missed Annie Laurie so much. It was actually amazing to witness these little souls working through their feelings caused by the absence of their mother. They seemed to understand that their mother was doing something that needed to be done; something that had been done for them at an earlier time. The children would take turns in our family prayers pleading that their mommy would be kept safe and come home soon. Then they would frequently add, "But if you need Mommy to stay longer to bring our brothers and sisters home, help us to be brave."

• •

—Annie Laurie

If you need Mommy to stay longer! Help us to be brave! Just words on a piece of paper, but for me and my family, they became our battle cry. For we were caught in a ferocious battle. A battle that would tear us apart and take us to the limits of our endurance and beyond. A battle against the evil in this country of Haiti where our five children and three grandchildren had been born and where there was a government that was corrupt beyond anything that I had ever witnessed or heard of.

One day we would be filled with hope, and the next we'd be starting all over again. Nothing was ever for sure. Everything was so confusing. To even try to explain this to anyone who has not lived through it is difficult, confusing, and just impossible. I would try to explain it to Brian over the phone, and he just couldn't understand it. It was not until he came to Haiti and spent a week with me several months later that all the craziness made some sense to him.

Things didn't move forward. Promises were never kept. I often wondered if anyone really cared about the children, or was it all just about money, more and more money.

The first week in January, we had moved into the orphanage. Micheline had begged us to just go home because it was not safe. She told us that she would let us know when it was all done and we could come back. But we both felt strongly that if we left we would never see our children again.

There was a great deal of unrest in Haiti at this time. It

was election time, and people were being killed, kidnapped, tortured, and rapings on the streets were becoming common. All the whites were sent home and chaos reigned. Was it safe? Were we being foolish? Would we ever make it home?

life in the orphanage

—Annie Laurie

What was life like in the orphanage? It was different than I would have ever imagined. Every day, everybody in the orphanage had a bath from a large bowl. I have to admit it was one of the cutest sights I have ever seen to look out there when all the babies had their bath time. They would all line up naked, and then those nannies would scrub every inch of their bodies and faces with soap. Some little ones would scream the entire time every single day. But those nannies didn't care. They scrubbed anyway, yelling at them the whole time. They could wash ten children in half a bowl of cold water.

Even with all the bathing, the stench of urine and decay was overpowering, especially in the rooms where the children slept. There was a big opening in the cement floor in the girl's room where there was a cistern underground that was the water supply. They would have big trucks come in and fill that cistern with water as often as they could afford it. That is what they drank, washed, and cooked with. While I was there, we had running water about once every two weeks, and it would last for about two hours. The rest of the time we hauled our water up from that cistern by the bucket full. I got really good at brushing my teeth, taking a bath, washing my hair and my clothes, and then cleaning the bathroom and flushing the toilet with one bucket of water. When we talk here in America about conserving water, we have no idea. We were lucky if we got a bucket a day. We learned to be very strategic in our toilet flushing.

They were very serious about their worship. We were awakened every morning before six to the sounds of loud singing and praying. They would sing, pray, and chant for about an hour and then the day would start. It was the same thing in the evening. Right before bedtime, they would all gather again and sing and pray for about forty-five minutes. I used to stand at the top of the stairs and just let the sound wash over me. I loved the sound of the children's voices.

Even though we lived in a house, there was no electricity, no running water, and no bedding except a sheet, and no decorations except the pictures we had the children color and put on the wall. Very Spartan; and there were bugs and ants everywhere.

Now I have this weakness. I love to read at night. It is a passion with me, and I read for hours. I had no light to read by, so I used a candle. I set it on the chair next to me on a coaster that I found. If I held the book really close to the candle, then I could see just fine. That meant that I would lie very close to the edge of the bed and pull the chair up really close. This particular night I fell asleep while reading. I don't know what woke me up, but I opened my eyes, and there were huge flames about two inches from my head. The chair was on fire and so almost was my hair. I was terrified. I had not realized that the coaster would burn. I was not very educated in things to do with fire. I frantically beat out the flames, yelling as loud as I could for someone to get some water. Fortunately we had some in our bucket.

When it was all over, the thing I was most upset about was the chair. The orphanage had to struggle for everything they had, and here I had carelessly burned one of their nicest chairs. I am afraid it took me about two and a half months to get up the courage to tell them. You will be glad to know that I learned my lesson, and I never burned anything or anyone else again.

Our children lived with us, and with fifteen in one room, we soon learned that the bathroom was off limits to the children. They may be able to sleep with us and play with us, but they had to go down and use their own buckets for their toilet facilities. Ours toilet would fill up faster than we had water to take care of it.

From as early as I can remember, I wanted to go to Africa and live in an orphanage. Well, I didn't quite make it to Africa, but I made it to the descendants from Africa, and I lived in their orphanage. I also lived every day with the reality of my experiences growing up in Alabama. And now here I was living in a country that was in the middle of a terrible rebellion with people being kidnapped and killed every day. I finally had to face my fears and decide who I was and what I was going to do with my experience.

I prayed daily that I would fall in love with these people and my fear of them would leave forever.

* *

—*Brian*

We were both frustrated because time was passing and nothing really significant was happening, and yet Annie Laurie was still in Haiti. Everyone wanted to be reunited as a family, and we constantly wondered if her absence was really necessary. Friends and family would frequently ask: "Why is Annie Laurie gone for so long? Is it really necessary that she stay in order to bring the children home?" There was even speculation among some members in our church that we had divorced. I should not have allowed this to bother me, but it hurt, nonetheless.

I could not get through to her on our anniversary, which was February 13. All Annie Laurie knew was that I did not call. The previous call was a rough one because it is so hard to communicate things of the heart when you are both hurting and there are thousands of miles between you. So for me, not to call was devastating to her.

On Valentine's Day, I went to pick up some building supplies and stopped in the parking lot in order to call Annie Laurie. Our vehicles were the only places for private phone calls because at home there were so many little ears that were waiting for any news at all about their mommy. As I sat there trying to get through the maze of international dialing and being cut off and dialing again, I saw something that cut me straight to the heart. I could see the mall parking lot across the street. I saw man after man coming out of the mall with their arms filled with Valentine's Day presents and flowers. So, here I am missing Annie Laurie terribly, watching other men, men with normal marriages, going home with presents for their wives and girlfriends. Here I was sitting alone in a cold van trying to reach my wife, knowing all the time that there was a good chance that we would only have more contention. But this call was going to be different. There would be a different spirit; this would be a turning point.

I finally got through, but I really do not remember clearly what happened or what we talked about. I only remember that Annie Laurie explained once again, as she had done so many times before, that she felt so strongly that these little children were ours and that God wanted them to be in our home. I don't know if it was something she said, but I do know that heaven intervened and my heart began to shift. A peaceful feeling began to wash over me, and I was reminded once again of something I had previously learned. We had a mission to gather these children. *We,* not just Annie Laurie; *we* included me.

From that point on, even though I missed Annie Laurie so much, I did not fight her or complain about the hardships. I began to encourage and support her. I soon began to feel like I was a part of a three-way partnership with God. Now, hopefully Annie Laurie would not feel alone in this journey to bring our starving and deprived children home from Haiti.

* *

—*Annie Laurie*

A partnership with God is exactly what we felt we were doing. I knew that Brian was going through some really hard things, and I wanted to be there for him emotionally, but my own struggles were so all encompassing that I was not able to give much. I think he was the same. We both needed the other to help lift our burden. Isn't that what married couples do? We tried, but in the end, it sent us both back to where the true help is anyway; right into God's arms.

It was a time of wonderful reflection on who I really was. I have heard that during times of peace is not when we show God who we really are, but it is in times of travail and trial that our true character comes to the fore. I desperately wanted my true character to be one that God would approve of. But it was so hard to remain faithful.

I honestly don't know how to explain what it was like. I have given descriptions of the waiting and wondering, and the frustration of not having things move forward, but as I read them, they in no way describe what went on inside. Every week we would set a new date for when we would surely be going home, and every week, we would find ourselves still sitting in that room. I had taped up my husband's picture on the wall, and every day I would look at it and weep and plead to go home. We tried positive thinking, we tried making bargains with God, we tried anger and ultimatums, but in the end, we were still always in Haiti in our room full of children with our other children at home who needed a mother. The guilt was huge. Was it fair to sacrifice all those at home for the eight that I was responsible for here in Haiti? Every time I was quiet enough to hear an answer, it was always the same. "I will tell you when it is time to go home. Stay and bring the children home."

I too, had my turning point in Haiti. I would take our children out onto that large balcony every night to sing and pray. I would take turns rock-a-byeing each child while everyone sang together. Then we would pray, and they would go to bed. Well it was around January 29, and we were out on the balcony doing our nightly ritual. Right in the middle, my cell phone started to ring. I answered the phone. I was rocking one of the children on my lap, but I froze with the news.

"Mom, I just need to tell you that Annie Laurie thinks that she is in labor. Mom, I think she is going to have this baby without you here."

Now, to some that may not seem like a big deal, but for me, for someone who had lost the ability to have her own children at such a young age, this was one of my most cherished moments with my daughters and daughters-in-law. I had been at every birth. And this was my firstborn daughter, and she really had hard births and needed me. This was also one of the bargainings I had made with God. *I will stay, but you have to get me home for my granddaughter's birth.* I was obsessed with the need to get home. Well, here was the call, and I was no closer to coming home.

I sat in that chair with those children who knew no English sitting around me and burst into sobs. I could not stop. They had no idea what was going on, but they all put their arms around me and held me as I cried. I think I scared them to death, but they were so soft and sweet. After a few minutes, I calmed down enough to tell Sarah—for she is the one who made the call—to call me back if there was anymore news. I also asked her to have Annie Laurie call me as soon as she could. I told the kids to go to bed, and I then went out to the front of the house and sat on the steps so I could be alone.

Annie Laurie called, and we wept together. I finally hung up and just sat there sobbing out my heart to my God. As I was thus pouring out my heart, I heard a slight sound close to me, and then I felt arms go around me. It was Christ-darling, who was one of the young girls in the orphanage. She was thirteen and taking a big chance being out there with me, as she could have been beaten for going outside after dark. But there she sat with her arm around me, and in her broken English, she asked me what was wrong. I briefly told her that I just wanted to be home with my daughter while her baby was being born, and my heart was very sad because I could not. She hugged me a little tighter and then started to talk.

"I have a family. I had six brothers and sisters, but we had no food, so three of them died. I really loved my mom, but we had no food, so she died too. I went to stay with my aunt, but they had no food and they beat me, so they brought me and my two sisters to the orphanage. We have been here four years waiting to be adopted. Do you think it will be soon?"

Before I could even say anything, she continued. "I know Jesus. I read about him in my Bible. Will you help me to read my Bible someday? Jesus really loves me and takes care of me. I know he will take care of you. You must just believe in Jesus." She got up and walked back into that orphanage where she had been living for four years waiting faithfully for her Jesus to give her a family, and I was left with the opportunity to take a really good look at myself.

Here I was, weeping and feeling so sorry for myself because I had to be in Haiti for a short while. I had a family to miss. I had a daughter that could give birth in a safe place, and my granddaughter would live and have all her needs met. I had a home that was warm with plenty to eat every day. I had children who loved me and a husband who cared for my every need. I had parents who had blessed my life abundantly, and I was crying and feeling sorry for myself! I don't know if anything has ever humbled me more quickly than that thirteen-year-old girl wrapping her arms around me and telling me God loved us. My heart was filled with love and gratitude. The tears that coursed down my cheeks were now tears of gratitude and joy. I was so blessed. I knew my daughter would be well taken care of. I knew my children at home would be well taken care of. But there was only me to take care of these children. God had sent me there on a mission, and I was going to fulfill that mission no matter what the cost. And I did. We all did.

I remember wanting desperately for Brian to understand this. How could I stay there if we were not together in our hearts? The few times we would get on the phone with each other, he was supportive in having me stay there for just a little bit longer. But he was very clear that I would need to come home after that. He didn't really want any more children anyway, and he just kept saying he felt nothing for these children that he had never met. And with every phone call he would let me know that he wasn't doing this again. There were no more children. It was an evidence of the kind of man that he is that he supported me at all when he was struggling so badly.

Our anniversary rolled around, and once again that had been one of our bargain dates. We will stay until...but then we must be home with our children. Well, there I sat on my twenty-sixth anniversary celebrating with our eight children. And my husband did not even call. I cried for hours that night. (You would think that the well of tears would finally dry up, but there always seemed to be more than enough ready and waiting). I was sure he had finally given up and didn't love me any-more. The problem is that I could come up with so many reasons why he wouldn't love me. I had led him down so many strange roads in our life together. I cried myself to sleep.

The next day was Valentine's Day. Would he call today? I waited and waited for his call. Finally, that afternoon, the phone rang. I didn't even dare hope. I answered, and it was Sarah. We chatted for a few minutes, and I hung up and cried some more. A few minutes later, the phone rang again. This time it was Brian. I could hardly contain myself. I was so grateful to just hear his voice. That call was a huge turning point for our mar-riage. It was also a huge turning point for our experience in Haiti. For the first time, Brian became the driving force behind our journey. I knew I could call him and cry on his shoulder when it got hard, instead of always being the one who made everything better. He was the one who, when I called frantic to get on a plane that very minute, would calmly say, "Annie Laurie, has God released you? Has he told you to come home?" I would answer that he hadn't. "Then you stay there, and you be strong. I know you can do this, Annie Laurie, bring our children home!" It was no longer my mission, it was ours.

⸱ ⸱ ⸱ ⸱ ⸱ ⸱ ⸱ ⸱ ⸱ ⸱ ⸱ ⸱ ⸱ ⸱ ⸱ ⸱ ⸱

We had become good friends with Pastor by this time. He was a great man. He had a temper that at first would scare us to death. But we soon learned that his bark was much, much worse than his bite. Anytime anything wouldn't go just right, he would rant and rave, fall to the floor, and shake his fists; he was really quite dramatic. We would just tell him we loved him and talk him through it. He was about my husband's age and a very small man. But his personality made up for his stature. What can I say, he was Haitian. I was learning to truly love the Haitian people. They were next to impossible to work with, but they were wonderful.

It was election time, and the world went crazy. We were in "lock down" at the orphanage, so no one was allowed in or out for over a week. We could see the rioting from our window. We heard gunshots every night. There was very little water and very little food. We began to ration the supplies in the orphanage, as we had no idea how long it would be before things would be safe again. Pastor was not able to get up to the orphanage, and all work on adoptions ceased for several weeks. We waited, hoping that things would change. It was at this point that my husband came through with flying colors. Everyone just kept saying, "What are you doing? Your wife is in danger. Why are you letting her stay?" He simply answered. "I am not letting her stay; I am asking her to stay!" This was a hard fought place for him. But we both knew it was right.

After several scary weeks, things began to settle down, or so we thought. One night we were sleeping when we were awakened by some loud chanting and drumming from outside. We looked out but could not really see anything in the dark. We would get glimpses of what looked like people in long, white robes. We heard gunshots and the wild chanting and drumming went on and on. They carried candles to light their way. We could tell that they were going up and down the streets that were up the mountainside from us. The noise was getting closer and closer, and we could tell that others were joining the group. They finally got to our road, and we watched as they walked in front of our orphanage. There were about a hundred people— some in long white robes, others in street dress.

They had musical instruments that we did not recognize and were singing, chanting, and shooting off guns. We watched from the safety of our room, wondering what was happening. This was truly a time when we were terrified. We were two white ladies in a land that had no love for Americans. We were some of the only white people in Haiti, and in that crazy world of fear, we wondered if they were coming after us. I was almost overwhelmed as they passed our home, and the relief set in.

We were safe! We found out the next morning that instead of a scary thing, they were actually celebrating. The president had been allowed to take office, and the rioting was at an end. Almost, anyway!

That next day, Pastor came up the mountain to the orphanage, picked us up, and took us down to the government offices again. Downtown Port au Prince is like nothing you have ever seen. Total filth and chaos! No traffic laws, no pedestrian laws, people absolutely everywhere and no one following any kind of organized pattern at all. You just go where you need to go and hope you are still alive when you get there. As we went downtown that particular day, we turned up a street, and all of a sudden our car was surrounded by hundreds of people of all ages. They were carrying signs, singing, chanting, and yelling. Pastor very quickly told us to sit back, smile big, and not to say a word. Not that we would have anyway. He started to smile and laugh and hoorah with them, and they slowly let us through. He told us later that it didn't matter whether we believed in what they were doing or not, the only way we got out of there alive was by acting like we were on their side.

It was shortly after this time that I started getting sick again. I have struggled with health most of my life. I was so grateful when our family started on Reliv. But I had not planned on spending half a year in Haiti. I had planned on two weeks. I was already rationing my supply, and I was taking minuscule portions so I would at least have a little bit every day. It was not enough. I had suffered with a heart condition for sometime before starting this product, but had been symptom free for over a year. I now started having problems again with my heart. I also came down with all the same symptoms that I had when we first arrived in Haiti. Could it be possible? Could I really have typhus again? Wasn't it enough that I was in Haiti? Did I have to be sick too?

I lay on my bed day after day in agony. The children would sit around and watch me until I thought I would go crazy. Everyone would be asleep at night, and I would be in so much pain. It was at this point that the heart condition came back, and I started having pains associated with that condition. I would lay there scared to death that I was never going to see my family again. There was nothing we could do. They wanted to take me to the hospital, but I would not go. If I was going to die, I would rather die in an orphanage than in a Haitian hospital.

I was just starting to feel a little better, and I mean a little, when because of my weakened state, I also contracted hepatitis A. I turned completely yellow. My eyes were absolutely terrifying. Could it get any worse? Never ask that question because it is as if someone out there just has to make a point that it can always get worse. On top of typhus, heart problems every night, and hepatitis A, I now got a skin rash that covered my body and never stopped itching. I would scratch myself until my sheets and pajamas were spotted everywhere with blood, but I couldn't stop scratching. I was so sick I could hardly move, and yet I could not hold still or I would go insane. My body was covered with thousands of scabs and the itching continued.

This was one of the lowest times in Haiti. I just kept wondering where God was. I would lie in that bed day after day in the heat, with ants crawling on my ravaged body, and would not even have the strength to weep. Tears would just continually trickle down my face and puddle in my ears and on my pillow, for I was too weak to wipe them. I would slowly roll over and put my face against the cool wall trying to find some relief from the heat and the pain. There I would lie for hours with the mold and peeling paint of that wall against my face but not caring. I would pray and plead hour after hour that I would either die or be delivered. I would rock my body hour after hour trying to do something to get away from how I felt, but nothing stopped the pain except one thing.

We had one CD with us, and there was a song on that CD that made me think of home. I played it over and over as my face was to that wall and wept out my anguish of soul at being so far away from those that I loved. I ate nothing for days and had the whole orphanage scared to death that the white lady would die. The older girls would come and sit on the edge of the bed and read scriptures to me or sing to me. Sometimes they would get rambunctious and play and wrestle and roll over the top of me. I let them, for I knew they were finding a place of peace in my little corner of the room where they felt loved and cared for.

Sarah finally heard how sick I was and decided that it didn't matter what it would cost to send it, I was getting back on Reliv. So she special delivered a huge package. It cost almost five hundred dollars to get that package to me. But as she so lovingly said, it was cheaper than paying for me to be sent home in a casket. I started feeding my body with nutrition, and I started to receive strength. Within two days I could walk around, and by the end of a week, I was almost my normal color. The scabs were healing all over my body. I felt like I had literally come back from the dead.

It was also about this time that the persecution started. In our experience, Haitian adoptions are different than other international adoptions in several ways. One of those ways is the time element. It can take up to three years for each adoption to be completed. Compare this with six to eight months for Vietnam. So once families found out who their child was going to be, they would come to Haiti and start visiting them at the orphanage periodically. Mothers and sometimes fathers would come over and stay for a few days and bring all kinds of gifts and really just spoil their child for a little bit. This was a sweet thing, but I was there to see what affect this had on the children in the orphanage.

It became one of their power plays between the children and even the nannies. It became a status symbol of who got the biggest and the best. I didn't see it necessarily creating bonds of love, just bonds of things. These children didn't know how to love and give their hearts to someone. That was too scary for them. So as the moms would come, the relationships were built around who got the most stuff. As long as gifts were coming, then everything was okay. You had status; you had your moment at the top of the pile. It was one of the reasons why there were problems with our children. They had the status of living upstairs, but their other expectation was to be given a constant stream of gifts. When that didn't happen, they were ridiculed by the other children and the other adoptive parents even used it as a source of measuring our love for our children.

We had become friends, or so we thought, with several of these parents. It was fun to have some other English speaking people in the house. Their process of adoption was as slow as ours, but they just went home to wait in between visits. They hadn't experienced losing their children at the other orphanage, and some of them started questioning why we would stay. I really don't know what they were thinking and why they even cared, but several were upset that we were staying. They felt it was wrong of us to be there, away from our families at home. They started some rumors about us that had absolutely no foundation to them. They sent them out on e-mail to all the adopting parents when they got home. I could never understand this, as really it was none of their business how we went about adopting our children. But once rumors start, there is no stopping what things are said. They started accusing us of taking the children up in our room and beating them. They accused us of doing ritualistic acts. This blew my mind, for here we lived in the voodoo capital of the world, and we were the ones accused of ritualistic behavior. My friend had made the mistake of buying a beautiful wooden statue. To us it was just a beautiful remembrance of Haiti. We had no idea that those statues were used in their voodoo worshiping. So obviously now we were worshiping statues in our room. Unfortunately we did not find this out soon enough, but as soon as we did, the statue went in the garbage. We did sing, and we did have a family prayer every night, but that was it.

Anyway, it started going around the orphanage and through the e-mail that we were unfit to parent. This was even harder to bear because we were already sacrificing everything we had to give, in behalf of these children, time, family, money, personal space, etc., and all that these parents could see was some woman's jealous lies.

We loved Pastor, and he believed in us no matter what anybody would say. He was constantly coming to us and saying, "I don't believe it but I must ask you ..." Then he would ask us the latest ridiculous thing that was said, and we would deny it. Haitian's lives are based on fear and superstition. So, when you start a rumor in Haiti, it is like starting a raging flood that just picks up force as it goes down the mountainside. Pastor's wife was very much involved in cult activities, and she started to make life miserable for us also. One day she would be very loving, and the next she would have exorcists outside our window at night singing the evil away. There were many times that she would get the whole orphanage up at four in the morning and have them stand and sing and pray for hours. We did not understand at the time, but they were trying to get rid of us and the spirit that we brought with us. I understand now, for evil does not like light and will do everything in its power to get rid of it.

We did have a few of the people we worked with there who really loved and honored us for who we were and for what we were doing. We would question them about what was going on and why there was this animosity toward us every time we turned around. They shed some light on the situation for us. They told us that when we were in the orphanage, there was a totally different feeling; that when we left for the day or a few hours, it was like the light left with us. They said that many had commented on the feeling that was with us, and they liked it, but over time it became scary because they did not understand it, and in Haiti if you don't understand something, then you fear it. Haiti is different than any place I have ever been. It is a country steeped in fear and the worship of evil.

Our children were told that if they came home with us that we would cut them up into pieces and eat them.

There were too many rumors. Pastor would come in and tell us how much he loved us and that we were by far his favorite parents. He said he could see firsthand the love we shared with our children. In fact, he said he had never seen mothers love children like we did, but he was too afraid of the people and what they would do to him if he let us adopt our children. My friend went into almost a comatose state with all the stress that we had had there in Haiti. She lay on her bed hardly speaking for three days. She hardly ever stopped crying, and this time it was her face that was to the wall. I think her will to fight just went out of her.

We stayed another week or so. They hadn't actually stopped the adoption process of our children, so we had hope that they would change their mind. We had now been in Haiti for over three months. Every week we thought, *This will be our last week here.* Every week we faced the disappointment of not going home. Every minute of the day was a challenge to stay happy and positive, to face the persecution and opposition with a strong heart and with our faith in place. It took every ounce of our strength. It was a time of stretching until we thought that we would break, and yet God just kept stepping in and carrying us.

It was now the first of April, and one night as I lay in bed, an impression came to my mind. I pushed it away, but it came again. I was hardly able to sleep that night because I was doing battle with the impression that just kept coming. That next morning, I couldn't wait to tell my friend. I just wanted to do my part and say it, and then everybody could say how dumb it was, and I would be off the hook.

I told her what I was thinking, and she looked at me for a minute and then said, "What do you think the men will say?" I knew what they would say: Absolutely not! What I was proposing was simply not feasible. We had no money, and the men would not be able to get off work anyway. But it was sure worth a try.

I called my husband first.

"Sweetheart, how would you like to spend a few days with me?" What could he say to that? He couldn't possibly say no. "How are we going to do that?" was the response. "Well..." I thought that I better say it fast, or I would lose my courage. "We could meet you in Disney World for a week and then we could come back and finish the process...?" My parents had given us both a year's pass to the Disney theme parks several months earlier before all of the additional expenses began to pile up, and the flights were fairly inexpensive at the time; it was a perfect plan.

Silence. He was learning. He didn't just say no, and would you believe it, by the end of the call, he said he would see if he could get the time off and that if my friend's husband agreed to go, he would do it. We were ecstatic. We were dancing around the room, hugging each other. Now we only had her husband to talk to, and he would be easy.

We used to make our calls in the bathroom, as that was the only private place we had. Later that day, my friend came out of the bathroom with tears in her eyes.

"He said no, he does not think it is practical."

What? How could he say no? We were desperate. *How could he say no?*

I got on my knees that night and promised that if we could have this help that we so desperately needed, I would come back and not leave until every child of ours was adopted.

The next morning, her husband called. This time, when she came out of the bathroom, her face glowed. "He said, let's go!" We danced again. We were leaving Haiti. Even if just for a short time, we were leaving. And who knows, maybe the children would be ready to come home by the time we got back.

We bought tickets that day and were on the airplane the next day. The feeling that came over us when we arrived in

America was indescribable. We wanted to kiss the ground, kiss the attendant; we would have even kissed Mickey Mouse himself, if he had been there.

Our husbands had not been able to put things together quite as quickly, but that was okay. I had called Sarah and asked her to come for the first week before the men got there. She had done so much. There is no way ever, if I spend the rest of my life trying, I can ever show enough gratitude for all she has done in our adoption journeys. She took over the school, our children, and my friend's children while we were gone. She kept me going with countless calls of support, called the children together to offer countless prayers in our behalf, sent paperwork as requested, paid for countless things that I don't even know about, and never once complained. She deserved a break. It was so good to see her.

She had never been in Disney World before, and we raced from one place to the next trying to show her all of it. We had a great time.

Brian came a week later, and we took Sarah to the airport, and then our honeymoon to end all honeymoons started. We had the most glorious time imaginable. The sweetness of that time was worth all the sacrifice until it came time to leave again. How could I possibly leave him? How could I go back into a place of darkness when I had experienced this kind of light? How could I go back to that orphanage where no one wanted me? Even the children had been so turned against us that they would hardly have anything to do with me. How could I leave my husband and go back. When I left before Christmas, I didn't realize what I was going to. Now I did! I just couldn't do it! I couldn't! But…

They were our children. I had promised God I would go back and stay until they were all adopted. I could not go back on that promise.

Brian was leaving the day before I was. I took him to the airport and drove away weeping. I could hardly see the road.

Fifteen minutes later, the phone rang. "Annie Laurie, are you there? I just got bumped. The flight was too full. I am not leaving until tomorrow. Would you like to spend another day together?"

Talk about tender mercies and miracles! Never was a tender mercy more needed. I couldn't believe that God had worked this kind of miracle for us. I broke all speed limits and rushed back to savor another miraculous twenty-four hours with the man I loved.

This time when I dropped him off at the airport, we couldn't even shed tears as we were so grateful for a loving Father in heaven and for his miracle that we just glowed instead. We would see each other soon. I was going to keep my promise to God since he had kept his to me.

My friend had decided that she just could not go back to Haiti and had gone home with her husband. I was going back by myself. I thought for sure I would be home in no more than three weeks.

back in haiti

—Annie Laurie

I walked back into that orphanage with a heart that felt like iron. No children came to hug me except my two grandsons, David and Daniel. It's interesting that through all of the persecution, those two boys stayed constant. They never once turned their back on me. They have such a special place in my heart. Anson, who was my son, didn't have a clue what was going on, he just loved being up in my room. But the girls had been told so many horror stories and even threatened with horrible consequences if they showed they liked me. They simply had no idea how to respond toward me.

I walked up those stairs and into my room. They had given me one of the smaller rooms as I was by myself and no longer allowed to have my children sleep with me. I walked into my room and closed my door, unable to face anyone. How could I stay there another day with the tangible feeling of animosity that was there? Why was I staying? That was a question I heard over and over from everyone that I talked to. My answer was always the same; it was what God had asked me to do. Later I found out that if I had not stayed, we would have lost every child. They would have been given to someone else. I just had to stay.

From that day on I was fed one meal a day. When I had been there before, they had fed us three meals a day. But with the feeling the way it was, I did not want any more from them than I had to. There were some of the nannies that were wonderful to me. They made sure that I had the noon meal with the children. One day a week it was spaghetti noodles with a wonderful fish sauce. The rest of the time it was rice with beans. I actually really like the food. I usually ate about a fourth of my food and then saved the rest to feed the children that night. I would line up all eight of our children and spoon the food into their mouths. I did this for several reasons. First, I wanted them to know that the food came from me. It would teach them very quickly that they could look to me for their needs to be met. It also made sure that everyone received equal portions.

But the best part was that it gave me a time to play with them and yet teach them obedience. I was always looking for ways to teach them to be obedient. They had to stand just so, they couldn't push or shove, and girls had to go first. If they weren't obedient, they missed their turn. And if they were real disobedient, they got sent back downstairs and lost the privilege to be in my room. At first, some of the children used this as a way to show they had the most power. In an orphanage, it is all about who has the most power. I had to show them, without being mean, that I was the one with the power. They soon learned that they would rather bend to my will than miss out on whatever happened in the room. During the day, the boys and I would wrestle and play card games. The girls loved to color and be tickled. Slowly I earned their trust and love again.

I set boundaries of when I was available and not available. I felt this was important, as they would have to go home to real life, and a mom is not always at a child's beck and call, especially as a playmate. Sometimes I would let them sit and do things quietly in my room while I was busy doing my own thing, and other times they were sent out to play. In the mornings they were not allowed in my room until I had finished my scripture study and prayers. It seemed that the more structured it became, the more they were able to give their hearts to me. But interestingly enough, this was the very thing that got me into trouble once again.

A mother and daughter came to stay at the orphanage for about two weeks. They were not adopting, they just wanted to serve a mini mission. They were Christian like me, but of a different faith. I have no idea what faith they were, as that really does not matter to me. We all worship the same God, and he loves us all. One of the things our country fought for so long ago was the right to worship according to our own conscience. I am grateful for that principle. But I guess these two did not feel that way. They hated me from the start and let me know it. If I would walk into a room, they would leave. They continually brought my children up to their room and gave them gifts and told them they were so sorry that the mean lady was adopting them. They would come and tell me that my children looked so sad and it must be my fault.

One day it had become so bad that I finally got the courage to confront them and asked them why they were so angry at me. This Christian woman looked in my eyes and, with her finger shaking in my face, told me I was from the devil. She said that my children hated me and she would rather see them die than be adopted by me. She told me I had no right to raise these children. I was not qualified to be a mother.

I have to stop here and say something in my defense. I have met people all over the world and told them our story. The response that I always get is tears and a thank you for caring and a hug, as they say what special people we must be to do this great thing. Now, I do not say that because we are anything special at all. We are just doing what we felt impressed to do. But I am saying it because every time I turned around in Haiti, someone who professed to be Christian was slandering our name or telling me I was evil. They just kept telling me that I was not qualified to be a mother either because I was not at home taking care of my children there or because I did not have these children in with me twenty-four hours a day or because I had them in too much. It didn't matter which, as long as they could find something wrong with what I was doing.

They finally left, but not until they had spread their opinions to the next group of mothers who were there. During those eight weeks, I hardly dared to come out of my room. It became my prison, my sanctuary. By the end, everyone but Pastor, the only one in Haiti that really knew me, had turned against me. He stayed perfectly true. I will be forever grateful for his loyalty. He has since been in my home, and we loved having him there.

It got so bad during this time that Pastor's wife would continually ask voodoo priestesses to stand by my door or under my window at night and chant the evil away. She brought the children into her room and told them over and over that if they went with me I would murder them. It was crazy, and I battled it the only way I knew how. I loved these people as much as I could love them. I prayed for them and stayed away from them.

I could not wait to bring my children home. I tried to make the time in my room happy and light so they would feel the difference. Near the end, they loved being with me, even though they too were persecuted for being with the "devil lady".

I have to share one of my most horrific experiences while

in that room. One entire wall was lined with built-in six-foot-high cupboards. Some of those cupboards had not been opened for months. This is where I had to put my things. When I first opened them, I saw several huge, and I mean huge, roaches race out of sight. That was it. I about fainted and then dropped to my knees. I told God there was no way that I could stay in this room with roaches. But no matter how I prayed, there was no other alternative. I put my things in that cupboard and prayed that somehow the roaches would find another home. It wasn't to be!

At night, as soon as I would blow out the candle, they would come skittering out and circle the room. These roaches were at least two and sometimes three inches long. I could see them in the moonlight. I would quickly light another candle in order to scare them back into the cupboard. Sometimes I would try to chase them and kill them, but they were always too fast for me. I could hardly sleep because every time my eyelids would close I would see them coming after me. I would jerk awake and start my vigil all over again.

After being there a few weeks, something changed. It must have been flying roach season. There were no windows to speak of and certainly no screens. So whatever was outside could come inside. So now on top of having roaches coming out of my closets, they started flying in through my windows. I think they must have sensed me cowering in my bed, for they would fly at me and dive bomb me. I remember one particular night. It was two in the morning, and several of these huge flying roaches had come into my room. I was running around my room dodging the dive bombing and crying so hard I could hardly see. I finally lost it and called Sarah at home. I couldn't get a hold of Brian. She happened to be with my daughter, Annie Laurie, that night. I woke them up, and as they answered the phone, all they heard was screaming and frantic crying. I knew they could do nothing, but I could not face one more second by myself without going crazy.

When they could finally understand what I was babbling about, they went and got Brian, and they all said a prayer that the roaches would leave me alone and that I would be able to sleep. It may seem to some to be a silly thing to pray about. But for me, I could not have stayed one more day if it had continued. Once again, I know the prayer of the faithful reaches God's ears, for that was the last crazy night. Oh, they were still there, but it was as if we became friends. Every night I asked them to just stay in their beds and I would stay in mine. I was finally able to sleep, and there were no more attacks or dive bombings. Prayer works.

That room became a little bit of heaven in the midst of the storm raging outside. I felt God's loving arms wrap continually around me to give me comfort. I felt the warmth of the Holy Spirit speak peace to a mind that was tormented with loneliness. I believe that the very jaws of hell were opened wide to make me turn away from my mission, but I would not be turned. Why? Because God knew I had made a promise and so did my family at home. I was not going to let either one of them down. My children were praying for me every day. They had sacrificed so much in order to have these brothers and sisters come home. How could I let them down? I couldn't.

How could I let my little Joshua down? He was only four, but he got up one morning and did not come to the table when he was called to breakfast. When asked why, he simply said, "If I fast and pray today, God will help Mommy bring the children home quicker." Much was learned in this refining journey, by all of us; lessons that I would not give up for anything. We went to hell and back, literally, and came out victorious with God's help.

. . . .

—*Brian*

Sometime in early spring, Annie Laurie informed me that we needed more money to pay additional adoption costs. We found more money in a home equity loan. That money was such a blessing, and at the time, we thought that was all we would have to spend, but that was not to be. A few weeks later, Annie Laurie let me know, with a lump in her throat, that we needed another $30,000. What a blow! How would I do that? Where would that money come from? To make matters worse, a few days later I discovered that we had an internal leak in our already very tight financial resources.

One of our daughters had been making overseas telephone calls without telling me. She had no idea that these calls had totaled to almost $7,000. When I got the phone bill, I was devastated. I wanted to quit. I just could not take one more set back, not one more problem.

I talked with my father-in-law and asked him for help. I told him that I could not pay him back. He covered more than half of the phone bill without even a hint of irritation or recrimination. Annie Laurie's parents were like angels out of the blue.

The $30,000 problem was still waiting for me after that smaller challenge had been resolved. I was beside myself and once again went to the place in my heart that I was so used to going. I just wanted to quit. I complained to God, cried a little, and figured that nothing could be done except to pack up and go home, figuratively speaking. I thought that maybe this part of the gathering journey just was not meant to be. It would have been so easy to walk away from the whole mess in Haiti, bring my wife home, and begin to rebuild our financial lives.

The answer to my dilemma was not an answer that I wanted, but it was nonetheless direction from heaven. Sometimes the sources of inspiration come from the most unexpected places.

In pondering our situation and our need, my mind went wandering on what seemed to be a mental vacation. You know, when you sometimes have thoughts so random they seem to have no connection to the problem at hand. I remembered a story about a prizefighter, James J. Braddock, and his wife who lived during the Great Depression. This strong couple had done everything they could possibly do to support their family of three children. They were out of money and food, but most importantly, money to pay their heating bill. Their heat was turned off, and the children had to be parceled out to relatives. As a last resort, this good man, had to request public assistance and beg for money from his previous associates in the boxing world. This must have been devastatingly humiliating for him. He and his wife had always stood on their own two feet and made it on their own. To ask for a handout was probably the most difficult thing he ever had to do, other than have his children taken elsewhere for warmth, food, and milk.

As I thought about this, I realized that this good man was fighting for his children and would do anything, within the bounds of integrity, for his children. This was a real fight. It was not for a purse or a title; it was for the lives and survival of his family.

I began to realize that it was my responsibility to fight for these children. After all, wasn't Annie Laurie fighting for them by staying in the orphanage, giving them hope by her mere presence? She was fighting by staying there, experiencing privation, hepatitis, food poisoning, typhus, no running water, and scant food. If she would have come home, the whole process would have come to a screeching halt and the children would still be there. Two of the children would be dead today if it wasn't for the courageous battle fought by my wife.

So now it was time for me to step into the ring. I wrote a letter to many people, explaining the situation, and then asked for donations. I not only asked; I begged, for the children's sake. Whatever feelings of egotistical pride I had before vanished with this letter. I made phone calls and wrote e-mails begging for money in order to continue the gathering journey for the children.

There were many people that showed interest and a genuine concern for the situation. There were people who had access to large sums of money; in fact, some of these good people could have donated the entire sum without even knowing it was gone from their checking accounts. However, for some reason, no one responded; except for some very close friends who donated $500. There was also the great generosity of two other men. These men would want their names left anonymous, but I must share that they donated $15,000 in cash. I don't know if they truly understand the miracle they made possible by this timely gift. The money was just enough to continue with the process and provided more time for us to figure out how to come up with the large amount of money that would still be required.

* *

—Annie Laurie

Things were getting increasingly worse at the orphanage. We were getting closer to the end of the adoption process, but we still could not get the last steps accomplished. I had wanted so badly to be home for Mother's Day, but there I sat in my little room by myself. I couldn't even face the children that day, so I just laid on my bed most of the day. My birthday was the next week, and I wanted to be home for that, too. Still nothing had happened.

In Haiti most of the children were not really orphans. Their parents put their children in the orphanage because they would otherwise die. You had to have their relinquishment when they were put into the orphanage, and then they had to go before the consulate after they were adopted and get their permission.

This is the point we were at by Mother's Day. They were all adopted, and we just had to go before the Haitian consulate with each child's parents and get their final yes. Never had parents said no at this point. I was good friends with all the parents. We had all visited many times, as they have "parent visiting day" every first Sunday of the month. I was so excited because we had finally made it, and we were just days away from going home. I did not realize at the time that someone had talked to some of the parents and threatened them if they said yes. I brought each parent to the consulate to make a statement that they were in favor of this adoption.

Laura's mom went through the door, and I stayed outside waiting. She came back smiling. All was well. Anson and Kaneasha's parents went through the door and came back a few minutes later and all was well. The mother of my three grandchildren went through the door, and she too came back smiling. Bethany's mother was nowhere to be found, but it was her grandpa that had put her in the orphanage and had custody over her. So he came and went through the door. I waited outside, and when he came back through the door, he was not smiling. The lady in charge came with him and said that his connection was not good enough. They would have to find the mom and have her come in. What? How do we find a crack addict who has been living on the streets for five years? Just put it in God's hands. That is all you can do. Right?

Okay, it was our little baby's turn. Our little Jislene. She was the little one that had been left in a corner to die; the one that would be crippled all the rest of her life. I had given her just a tiny bit of my Reliv every day, and now she ran, laughed, talked, and was the joy of the orphanage. They all called her the miracle baby. I loved her so much, and she loved me. Her dad walked through those doors, and I was excited. We would figure out Bethany's mother later, but all the rest would be finished and ready to go to the American consulate as soon as he came back through that door.

The door opened and once again the lady in charge was standing there with Jislene's father. "He said no, he does not want you to take her to America. I'm sorry." I stood there with my mouth hanging open. After all I had been through the answer was *no?* How could this be happening? No one said no at this point. Would this nightmare never end?

I left that place as fast as I could. The rest of the parents had left, but we had to take the children all back with us to the orphanage. We also had to take the father of Jislene back to the orphanage. When we got there, I took Jislene in my arms and I held her close and wept. I then carried her to the father and put her in his arms. I told him that if he would not let me take her to America, then he had to take her home and watch her starve. In Haiti, I was now legally her mother. I just could not get her out of Haiti without a passport, and I could not get a passport without his permission. He held his little girl as she screamed and reached for me. It was one of those gut-wrenching moments when all I could do was turn around and walk away. I could hear her screaming for me all the way to my room. I just sat on my bed and wondered why. Why? Why had God brought me all this way to lose her in the end?

We talked many times to the father, and each time he said that he wanted his daughter to go with me to America. He just wanted to still be her dad. Three times he said he would say yes at the consulate, and we took him back. Each time in the end, he would say no.

It was after one of these trips to the consulate that I came home and finally completely folded. I called home sobbing out loud. I could not do this another day by myself. I was either coming home or something had to change. My sweet husband, who was so worried about money, was on a plane the next day to join the battle in Haiti.

· · · · · · · · · · · · · · · · · · ·

—*Brian*

I was about to travel to Haiti. After five months I would have the opportunity to share with Annie Laurie what she had endured. The moment the airplane doors opened, I could feel something; I don't quite know what to call it, but it was unlike anything I'd felt while traveling in any other country. It may have been a feeling caused by the extreme and crushing poverty.

I quickly shrugged off this oppressive feeling as the realization began to flood in that I would be holding Annie Laurie very soon. As I pictured our first embrace, her touch became so real, but just then the reality of this trip's purpose began to wash away my romantic fantasies. I was about to meet five little human beings that were soon to become my children. Would I be able to measure up as their father? Could I love them with the same intensity that I love my other children?

I needed yet another miracle of the heart, and I needed it fast.

After several hours waiting at the airport, using the term *airport* very loosely, Annie Laurie arrived. She looked and smelled and felt so good. I had missed her terribly. After a thirty-minute drive, we pulled up to a large, solid iron gate. The driver honked and the gate rolled back. We entered a courtyard filled with children, nannies, and a huge golden retriever.

As the car rolled to a stop, we became surrounded by curious and suspicious children. We got out, and Annie Laurie smiled at me, hugged me, and pointed to a very small girl while she exclaimed, "Brian, I want you to meet your daughter." I looked down and beheld a very skinny and tiny girl. This was our little Kaneasha. She was then, and is now, so beautiful. She stood staring at the ground, not daring to look up at me or even smile. I picked her up and held her high above my head. I simply said, "Sweetheart, I'm your daddy." I lowered her just enough to hold her next to me, and while looking at her face, I saw it for the first time—a shy little smile. This was my daughter.

I was next introduced to a tall, slender, almond-eyed, beautiful girl. She gave me a perfunctory hug, but when she smiled, *wow*, life just seemed better. Her name is Laura.

The next little soul was a very reclusive, almost non-responsive girl standing in the shadows of the car port, about ten feet from me. As I approached her, she did not recoil or back up. She simply stood there motionless, almost lifeless. Maybe a better description would be spirit-less. There was no smile, no spark, only necessary movements like shifting her weight and a quick glance. Sometimes she would not even brush the flies off her face. It became very obvious that something was definitely wrong. Annie Laurie leaned over to me and whispered, "I'll talk to you later about Bethany".

I had noticed a group of young boys playing their version of soccer with a small rock when the car first pulled into the orphanage courtyard. Annie Laurie called out, "Anson, please come here." A small but athletic ten-year-old came and stood very close to Annie Laurie, eyeing me carefully. She simply said to me, "Brian, this is Anson." I knew that he asked for an American name, so we had chosen the name of an American pioneer from the 1800s. Anson Call was the name of one of our ancestors, and this little boy received this special family name, and he was thrilled. I hugged him very briefly, for that is all he would allow, and then he returned to his rock soccer game. I also met our new grandchildren and was excited to get to know them as well.

After some brief introductions to some of the nannies and others, Annie Laurie led me to her room. As I looked around at the empty and aging rooms, I realized this is where my wife had suffered so many physical and emotional pains. This upper floor of the orphanage was also the place where she had suffered emotionally and spiritually, due to the prejudice and religious intolerance of so many.

These children were strangers to me, and I was a stranger to them. I had no emotional or inspired feelings toward these very needy children. So what do you do when your heart is not in the right place for the tasks given by heaven? I have only two answers: I began to pray as if everything depended upon God, because really it does. Then I go to work.

I threw myself into the process. I began to play with the children. I attempted to communicate with them. I laughed with them, teased, and tickled them. I showed them my lame magic tricks, played soccer, cars on the floor, and fed them. I knew Annie Laurie had gotten hepatitis from one of the children, so I was kind of scared to touch them. That lasted about three seconds, because the mission at hand would not allow fear; it only had room for love.

I wanted the children to understand that I was a safe man, one that was gentle and would not hurt them or take advantage of them. For me, little Bethany was hard to love because there was little or no response. I continued to build bridges to these little children's hearts under Annie Laurie's experienced tutelage. I only had about seven days with the children and Annie Laurie. After several days of continuing this work of love, I still had no feelings toward little Bethany other than pity and compassion, and she needed so much more than this. This little girl had been damaged by the ravages of pre-natal crack-cocaine and malnutrition. I also had a feeling that she was not treated well by the other children and the nannies in the orphanage. Bethany also had autistic characteristics, which had made her situation much more difficult. How would this little one fit into our family? Did she even have a promising future? She acted as if she wanted to be invisible or not even exist.

How could I ever do more than just have compassion for this frail little soul? I began to pray more and more about Bethany. I found myself wondering if the adoption was right, or more correctly, was I right for Bethany? Raising her and helping her to heal was going to take an immense amount of love because of the constant emotional investment involved. I was feeling pretty desperate because I just kept drawing emotional blanks about this needy little girl. I began to pray with more fervor and energy. I could not have stopped praying even if I wanted to; the prayers just flowed out of me by themselves. I was pleading, not so much for a change of heart but a multiplying of love in my heart.

As I was kneeling and praying, during one of the rare moments of privacy, my mind began to wander. At first I tried to bring my thoughts back in line with the task at hand, but my thoughts refused to stay focused on Bethany, or so I thought. In my mind's eye I saw a mental video. I saw a young couple embracing; perhaps they were dancing very slowly in a close embrace. The young woman seemed to be in her mid-twenties and her back was toward me. She wore a white wedding dress, and the young man was clothed in a fitted dark suit. He was a strong and handsome young man, with beautiful dark skin and clear eyes. He was looking at the young woman in his arms with such adoration. Then, all of a sudden, the young woman turned her head and looked straight at me. Her smile was so beautiful and full. Her white, straight teeth gleamed. With tear-filled eyes, she mouthed the words, "Thank you, Daddy." This scene struck me with such force, straight to my heart, that it pierced through all of my concerns, fears, and feelings of inadequacies. The young woman was a mature and grown up Bethany. When that realization became clear, I knew it was unmistakably this little girl as she would look as a young woman. It was without doubt our Bethany.

Ever since that experience, I have known that no matter what the path of gathering Bethany would require, we had to do everything possible to travel it. Her life is still very challenging. The probability of this little girl ever marrying still seems unlikely. But hope is what we are banking on when it comes to Bethany's future. Hope may be the force that will continue to bring about the miracles that Bethany will certainly have to hang on to. Her full name is Bethany Hope. How appropriate for this precious little soul who has come so far.

* * * * * * * * * * * * * * * * * * * *

—*Annie Laurie*

It was time for Brian to go home. We had worked all week to finalize the adoption proceedings. He had promised himself that he would not go home without me. But at the end of the week there were still a few things to do. Brian had talked to Jislene's daddy and once again he had said yes he would like her to go home with us. We had taken him in again to the Haitian consulate. Once again the lady in charge came through the door and told us that he had said no. I was undone. What in the world was going on? Why was he doing this? I just could not understand the Haitian mind. Jislene had come back to me when he had last agreed to go ahead with the adoption, but I made him take her again after this. Each time this tore me apart. I had hoped that Brian would have made a difference but …

It was now time for Brian to go home, and as I said, not everything was done. He would not leave me there alone after seeing and feeling the conditions there at the orphanage. So, my good Sarah dropped everything and got on a plane and came to Haiti. It was a strange moment in time, for as I dropped Brian off at the airport, Sarah arrived. All three of us were at the same airport at the same time, but in different places. There is nothing like family on this earth, other than our walk with God.

I had been dropped off at the airport by Pastor and left to wait for Sarah to come. I had to wait for several hours, as it takes forever to go through customs. In the meantime, Pastor had called and said that he could not get back to pick me up and could I find my own way home? In all the time I had been in Haiti, in all the different and crazy experiences that I had gone through, I had never been left on my own to go anywhere. We had even had one of the president's assistant's come and escort us to a meeting with a high government official. But I had never been on my own. I went over to where the taxi drivers were and tried to explain where I needed to go. He asked for an outrageous price because, of course, I was a foreigner. I didn't have it. I finally got him to take all the money that I had, which was half of what he asked for. So when Sarah finally came out, we both got in his car. Just before he pulled out, another very large man got in the front of the car also. He seemed to be a friend of the cab driver.

All of a sudden, I realized that I was in a car with two men whom I did not know or trust. There was not a thing I could do if they decided to harm us, kidnap us, or whatever. I started praying and told Sarah to do the same. They could also drop us off anywhere they wanted because I had no idea how to get to where we lived. Yes, I had been all over Port au Prince in the back of Pastor's car, which, by the way, was just like an Indiana Jones vehicle, except I don't think even he would have allowed all of the roaches in his car that were in Pastor's car. There were hundreds of them, and they would fall on us when we went over bumps or turned corners, and that is all you did on Haiti roads was go over bumps and turn sharp corners.

Anyway, there we were at the mercy of these two men, and I was scared. No, I was terrified! All of a sudden the big man turned around and said they wanted to be paid the larger amount of money that they had at first asked for. I didn't know what to do. I had no more money. Not even back in my room. I just kept praying and very calmly and strongly told him that we had a deal and he would not have honor if he changed that deal. I was shaking, but I know God gave my voice a power and confidence that I did not have. He scowled at me but didn't say any more until we finally pulled up in front of that lovely iron gate of the orphanage. As soon as we got out of the car, he began to yell at us. He threw Sarah's luggage on the ground and continued to yell at us that we owed them more money. I was frantically knocking at the gate, hoping someone would come to let us in, while at the same time trying to look stern and immovable. The gate finally opened, we waved, said thank you, and disappeared. I could hardly stand as relief swept over me. We were still alive and safe.

It was wonderful having Sarah there with me. I loved watching her reunion with her children. They were so excited. Her dad had told her that no matter what, she was not to leave until I came home. I have to admit I was grateful to hear it.

Those last two weeks were busy as we worked on the last few things necessary to get these children home. Everything was finally falling into place. We had even found little Bethany's mother. We took her into the consulate, excited to have the process complete. We waited anxiously for Bethany's mother to walk back through that door. Instead, the woman in charge came out through that door. She told us that she appreciated us finding the mother, but that we did not have sufficient proof that she was the mother, so we were going to have to pay for DNA testing. That process would take another month. I just sat down and wept again. How many tears had Haiti seen me weep? After all my efforts, I had at the last minute lost my baby, Jislene, and now Bethany would take at least another month. *What do I do, Father? I just can't stay any longer. It has been six months since I have seen my children at home. Please, what do I do?*

I just didn't know. I had made a promise, but how could I stay any longer? I begged that woman, I cried, I stood and stared with all the feeling of a mother's aching heart written on my face, but she was unmovable. I turned and walked out. This would not only mean more time but more money. Another thousand dollars from somewhere. Who knew where? I didn't care. I just wanted to go home.

We spent the next few days finishing up the rest of the adoptions and applied for passports. Of course we paid horrendous fees for them so that they would be expedited. The high government official working with us promised we would have them. We bought plane tickets. I had stayed until the very last day possible. For a year there had been a huge family reunion planned at my home on the 15 of June. Family was coming from all over the country, and even from Germany. It was at my home, and I was in charge. I had to be there! That day was my drop dead date, no matter what it looked like. We bought tickets that would get us there on that very day. We purchased tickets for the children just in case. On the fourteenth, we still did not have passports in hand for a single child. Sarah sat at the American consulate, and I sat at the Haitian consulate. We had all the children with us, and we just kept shuttling papers to each other as fast as we got them. Whoever we received a passport for by two we could take home. The rest would have to wait for me to come back. What a day that was. I could not believe that all my efforts were ending like this. We never stopped praying, even for a second. I knew whoever I left behind would not be coming home for a very long time. I knew Haiti; if they said a month it meant six. *Why, Father? Why did it end this way?*

At two, we had David, Daniel, and Kaneasha's passports and visas in hand. I was the one who had waited six months, and only one of my children was going to come home with me; one out of five children that I had been working on for over three years. I was trying so hard to be excited for Sarah, but my heart ached. At two thirty, I had Laura's passport. I took it to the American consulate and begged them to try and put just one more through the system. You see their computers that produced the visas, worked with American computers and when the American computers shut down so did theirs. They had no control over it. The computers were just never on after two.

"Please try, please!" *God, please make him say yes.*

"I don't believe it. The visa went through. You can take your daughter home!" God had heard my prayer. We had our miracle.

Now it was Sarah's turn to be disappointed, for thirty minutes later, her little girl, Fayetta, received a passport too. But there was no way to push it through. It would take one year to accomplish what could have been done if we had one more hour, one more day. This was a time of trusting God, that he knew what was best. I knew he could have brought all of them home, but for some reason he choose to only bring two of mine and two of Sarah's. The rest would have to wait.

That night as we packed, it was very hard to say good-bye to Fayetta, Anson, and my sweet little Bethany, who once again was being abandoned by her mother. Would she ever trust me? Only God knew the answer to that. I had already said good-bye to my Jislene. I was told I would never be able to get her. I looked in Pastor's eyes and said, "Oh yes I will, God has told me she is my little girl. I'll be back."

I have wondered over and over and been asked by many why the gathering of each child has been filled with so much turmoil, heartache, and opposition. I can answer that at least in part now that I look back and as I watch my children every day of their lives. Each child knows their story. Each one of them knows that they had parents and family who have given everything to have them come home. Each child has no question in their minds that their parents will go to the ends of the earth and back if necessary for them. They also have no question that God wants them in this family. Their journeys have given them the confidence that they need in order to have peace where they are at. They have felt the love that has been shown by the sacrifice of the rest of the family in order to bring them in and that has created a bond that is hard to get in a family like ours. The harder the journey, the greater the gift and the ability to find joy. We have been given the gift of building a family through pain, challenges, serving, joy, and walking with God. I wouldn't have it any other way, for the children's sake.

We boarded the plane that next morning, holding tightly to our four new little ones, and I felt like I had let God and the children back home down. But as we flew home and I prayed and struggled, God spoke peace to my heart. I had the clearest impression come to my mind.

"I release you, Annie Laurie. You did what I asked you to do, and you kept your promise. All your children are adopted, and you are bringing children home. I will take care of the others until you can return for them. Well done, my good and faithful servant."

Incredible peace filled me and every step of that journey, that incredibly hard, long walk became sweet to me. I had done it, and God was pleased. I could go home and witness to my family that their offering and sacrifice had pleased God. They had done it! God had done it!

Only a fraction of the story is told here. There were so many more miraculous gifts and tender mercies, but hopefully we have shared enough that many hearts will understand.

The first activity of that family reunion was at the airport, where after six long months, we were finally reunited as a family. It was glorious!

kyrstin

—Brian

This part of the gathering journey came out of the blue. It was so unexpected, but not unwelcome.

By the first of May 2007, we still did not know if Anson, Bethany, and Jislene, or our granddaughter, Fayetta, were going to make it out of Haiti. We believed it, and we hoped with all of our hearts, but their little calloused feet were not yet on American soil.

It is amazing to me that during all this time, not only was Annie Laurie gathering children, mothering them, and teaching a school, she was also running her own business. This may sound like a paid commercial announcement, but it's not; it's just the plain truth. She felt so passionate about the changes that occurred in our health situation with Reliv that she started sharing it as a business. She worked as hard in this as she did in everything she does, and it quickly became very successful, and soon her income topped my teacher's salary.

· ·

—Annie Laurie

Sarah was also doing the same business that I was. She had a daughter with cerebral palsy, and when she saw what it did for her life, she too felt a desire to share with people. I had always told my husband that I could never just go get a normal job. I had done temporary work as a receptionist and loved it. But I couldn't keep doing it, for I longed to be changing lives somehow. In my business, I felt I was doing just that. One of the other reasons I loved it was because Sarah and I always did it together. Except for one particular day when I was out of town.

Sarah had gone to talk to a woman that someone else had introduced her to, so she really did not know anything about her. She just knew she was interested in hearing about our product. So Sarah went to her home to talk to her about it. As Sarah was about to leave, the woman looked at her and said, "I don't quite know why I am bringing this up, but do you know anyone who would adopt a little eight-year-old girl?" Sarah just looked at her for a minute and then said, "As a matter of fact, I think I do! Can I call you later today?"

Sarah walked out of the house, went to her car, and called me that very minute.

"Mom, you are never going to believe what just happened."
Oh no, here we go again. We don't even have all our children
from Haiti and here was another child needing a home.

"Tell me her story," I said, not really wanting to hear but
knowing that I had to at least be willing to listen.

She had been adopted at the age of eighteen months. She
originally came from Bolivia. They found out that she had some
pretty serious mental and emotional challenges, and her adoptive parents did not know how to deal with them very well.
After five and a half years, DCFS had become involved. She
needed a home. *Oh, Father, can I help her?* She was out of control in her behavior and did not know how to be in any kind of
a relationship situation. DCFS felt that she would do best in a
home where she was the only child.

My first reaction to that was, "Are you kidding? What she
needs is a houseful of children who know how to love. Children
who have come from hard places so they understand *her* hard
place. She needs us!"

Oh dear, what was I saying? If she needed us, then that
meant we needed her. Once again I had to face a phone call with
my husband.

I have to admit that I was shocked into silence when after
having shared with him the story over the phone, he simply
said, "We have a home, we have love, and we have safety for this
little girl. Let's move forward."

* *

—*Brian*

Annie Laurie came to me about a little girl that no one seemed
to want. When I found out the circumstances of her life, a
thought came almost immediately: *How can you withhold what
you have from this little girl?* Whoa, wait a minute. What do I

have? Our home is going to be put up for sale as soon as I finish it. We're living in a large basement apartment that I finished, belonging to Annie Laurie, our married daughter, and I don't have insurance. We're in so much debt I can't even see the top of the financial hole we're in. The thought persisted, *You cannot withhold what you have from this little girl. She needs your family. She needs to have Annie Laurie as her mother. She needs you as her father.*

I figured I had better listen pretty quickly this time as compared with all of the other times in this gathering journey where I had stopped or slowed the process by complaining, worrying, being negative, and whining. This time I was going to do it right, so I responded immediately to the thought. It was like God's spirit was enticing me. Perhaps the thought came from the whispered pleading of this little girl's heart and was carried into my mind on the wings of heaven. I really don't know the mechanics of exactly how such things work; but I do know the thoughts were powerful and clear. Clothe the naked, feed the hungry, and take care of the fatherless. Kyrstin was not physically naked, but as far as having a permanent family, she was certainly uncovered.

It was obvious that she had been eating plenty of food. She was a little bit chubby. But you could see the emotional hunger or near starvation in her eyes. She had been beaten, humiliated, abused, and starved in her original home, and after five years in that home, she was then removed and put into the foster care system. She was at a crossroads now, because her loving foster mom could not continue to care for her, on account of her husband's deployment to Iraq. DCFS had placed her in several foster homes on a trial basis, but they all just sent her back with a "no thank you."

Maybe I should have prayed to get an answer about the rightness of bringing her into our family, but I didn't; at least not until months later, right before the final adoption proceedings. When I finally did pray, the answer was the same:

"Feed the hungry, clothe the naked, protect and take care of the fatherless."

Kyrstin was placed in our home as a foster child, with the plan that in six months the adoption would be final. There would be a few technical difficulties, but DCFS took care of every road block. Our experiences, with DCFS several years earlier were very difficult. This time, our workings with DCFS were wonderful. We are so grateful that this little Bolivian orphan, who was almost literally let go of by the world, was picked up by DCFS.

So where were the miracles of Kyrstin's gathering? The miracle was in the changing of this father's heart in a split second. The miracle was in the ease with which she was brought into our home, when we simply could not bear another long walk in the gathering journey. Are miracles alive and well? Of course they are!

Kyrstin was adopted on her ninth birthday, January 5, 2008. She still has more than her share of hurdles, including intellectual and emotional challenges. However, she is in a home now, where she is fighting to overcome and learn instead of being overrun by the challenges. She is overcoming and winning. She is part of our family now. She is our daughter just as much as every other child, and whether brought to us through the labor of birth or the labor of adoption, to us they are one and the same.

the ordeal ends

—Annie Laurie

The four children we had brought home from Haiti were wonderful. David and Daniel, our grandsons who were nine, were such sweet boys. They fit right into a family that already had four children ages four and under. They were such a help to Sarah.

Our two, Laura and Kaneasha, could not have been sweeter. They learned the language so fast and fit in so well we were amazed. There is always an adjustment time when new children come into the home. Sometimes this adjustment on all sides is harder than others. With these two it had been by far the easiest adjustment we had. Katurah and Laura became bosom buddies immediately and have never been separated since. Kaneasha was very shy at first but now is a little spitfire. They have been a joy to have. Kyrstin came in May, and that adjustment was a little bit harder and longer for all of us. But after being in our home five weeks, her social worker came into the home and said she would not have recognized her if she hadn't already known who she was. She was a completely different girl.

And now it was time to bring our four precious Haitian children home, three more for us and one for Sarah.

I had been home almost a year, and the thought of going back just about sent me into a nervous breakdown. We had been in contact with Pastor, but everything had been lost, had to be started again, paid for again, etc. Just Haitian red tape! But now everything was in order except for Jislene's dad's permission. Pastor called and told me to please get on the phone with him. I found a translator, and we called him. We told him that we were coming again one more time to Haiti and we would love to bring his daughter home with us, but he had to go to the consulate and say yes. I guess he finally realized this was the last chance for his little girl. He had put her back in the orphanage, and she had almost died. He told us he would go.

I told Pastor to call me as soon as we had the go ahead.

He called me a few days later and said everything was done, but I would have to come and get them. I was terrified. The emotion that this caused in me was awful. I dreamed that night that I landed in Haiti and these big arms reached out and grabbed me and I was never able to leave again. I woke up in a cold sweat. Could I really go back? I told Pastor I would come, but I would not go back to the orphanage. He had to bring the children to me.

Brian did not want me to go back. He was scared to death to have me go. He wanted me to stay on the airplane and not even get off. "Just have the children brought onto the plane, or better yet, have them brought to Florida," he said. Unfortunately, that was not possible. I was going to have to go back. I told Sarah, and as usual, this wonderful daughter stepped up to the plate and said she would go with me.

We got on that plane, and I was literally shaking. I am usually pretty solid. Nothing much deters me when I know what I need to do, but this was hard. We had to stay overnight in Florida. That part was fun. But the next morning I had to get on the plane that would take me the final leg of the trip. The only thing that got me on that plane was my love for those children, and I knew that God would bear me up and protect me. Sarah didn't even dare talk to me. She said my face was ashen and that I looked more afraid than she had ever seen me. But guess what? God did bear me up. I walked off that plane onto Haitian soil and walked across the runway into the building and through customs and got our luggage and then walked outside, and there was Pastor. We hugged and laughed, and then he took us and dropped us off at our hotel, where I threw myself on my bed and started once again to breathe. I had done it. We had done it. We were here, and I was going to bring my children home!

Sarah and I had a wonderfully relaxing evening in an air-conditioned room with running water and electricity. It was still a bare bones room, but it seemed like a palace to me. The hotel served a wonderful buffet that we ate until we could eat no more, and we slept like babies. This wasn't so bad!

The next day, about four hours before our plane was to leave, the children and their parents arrived. We all piled in the roach-filled car that I remembered so well and headed for the airport. We said our quick good-byes to everyone outside the airport, hugged them, and then off they went to head back to their homes. We quickly got in line and headed into the airport. I couldn't believe it. We had done it! We had our children.

Anson looked great. He was excited and jumping around. Fayetta was doing great. A little overwhelmed with all the excitement but doing fine. Jislene just clung to me as if she would never let go of me again. But our little Bethany broke my heart. The nannies thought that she was possessed, and so they would not feed her. She is our crack baby, and without good nutrition, has terrible hallucinations at night. She sees big spiders everywhere. She goes pretty crazy. I used to hold her in my arms while she had these fits. But the nannies would just beat and starve her. I have never in all my life seen a body that looked as emaciated as hers, and I have seen some pretty horrific things. I just cried the first time I gave her a bath. I wondered if she would even make it home, she was so frail. It was almost more than I could take. It was worth going back. With all my heart, it was worth going back! Never again would my little Bethany Hope be subjected to that kind of horrific life.

As we sat on the plane heading once again for America, my heart was filled with so many profound emotions: relief, love, gratitude, and a wonderful hope in a future for all of our children. And then the incredible peace came as I felt the loving approval from above. Our family had not quit this long walk until the journey was complete.

We spent the night in a hotel again in Florida and got them all washed and dressed in new clothes. Then we started our final journey home. What a sweet reunion that was as we all greeted each other at the airport knowing that the challenges of Haiti were finally being brought to a close. How grateful we were that we had not quit. We may not have changed a nation while I was in Haiti, but we brought joy to eight little ones. Is there any sweeter victory in life than that?

our little girl comes home

The final journey of this "gathering story" was about to take place.

—Annie Laurie

Kyrstin had been with us for a week and things were just a bit crazy. To be honest, this was the first time I didn't know if I was going to be able to parent a child. I knew I was supposed to, but I didn't know if I could. Her heart had been so shattered and she was so tormented with voices in her head, inappropriate behaviors, and so much anger. I wondered if I had finally taken on more than we as a family could handle. But in my mind I did not have a choice. God would just have to show us how to do this thing. And over the last year and a half, he has. Time and again he has shown us how to take this damaged flower and help her to bloom.

We were also just a few weeks away from heading back to Haiti to get our last 4 children.

But this sweet morning in May it wasn't about Kyrstin, or about 4 children in Haiti, it was about a little baby. I received a phone call.

"Annie Laurie, this is a friend. Are you still interested in adopting children?"

Yes, I was, because even with all the children that had been brought into our lives, I still had not found my little girl; the little girl that I had been promised years and years ago. I answered yes and asked her why.

"I know a young woman who is pregnant but not married. She wants to give this baby to a family who will really love her. I thought immediately of you. Would you like a baby? You would be able to get her straight from the hospital." Pause, "Annie Laurie, are you there?"

I was crying so hard I could not answer. I was so filled with the knowledge that I had done all I had been asked to do, and this was my personal gift from God. It was finally time for my little girl to come. She had waited until all the other children were brought home, and now it was her turn.

"Yes, I'm here, and yes, I'm interested." I squeaked out. "What do I have to do?" It didn't matter what I had to do, I would do it. She informed me of the conditions and my heart sank. Brian would never say yes, never. He was too distraught about our financial state. *Father, why now, when every last resource was gone and beyond gone? Why?*

"Please, let me talk to my husband, and I will call you back."

"You have fifteen minutes, and then I am going to be calling someone else. I need to get this baby placed."

Phone calls that change your life. There had been so many phone calls, so many long walks, so many miracles; what did our future hold this time? I called my husband.

—*Brian*

Have you ever thought you had changed a characteristic you felt was undesirable? You think you're a different person, and then out from seemingly nowhere your old self comes right back as if no change had occurred.

Annie Laurie informed me that part of the package of adopting this little girl who was yet to be born was to provide support for the mother during her pregnancy at the rate of $1,000 per month for seven months. It was really a very reasonable and fair request, and legal in the state of Utah. But seven thousand dollars was completely untouchable for us. When Annie Laurie called, I said, "No! We cannot go forward with the adoption. We'll just have to say no." I knew that this was breaking Annie Laurie's heart. "We simply do not have any resources left to borrow money or even cover another payment if we could borrow." I told Annie Laurie that I wanted to adopt this little unborn baby, but I needed to be shown the way, because I had come to a dead end.

She quietly asked me, "What if this is finally our little girl we have been waiting for? Isn't that more important than money?"

I replied, "Yes, of course she is more important, but I don't know what else to do."

I just want to go back in time and reason with myself and, if needful, give myself a swift and well-placed kick! I want to go back and tell myself to do whatever it takes to raise the money. If I could go back, I'd sell everything we had that wasn't absolutely necessary for survival to meet the requirements for our little girl. I now would literally lay down my life for this precious little daughter. Boy, would I do it differently. But now is not then.

• • • • • • • • • • • • • • • • • • • •

—*Annie Laurie*

I hung up the phone, and it felt as if all the pain of all the times I had been told no by my husband came back in one horrific blow. I could not stop sobbing. At this time, we were living in my daughter's, Annie Laurie's, basement, and Sarah was living in the upstairs while Annie Laurie lived on the main level. We were finishing up our home to get it on the market. Sarah and Joseph had been living beside us but had already sold their home. We were trying to buy a ranch in Missouri, and Sarah and Joseph were going to do that with us. There were thirty-seven people living in that home. Crazy, I know! I certainly could understand Brian's concern. But that did not make it any easier. My two girls, Sarah and Annie Laurie, were there with me, and we all cried together.

My Annie Laurie held me in her arms as I wept. Our tears mingled as we prayed right there that somehow God would work one of his mighty miracles. She just kept saying, "This little girl is yours, Mom. God isn't going to let you lose her. I know she is yours. He'll bring you the money, don't worry." She understood very clearly what I was going through having walked her own journey with adoptions and all that comes with it.

Then my sweet Sarah put her arms around me and told me not to worry. They would pay the $7,000 and not to worry about even paying it back. She told me to get on that phone and to tell my friend we wanted that little girl.

· ·

—*Brian*

Heaven was not ignorant of our need, and it became apparent that God had prepared someone to help with the needed miracle. It came from my son-in-law, Joseph, and daughter, Sarah. They stepped forward, without being asked, and simply, quietly paid the $7,000. Their attitude was kind and generous. They really did not have excess money; in fact, they had recently lost a significant amount of money on the sale of their home. But there it was in our bank account, the miracle we needed.

The only redeeming ingredient in this experience is the deep gratitude which grows every day in my heart toward Annie Laurie, Joseph, and Sarah for bringing this little angel into our family. Thank you, Annie Laurie. Thank you, Joseph and Sarah.

· ·

—*Annie Laurie*

"The birth mother is going to have an ultrasound. Do you want to know what the baby is?" Yes, of course, but really, I already knew. It was a girl. Sure enough, I got a call the next day, and we were having a baby girl. My daughters and I went straight out and bought a little outfit for her. *A girl, my girl.* I had a houseful of my girls. But the search for this little girl had made all the others possible. It was in large part our unending quest for this sweet little one that fueled the fire of the gathering, which has brought together these precious souls we now call family.

The whole family was so excited. It was really quite cute because the big question was, "Is this going to be a white baby?" When I would say yes, they would look at me and say, "Do you know how to take care of a white baby?" Color of skin in our family is fun. I love sweets! So my blackest children are dark chocolate, the brown ones are milk chocolate, the Vietnamese are caramel, and the whities are vanilla. They all know that dark chocolate is my favorite, so I just have to eat on them more. (That means kisses all over the face.)

I have to tell this sweet story about my Katurah. I really think her brown skin is so beautiful. We spend all summer trying to get our skin to be their color. But when my Katurah was little, she would sit by me and we'd put our arms by each other and she would sigh. Then she would rub my arm over and over. I finally asked her what she was thinking about when she did that. She turned to me with her big beautiful eyes and said, "Your skin is so beautiful. I wish I was white like you." I looked down at my arm with all the freckles and age spots and knew that love was blind. Now, years later, there is no way she would give up her perfect skin.

I have to tell one more story about my Esther and Emily. Shortly after Esther arrived in America, we had a fluke snowstorm in New Mexico. She ran outside without a coat on and just stayed out there. I didn't think much of it at the time. We then moved to Utah where it really snows. That first winter, she and Emily went outside every time it snowed. Finally, one day they came up to me and said, "When is it going to happen?" I replied, "When is what going to happen?" They looked at me with their innocent eyes and said, "When are we going to turn white? We play in the snow every day, but we are still brown." We all laughed and then tried to explain to these two precious daughters just how beautiful they were.

But this time we were going to have a white baby, and everyone thought this was great. She was due in November, and we had to go to Maryland to get her. We headed to Maryland a few days before the due date. We were going to have to stay in Maryland for a few weeks, but we didn't care. We would have our baby to play with all day long.

. . . .

—Annie Laurie—our twenty-eight-year-old daughter, one of the twins

When I heard that my mom and dad could possibly be bringing another little baby girl into their home, it was a great moment for me. It was the culmination of twenty-three years of waiting, wondering, and praying our hearts out that our mom would be brought home safe from her many gathering journeys and that somehow one of those journeys would give her the little girl she so desperately wanted. To see them walk through the door with this last brand new baby girl was going to be unforgettable.

As the oldest biological daughter, I was one of those blessed to see this process from the beginning. I remember sitting at the kitchen table when I was eight years old. My mom was going through the phone book looking at adoption agencies. I got really excited about the whole process. I wanted to know every detail about what would happen. It would be a long time before we actually had anyone join our family through adoption. But it was then that adoption entered my heart.

My parent's first adoptions took place after I was married and already wanting to start my own family. To watch your own mother go through feelings of doubt, fear, and heartache over searching for her children is life changing. It has created a bond of love and sisterhood that is unbreakable.

My mom was going through what I was going through. We both knew what it was to wait by the phone hoping you'll get that call. We both looked longingly at babies as they were carried by in their parents' arms. We both felt that deep need inside to *search* for your child. We have cheered and cried for each other. My mom was there for me in the hard times.

I was pregnant with my second biological but third child, or so I thought. I had a little boy whom I had given birth to, and I had already adopted a little crack baby from the DCFS system.

So here I was seven months pregnant, and we finally receive the call that there were twins in Kazakhstan who were available. They were nine months old. We had been trying to complete our foreign adoption for two years.

How do you go to a foreign country by yourself when you very well could deliver before it was time to come home? I had no choice. I had to go and bring my children home. I had to stay six weeks in that country. I spent my days at the orphanage and in my hotel room. Near the end, my husband was able to join me, but there were many times when I could not help but wonder what was going on. I was all alone and eight months pregnant in a foreign country. I couldn't help but ask, "Why am I here? Am I doing the right thing? Maybe everyone else is right, this is crazy!"

I thank God that I had a mother who was praying for me and had experienced the same kind of journey and could walk me through all those hard times. I brought those twins home, and two weeks later, instead of giving birth to number three, I gave birth to number five; all of them three and under. I needed a mom who understood. I am thankful every day that I had one who had already walked the walk and could show me the way.

We have helped each other with unfailing love and support. Having support as you bring another child into your life is crucial. It was an added gift for me to build my family at the same time my mom was building hers.

What began around our kitchen table so many years ago has grown into something so big none of us could even have begun to imagine it. My mom's first desire for another baby girl has brought so many children into my heart, indeed, into all of our hearts. It has opened so many doors into my soul and made me who I am. And now it was my mom's turn to have her heart filled. She had filled so many others throughout the years. But as I saw her with that little baby girl in her arms and witnessed the joy in her face. I knew that the gift for all of her unselfish labors was now being given to her.

Only as a parent can you begin to fully appreciate what your parents have done for you. Mom, thank you. This journey has been and will continue to be a cherished moment shared by a mother and daughter who placed their loving hearts in harmony with each other's song.

* *

—*Annie Laurie*

The day after we arrived in Maryland, we got a call. "Your little girl has been born and she is beautiful. We are making arrangements for you to pick her up day after tomorrow." *Okay, just breathe! Come on, Annie Laurie, just breathe.* It had happened. Those two days were nerve racking. I had lost enough children that I was still scared to death. But…

Can't you drive any faster? We only have a few minutes to get there! Oh, can this possibly be happening? It was so hard to believe that it was actually true. But it was. After twenty-three long years of waiting, our little girl was about to be placed in my arms.

* *

—*Brian*

As we entered the attorney's office, there he was, awkwardly, very awkwardly, holding this little two-day-old treasure. This moment formed a visual picture that is burned into my memory forever. This was a sacred moment when Julianna was placed into Annie Laurie's arms. The gathering journey was coming to a close. After years of gut-wrenching struggles, almost half a million in adoption expenses, months of separation, hours and hours of pleading prayers on our knees and silently in our hearts, this was it, and there she was.

How do I describe this miracle? This little baby's middle name should do it all—Joy! Annie Laurie felt impressed that her name should be Julianna Joy. She is truly a joy. Even through all of the toxic waste diapers, the teething episodes, the spills and messes, and the sleepless nights, to name only a few, I have experienced an intense joy that fills me from the top of my head to the soles of my feet. We experience Joy, Julianna Joy, every day.

•   •

—Annie Laurie

As I held her for the first time, I could not hold back the tears for the memory of the journey to get to this moment came flooding back to my mind; Haiti, camping in the Marshall Islands, orphanages of Vietnam, DCFS, tears of loss, and tears of joy. And now I held my Joy, my Julianna Joy, our family's gift from God.

•   •

This is our story.

epilogue

—Annie Laurie and Brian

Some miracles come when least expected and without any warning. We are on the down side of the hill called middle age. We are in our fifties. I guess this is when ordinary people just like us are busy loving their grandchildren and having their mid-life crises, whatever those are. We did once own a little white convertible a few years back, but we traded it in for a twenty-one passenger bus out of necessity. And we have twenty-one grandchildren that we do enjoy.

But here we are, at our age, loving every minute of having a ten-month-old baby girl; we are so very grateful.

One morning recently, Brian retrieved Julianna from our bedroom to prevent her from awakening Mommy from her precious and often rare sleep. He had gotten up early to work on this book and had brought Julianna downstairs with him. He placed her in his lap and wrapped his arms around her in an attempt to continue writing on the laptop. She placed her little head against his chest and stayed there for a moment or two. She lifted her head and looked up at him, into his eyes, and down into his heart. She held his gaze for about a minute and then returned to resting her little head on his chest. We ask you, "Was it worth it?" Every minute, hour, day, week, month, and year of struggle, uncertainty, near poverty, and loneliness was all worth it; every tiny bit was worth it!

That which has become of most worth to us, however, is not the fact that we are the parents of twenty-four children. No, that's not the best part or the most miraculous dimension. The best and most miraculous is how God changed us. He made us into a better man and woman through this whole process. He made us into people who love and care more deeply than we ever would have been able to do on our own. He took us out of our comfort zones so many times that the zone hardly exists anymore. He has given us the privilege to sacrifice everything in order to bless, protect, and help others. We have had the precious and rare experience to feed the hungry, clothe the naked, and protect the fatherless. Even though our children are no longer fatherless, we get to feed, clothe, and protect them every day, until the day that we leave this beautiful green earth.

So did we set about to change the world? No, we just saw some little people in need—desperate need. Did we change the world? No, we did not. But we did change nineteen children's lives forever. Each one of us have been surrounded by wonderful souls who have all been gathered by love, miracles, and the tender mercies of our God.

—Brian

Are the whisperings now silent? I don't think so. This wonderful and courageous woman at my side still has ears to hear and a heart ready to give. Only this time, we will be listening and giving together.

endnotes

1   Go Bring Them in From the Plains

Words and music: Dan Stirling, Nancy Hanson, Sam Cardon

2   Be Still My Soul

Text: Katharina von Schlegel

Music: Jean Sibelius

further information

For additional information about *The Gathering*,

please visit:

http://thegatheringplace.tatepublishing.net

listen|imagine|view|experience

AUDIO BOOK DOWNLOAD INCLUDED WITH THIS BOOK!

In your hands you hold a complete digital entertainment package. In addition to the paper version, you receive a free download of the audio version of this book. Simply use the code listed below when visiting our website. Once downloaded to your computer, you can listen to the book through your computer's speakers, burn it to an audio CD or save the file to your portable music device (such as Apple's popular iPod) and listen on the go!

How to get your free audio book digital download:

1. Visit www.tatepublishing.com and click on the e|LIVE logo on the home page.
2. Enter the following coupon code:
   7c24-0635-9069-96c4-c1f6-6240-c8cc-2f32
3. Download the audio book from your e|LIVE digital locker and begin enjoying your new digital entertainment package today!